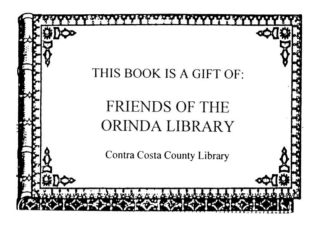

Ovid: The Poet and His Work

OVID

The Poet and His Work

NIKLAS HOLZBERG

Translated from the German

by G. M. Goshgarian

Cornell University Press

ITHACA AND LONDON

Original German edition, *Ovid: Dichter und Werk,* copyright © 1998 by
C. H. Beck'sche Verlagsbuchhandlung, München.

English translation copyright © 2002 by Cornell University

The translation of this work was published with the assistance of Inter
Nationes.

First published 2002 by Cornell University Press
Printed in the United States of America

Library of Congress Cataloging-in-Publication Data
Holzberg, Niklas.
   [Ovid English]
   Ovid: the poet and his work / Niklas Holzberg ; translated from
the German by G.M. Goshgarian.
       p. cm.
   Includes bibliographical references and index.
   ISBN 0-8014-3754-7 (cloth : alk. paper)
   1. Ovid, 43 B.C.–17 or 18 A.D.—Criticism and interpretation.   2.
Epistolary poetry, Latin—History and criticism.   3. Didactic poetry,
Latin—History and criticism.   4. Elegiac poetry, Latin—History and
criticism.   5. Mythology, Classical, in literature.   6. Rome—In
literature.   7. Love in literature.   I. Title.
   PA6537 .H65 2002
   871'.01—dc21   2001006502

for
Stefan Merkle

Contents

Preface to the First German Edition

"As far as the power of Rome stretches over the conquered lands, I shall be read out from the mouth of the people." These words stand at the end of Ovid's major work, the *Metamorphoses*. Clearly, the poet here sees himself changed into a new form—that of a book. Indeed, today we essentially know him only as a book, that is, in his work; of the individual named Ovid, we can say virtually nothing. We are relatively well informed about the times in which he lived and wrote; but we know Ovid himself only in the forms and figures into which he transformed himself in his poems. Whenever he pronounces the word "I" there, whether as elegiac lover, professor of love, teller of myths, or commentator on the calendar, he comes before the reader in a role. He does so even as an exile living in Tomis on the Black Sea coast. And, in one of his works, he slips into the roles of mythical men and women whom he imagines writing letters.

This book will accordingly present the poet as he is reflected in the various roles he plays in his work. The role-playing he engages in is literary role-playing; it refers constantly to Greek and Roman texts that readers of Ovid's day were familiar with. We are still familiar with many of them today. I shall show how Ovid skillfully and also wittily adapts certain themes and reflections he finds in these writings to the intellectual world of his own texts. But Ovid's poetry also repeatedly alludes to the events and personalities of his day. I shall therefore be discussing the poet's ongoing debate with the Rome he wrote for, that is, the Rome of Emperor Augustus. Of course, modern readers are above all interested in Ovid for the timelessness of his character descriptions. I shall try to give the reader some sense of the way Ovid's wit and his capacity for psychological observation combine to yield a fascinating talent for the depiction of human behavior. In particular, Ovid tells vividly realistic stories about people in love.

Ovid not only played many different roles, but also published his works in many different rolls. For, in his time, books consisted of papyrus rolls attached to a rod that the reader had to unroll as he read. Almost all of Ovid's works are made up of several books, the papyrus rolls of an earlier day; we shall be examining them in chronological order and shall unroll them as best we can ourselves, like his Roman readers. I would, then, like to go through these works one by one with an eye to their structure, treating them, to the extent that I can, in their entirety. We shall see that, when they are approached in this way, they can be read like novels. And we shall also clearly see that this literature, although it is two thousand years old, is not really all that different from the kind most often read today.

Because Ovid's works are so "modern," this book tries to address as wide a readership as possible. Quotations from Ovid are therefore given in translation—not in a metered verse translation, but in one that hews as closely as possible to the original, following its lineation and even adopting its word order whenever that can be managed. Those who would like to read a Standard English prose translation should consult the complete edition of Ovid's works in the Loeb Classical Library, which also provides the Latin texts and includes fragments and works of uncertain attribution. Of the existing German prose translations, I shall here mention only those by Michael von Albrecht and Friedrich Walter Lenz in the two series Reclams Universal-Bibliothek and Schriften und Quellen der Alten Welt, both of which also provide the Latin text. To readers wishing to consult a critical edition of Ovid, I recommend the editions of the *Amores, Ars amatoria,* and *Remedia amoris* in the Bibliotheca Oxoniensis (E. J. Kenney), the edition of the *Epistulae Heroidum* in Volume 6 of *Texte und Kommentare* (Heinrich Dörrie), and the editions of the *Metamorphoses* (William S. Anderson), *Fasti* (E. H. Alton, D. E. W. Wormell, and E. Courtney), *Tristia* (John Barrie Hall), and *Epistulae ex Ponto* (J. A. Richmond) in the Bibliotheca Teubneriana. I shall explain all Latin words that I discuss as well as any concepts that pertain specifically to ancient culture. The reader also will find short explanations of these words and concepts in the Glossary.

This book is based on a review of all the pertinent secondary literature at my disposal and is thus addressed to specialists too. However, I have deliberately avoided scholarly commentary as well as discussion of controversial problems. Yet I do often refer the reader to studies that prompted some of the reflections I here offer on the interpretation of Ovid's works, mentioning only the author's name, year of publication, and, where relevant, page number in the text, since all of the studies cited are listed in alphabetical order in the bibliography. Because we now have an enormous mass of criticism on Ovid, the bibliography mentions only those studies that have taught me something directly relevant to this book. I have also included, in the bibliography for this English translation, material published after the second German edition appeared. I here single out for special mention the books and essays by Alessandro Barchiesi, Gerlinde Bretzigheimer, Gregson Davis, Siegmar Döpp, Bardo Gauly, Stephen Hinds, Alison Keith, John Miller, Sara Myers, Betty Nagle, Carole Newlands, Gianpiero Rosati, Ernst Schmidt, Alison Sharrock, Friedrich Spoth, Wilfried Stroh, Stephen Wheeler, and Gareth Williams.

I would especially like to point out that in reading and studying Ovid more closely than ever before over the past few years, I have modified many of my earlier views. Thus Ovid has put me too through a metamorphosis. This explains why, on certain points, I defend views different from those I put forward in earlier works on Ovid. I have of course not indicated this anywhere, as I have no desire whatsoever to engage in scholarly debate with myself. "Everything flows," say both Heraclitus and the Pythagoras of the *Metamorphoses*. That holds for the interpretation of literary texts in particular. Thus, on certain issues, I have not expressed as clear-cut an opinion in this book as I did a few years ago.

My work on this book went hand in hand with seminars and tutorials that I directed at the University of Munich in 1994–1996. I owe a large debt of thanks to the participants for their simulating remarks. Herbert Neumaier, Helmut Prechtl, Martin Schröder, and Christian Zgoll wrote helpful essays. Also of great use to me were the partly oral, partly written discussions about Ovid that I engaged in then with the following colleagues: Alessandro Barchiesi, Gerlinde Bretzigheimer, Siegmar Döpp, Brigitte Egger, Claudia Klodt, Werner von Koppenfels, Hartmut Längin, Stefan Mairoser, Stefan Merkle (the three last-named colleagues also cheerfully took on the chore of reading through the manuscript), John Morgan, Carole Newlands, Hans-Peter Obermayer, Bryan Reardon, Gianpiero Rosati, Friedrich Spoth, and Michael Zeller. I thank them all cordially for their contributions to my work on Ovid.

I owe special thanks to Stefan Merkle, an old friend and colleague; that is why I dedicate this book to him. He took a constant and never-wavering interest in its production, endlessly discussed it with me, and undertook several painstaking readings of the manuscript. I would also like to thank him here for his long-standing collaboration in the Munich branch of the Petronian Society.

Munich, September 1996

Preface to the Second German Edition

A number of errors and omissions in the first edition have been corrected here. I thank Herwig Aulehla, Guy Lee, and Maaike Zimmerman for helpful suggestions.

Munich, December 1997

Ovid: The Poet and His Work

Approaches to the Work:
Ovid and His Readers

A New "Age of Ovid"

Aetas Ovidiana—that is what the medievalist Ludwig Traube called the Latin literature of the twelfth and thirteenth centuries. But we can extend the notion to cover the whole of the literary culture of Western Europe in this period, for no writer left a deeper mark on its literature than the ancient Roman poet Publius Ovidius Naso. It is true that, with the development of the vernacular Western European literary tradition from its beginnings in the twelfth century down to the present day, the influence of the authors of antiquity has steadily waned. Ovid, in particular, was relegated to the margins in the Romantic period and for a long time thereafter. Yet, since the mid-1980s, he has become so popular, not only with classicists and other lovers of Greek and Roman poetry, but also with poets and prose writers, that we may once again speak of an "Age of Ovid," at least as far as the literary afterlife of antiquity is concerned.

Let me mention only the most compelling evidence of the new Ovid renaissance. The poet is the protagonist of a number of novels and stories; some have enjoyed considerable success, including Luca Desiato's *Sulle rive del Mar Nero,* Derek Mahon's *Ovid in Tomis,* David Malouf's *An Imaginary Life,* Christoph Ransmayr's *Die letzte Welt,* and Antonio Tabucchi's *Sogni di Sogni.* Ovid's greatest work, the *Metamorphoses,* has inspired contemporary authors in several English-speaking countries, among them such well-known writers as Seamus Heaney and Ted Hughes, to publish retellings of certain of the poet's stories of transformation; these were gathered together in a 1994 anthology (*After Ovid:*

1

New Metamorphoses), where they appear in the same order as their models in the ancient text. One sign that classicists have suddenly begun to take a special interest in Ovid is the fact that nearly every new issue of the many specialized academic journals contains an essay devoted to him. What is more, substantial monographs have begun appearing on works of his which, until recently, were all but ignored. Thus four books were published on the *Fasti* in the space of five years (Miller 1991, Barchiesi 1994, Herbert-Brown 1994, Newlands 1995). Again, feminist Latinists have repeatedly singled Ovid out for special attention, as they do, for example, in a collection of essays on the poet by the Women's Classical Caucus of the American Philological Association (*Helios* 17/2 [1990]). And translations of Ovid top the list of the most popular new publications of ancient works on the recent book market. In 1995, for instance, a major German paperback publisher launched a series that aims to make the classics of world literature available to as broad a public as possible at unusually low prices: the first and, to date, the only classical text included in the series is Ovid's *Art of Love*.

What explains this popular interest in a classical writer? As late as the end of the 1970s, nothing led us to expect it. For ours is, after all, an age that has precious little use for the Greek and Roman classics, not least because it is no longer prepared to take the humanist educational ideal as a touchstone, an ideal that usually goes hand in hand with an appreciation of this literature. Yet it would seem that it is precisely *not* something specifically classical that fascinates Ovid's contemporary readers. For it is striking how often his interpreters make the claim that he is distinctly *modern*. And it is true that we discover at every turn in his work, expressed with a freshness that has, astonishingly, come down through two millennia unimpaired, a critique or at least a questioning of certain values commonly regarded as conservative and hence unmodern. For example, when a voice that speaks to us from Ovid's verse—whether it be that of the first-person speaker or another character—associates a pronounced distaste for the business of war with a make-love-not-war philosophy, it is only natural that we should be reminded of "progressive" contemporary texts with related themes. Again, it is no wonder that when Ovid portrays a woman victimized by a man's abuse of his power and physical strength, contemporary female readers too are strongly inclined to identify with her.

Moreover, when Ovid tells a story—and, of the various modes he employs, narrative is the one that most powerfully affects his contemporary audience—he manages to present even the oldest Greek myths in such a way as to make us feel that we are reading about the everyday experiences of characters in a modern novel, not the adventures of legendary gods and heroes. Take, for example, his version of the myth of the Caly-donian Hunt in Book 8 of the *Metamorphoses* (260–546). Here the great-est heroes of the generation preceding that of the Trojan warriors have teamed up to hunt down and kill a monstrous wild boar. Yet, contrary to expectations, all these heroes taken together find themselves almost hopelessly outmatched by that one animal for hours on end. For it is only after the boar has killed one of them, injured three more, terrified still others or dodged their (as a rule) ineptly cast spears that he is, at last, ever so slightly wounded, by—how humiliating for our warriors!—the only woman in the hunters' ranks, Atalanta. Before the beast is fi-nally bagged by Meleager, who has organized the hunt, yet another hero is killed, two more spears miss their mark, and Nestor, who one later finds among the ranks of the fighters at Troy, turns in a particularly dis-tressing performance in the context of this unheroic boar hunt. We are told—and this is to be found nowhere but in Ovid—that

> . . . sumpto posita conamine ab hasta
> arboris insiluit, quae stabat proxima, ramis
> despexitque, loco tutus, quem fugerat, hostem.

> . . . setting the spear upright and using it as a support,
> he leapt up onto the branches of the nearest tree,
> and looked down from his refuge at the foe he had fled.

(366–368)

The way high heroism is here stripped of its luster and high drama—indeed, made to seem ludicrous (Horsfall 1979)—like the fact that the all-too-human behavior of these demigods peaks in a remarkably preco-cious example of a pole vault, is by itself such as to impress readers of our day as anything but old-fashioned and, in that sense, modern.

As a rule, today's general reading public can enjoy a translation of Ovid as easily as it would a contemporary text that satirizes heroic pos-turing, if only it is provided with a few notes identifying names and fill-ing in background information. As for those who read Ovid in his own day, we may take it for granted that they too delighted in his imperti-nent treatment of a venerable mythic tradition and the values it con-veyed. But can we assume that readers of Ovid in the early Empire are comparable to the contemporary reading public in that, just as today's readers need not be classicists to follow the poet, so ancient readers did not need to have very extensive background information at their finger-tips? Is it likely that, even in his own time, the Roman poet appealed to readers of all social strata? I shall go on to show that this is most improbable—to begin with, because Ovid, like all major Roman writers since Catullus' time (c. 84–54 B.C.), was ranked by his contemporaries as a *poeta doctus* (learned poet) and thought of himself as such.

Ovid, a Poet between the Texts

Needless to say, even in the Rome of Emperor Augustus, people did not have to have the kind of knowledge only higher education could provide in order to laugh over Nestor's unheroic pole vault in the passage just cited. Yet poets like Ovid simply took it for granted that they were writing for readers who had acquired such an education: in a word, for members of the upper class. And such a public patently expected— at least, recent analyses make this seem quite likely—that a poetic text would not only yield up a meaning that everybody could fathom without further ado, but also contain another that could only be made out between the lines. For example, the hidden meaning might emerge from an indirect reference to another literary text.

Precisely that holds for our passage from the *Metamorphoses*. Shortly before Nestor performs his athletic tour de force, we are told that the hero, who, as the reader of Homer's *Iliad* knows, will take part in the battle for Troy in his grand old age, was still relatively young at the time of the hunt for the Calydonian Boar (313). Anyone who truly knows his Homer—and Ovid's educated contemporaries were eminently familiar with the Greek poet's work—will remember that the Nestor of the *Iliad*, whenever, as sometimes happens, the war takes a turn that is not to his liking, favors his fellow warriors with a long speech in which he waxes rhapsodic about the heroic deeds of his youth. "If I were as young as I was when . . . ," is how he begins—11.670 provides an example. And he claims to have done his magnificent deeds with, precisely, his spear (Watkins 1983). But since, even in Homer, the old man is already as boastful as he is garrulous, Ovid has the opening he needs: he can "at last" let his readers in on the secret of what Nestor, in his younger years, "really" used his spear for.

What makes for the special charm of Ovid's lines about Nestor's curious contribution to the Calydonian Hunt is something modern literary criticism calls "intertextuality." In the present instance, this generally very complex literary phenomenon takes the following very simple form: between Ovid's text and another, there exists a relationship, established by Ovid, thanks to which his text conveys a second meaning that emerges over and above the one accessible even on an ordinary reading. Thus the text addresses us on several parallel levels simultaneously. It might be compared to a piece of polyphonic music. One can adduce other examples of intertextuality in Ovid to show that the polyphony of his verse often results from the superimposition of *more* than two levels of meaning.

Of course, Ovid was neither the first nor the only ancient author to make a text polysemous by bringing it into relation with others. From its origins to late antiquity, all Greek and Roman poetry was predisposed to polyphony by dint of the fact that it relied heavily on stock themes and motifs. For example, as early as the fifth century B.C., when a tragedy that dramatized an episode from the Trojan cycle was staged in Athens, the audience could hear, behind many of the lines, the substance of a line from Homer. Ovidian intertextuality was, however, different: in Ovid and even in his predecessors among Roman poets from Catullus' generation onward, open or veiled inclusion of other authors' texts in one's own often took the form of a highly artificial game. The objective was to serve up intellectually stimulating entertainment to literary gourmets who had to know a great deal more than, say, an Athenian theatergoer in the classical period.

Intertextuality as a veritable end unto itself made its first appearance in Greek literature in the work of Hellenistic authors living in Alexandria, the seat of the Greek kings who had ruled Egypt since 305/304 B.C. These authors wrote for a pampered courtly public that was steeped in aesthetic pleasures and had correspondingly high standards. It is in Alexandria that we find the oldest breeding ground for the *poeta doctus* later incarnated by Ovid (and others) in Rome. The foremost Greek representative of the category was undoubtedly the writer and scholar Callimachus (c. 300–240), whose poetic style exercised a decisive influence on both the late Republican and early Augustan verse traditions, particularly on their subtle play with its pre-texts. We need, then, briefly to consider this Greek poet.

Typical of Callimachus and the other Alexandrians was the fact that, while constantly drawing on the classical Greek tradition in their own poetic work, they radically altered both its form and its content. As far as form was concerned, they replaced the full-scale epic with either the *epyllion* (miniature epic) or the verse narrative in elegiac couplets (regularly alternating lines of hexameter and pentameter), often grouped with other elegiac narratives to create a "collective poem." Thus it was "minor" genres that poets preferred in this period, which consequently also saw the first flowering of the epigram. In this spirit, when Callimachus programmatically declared that a "big book" was like "a big evil," he was not only demanding that poems be kept down to modest size, but also calling, in matters of form, for a carefully crafted language of the utmost refinement, one that would substitute wit and irony for archaic emotionalism and be as rich as possible in stylistic nuance, allusion, and *trouvailles*. And, on the thematic level, Callimachus pulled the old mythical figures who had earlier served as the subjects of poetry down from the pedestal of the early Greek heroic age and into the world of the Hellenistic capital his public lived in, the everyday world of urban life with all its problems. Among them were the trials and tribulations that erotic passion could bring—a favorite Alexandrian theme.

It is true that the theme which serves as a frame for Callimachus' miniature epic *Hecale* (like most of the poet's works, *Hecale* has survived only in fragmentary form but can still be followed to a certain extent) was an illustrious exploit by the Athenian hero Theseus—his triumph over a monster, here the bull of Marathon. But the centerpiece of the narrative is a description, painted in loving detail, of the idyllic visit the hero pays the epic's titular figure, a poor but hospitable little old lady. Here as elsewhere, Callimachus arranges to treat a theme that is as far off the beaten track as possible, and, in that sense, unclassical. In the process, he calls on the full range of the artistic techniques that recur constantly in Roman poetry from Catullus to Ovid—among them, precisely, the creation of polyphony on the plane of the textual enunciation. In Callimachus as in his successors, this is sometimes pursued to the point of riddling, so that the reader ultimately finds herself in the position of a detective searching for all the levels of meaning in a given line. What is more, considerable erudition, veiled or flaunted, is often incorporated into the text; we see this, for example, whenever the poet explains a custom, religious holiday, or name by recounting a myth. It was by way of a collection of such *aitia* (explanatory legends), entitled just so, *Aitia,* that Callimachus exerted a profound influence on all of Augustan poetry, Ovid in particular.

Thus those who read Ovid in his own day—the subject before us is still the knowledge they brought to their reading of his work—found themselves dealing with a relatively long-standing literary tradition when they saw the Roman poet playing with and "between" texts. They would accordingly have been willing—indeed, eager—to give Ovid's skill in this domain the appreciation it deserved. However, contemporary readers, specialists aside, can hardly do so without the help of scholarly commentary. They are just as hard put to appreciate another form of polyphony in Ovid's works, one akin to intertextuality: the kind a poet generates by making more or less veiled references to the events and institutions of the day—that is, by lacing his text with political allusions. This was another of the methods classical literature had, since its inception, consistently called on to produce polysemous discourse. As a rule, it meant that an author would write in such a way that his contemporaries could also read the political goings-on of the day between the lines of his texts.

Thus one has every reason to suspect a latent link to the Roman present when, in a myth in Ovid, one comes across a god or hero who is an autocrat like Augustus, the emperor who ruled Rome during most of Ovid's lifetime. In Book 1 of the *Metamorphoses,* for instance, where the poet describes how Jupiter conducts a meeting of the gods (163–252), even drawing a direct comparison between him and Augustus (204–205), he may be alluding to a meeting of the Senate convened by the emperor at one time or another. Or perhaps he is alluding to what he thinks typically goes on at such a meeting. But those of today's readers who lack the specialist's knowledge of the Augustan period are not the only ones who have trouble verifying their interpretations of this kind of polysemousness; even historians of the ancient world have a hard time of it, simply because not enough really exact knowledge of the course of political events in the period has come down to us. What we do know is based mainly on the reports of a few historians and biographers of the first three centuries of our era, who usually serve up anecdotes rather than solid facts and give their texts a tendentious cast into the bargain. Like literary texts, these texts therefore require interpretation. Thus it is no wonder that the specialists disagree as to whether Augustus' policies should be regarded as those of a high-handed dictator, a responsible ruler devoted to preserving the peace, or something of both. There are, accordingly, three diverging interpretations of Ovid's attitude toward the emperor among the poet's critics. Some hold that he was one of the sovereign's partisans, that is, pro-Augustan; others consider him a critic of the regime, or, in other words, anti-Augustan; the third party plumps for a compromise, arguing that Ovid took no interest in politics and must consequently be regarded as "un-Augustan."

One can see why today's reader of Ovid stands on treacherous ground in his search for political intertextuality in the Roman poet's work and why he constantly risks being carried away by a subjective judgment. It goes without saying that those who consider Ovid anti-Augustan have so far unearthed the greatest number of what they take to be veiled references to the emperor's policies. But the readers of Ovid's day may well have proceeded in much the same fashion. We have three reasons for thinking it highly probable that they expected the poet to make veiled allusions to contemporary events. First, the Latin language lends itself particularly well to wordplay and the use of coded language; indeed, polysemousness is one of its most conspicuous features. Second, it has been shown time and again that certain lines in dramas of the period were understood as allusions to well-known political personalities.

Third, the delight Ovid took in playing with different levels of meaning in a line of verse makes itself felt, as I have noted, in the way he handles his literary pre-texts. Even readers of his day, however, may have been unable to say with certainty whether this kind of playfulness included the making of coded political statements and, if so, what the general drift of those statements was. For the purpose of camouflage—and that may be what was involved here—is precisely to prevent certain people from immediately seeing through it.

The Ovid scholar is therefore best advised to bring allusions to contemporary events into her interpretations of a text only when they can be identified with certainty. I shall attempt to do so in discussing individual works. For the moment, however, we are still trying to develop approaches to the polyphony of Ovid's texts. Since I pointed out a moment ago that such polyphony can also be generated at the linguistic level in Latin, and quite easily at that, we shall proceed to examine this third and, for us, last level at which Ovid plays with and "between" texts.

As I have stressed from the outset, the present book is also and indeed especially addressed to readers who, because they have little or no Latin, can read Ovid only in bilingual editions or in translation. But, precisely for that reason, I need to begin with a general indication of what such readers will miss. For even if there is some doubt as to whether Ovid wove veiled political allusions into his verse, and, if so, how, one thing is beyond question: as a writer who dealt mainly with erotic subjects, he constantly exploited the ambiguity of Latin words to lace his texts with obscene double entendres.

Let us again take an example straightaway, from the *Art of Love* this time. Ovid, who slips into the role of a professor of "applied sexology" in this work, likes to shore up his arguments with mythological exempla. In his rendition of a Greek legend in Book 1 (681–704), he tells how Thetis, Achilles' mother, dresses her son in woman's clothing so that he will not have to go off to fight in the Trojan War. We next find him disguised as a woman and carding wool in King Lycomedes' palace in Scyrus with the king's daughter Deidamia; he capitalizes on the situation to rape her. There are only allusive references to the fact—something not directly relevant to the matter at hand, and known, moreover, to every reader of the day—that Achilles would soon be tricked by Odysseus into taking up arms and sailing for Troy with the Greeks after all. The lesson to be illustrated is that someone courting a woman's favors can count on receiving a positive response even if he resorts to force to achieve his ends. Let us see how matters stand with Deidamia:

Viribus illa quidem victa est (ita credere oportet):
   sed voluit vinci viribus illa tamen.
Saepe "mane," dixit, cum iam properaret Achilles;
   fortia nam posito sumpserat arma colo.
Vis ubi nunc illa est? Quid blanda voce moraris
   auctorem stupri, Deidamia, tui?

By force, to be sure, she was vanquished (that's what one must believe),
   but she really wanted to be vanquished by force.
She would often say, "Stay!/Wait!" [*mane*] when Achilles was already
   hurrying off,
for he had laid the distaff aside and taken up powerful arms [*arma*].
Where is it now, that force? Why do you detain, with a coaxing voice,
the man who has defiled you, Deidamia?

(699–704)

One might, at first blush, simply read the text as follows: Deidamia, raped by Achilles, not only enjoys her first union with the hero but also frequently begs for a repeat performance; she does so even after it is too late, because Achilles has already taken up arms [*arma*] and is hurrying off to Troy. On this reading, the word *mane,* which Deidamia uses in imploring Achilles to put off his departure, would mean "stay!"; we might accordingly imagine a touching seaside scene of farewell. But, in Latin, the *arma* Achilles grabs can also be understood metaphorically—as is attested in numerous passages—to mean his penis (which has already gone into action); in that case, the scene is taking place in bed. But, in bed, Deidamia says not "stay!" but "wait!" because she doesn't want Achilles to hurry to reach what she wants to reach with him: climax. Thus this woman, "detaining" (703: *moraris*) a lover who is racing out of control, is already—as S. J. Heyworth (1992) has rightly observed— referring Achilles to a specialized subdiscipline of the *ars amatoria,* one the professor of erotics will, at the end of Book 2 (725–728), enjoin all lovers of both sexes to learn: the *ars moratoria.*

As is shown by this example of a type of ambiguity found in much of Ovid's verse, our search for approaches to his work has brought us up against a dilemma. We began by observing that Ovid still has something to say to modern readers, that, indeed, he even frequently appears to *be* modern. Our first look at a text, however, has confronted us with the phenomenon of a polyphony generated by literary and perhaps also political allusions as well as double entendres. Although these could be recognized by contemporary readers and can still, by and large, be appreciated by classicists, most of them will, on an ordinary reading, remain invisible for the general public of our day. If today's readers are to understand the multiplicity of levels of meaning in Ovid, they need to be provided with a mass of background information by specialists. Of course, a book like this one cannot accomplish that task.

Naturally, I cannot content myself with establishing the intertextuality of Ovid's works using examples like those I have just cited and then make no attempt to bring out the "polyphonous" message of the individual poetic works, all of which I intend to interpret in their entirety here. For to proceed in that fashion would be to ignore something that was by no means unimportant for the author and his contemporary audience. But rather than focusing on short passages or individual words, one can bring out the polysemousness of Ovid's texts by attending to wider frames of reference, represented in the literary domain by, for example, genre. It is, indeed, particularly appropriate to take genre as one's starting point in discussing polyphony in Ovid's texts. For if, in reading Ovid, we remain alert to textual references to the subgenre "erotic elegy," then not only will our eyes be repeatedly opened to literary intertextuality, but we will even occasionally notice puns and references to contemporary events. It is, then, well worth taking a brief look at the elegiac system, as we shall now go on to do.

The Elegiac System

In antiquity, communication between authors and readers was essentially governed by the fact that an author situated his work in a particular generic tradition which his readers recognized as such. Even today, when the reader of a detective novel, for example, sees the author first conceal the murderer's identity and then invite him to solve the mystery along with the detective, he has the sense that he is being asked to play a kind of parlor game with clearly defined rules. Stock structures and themes guide author and reader down their common path through the novel; so do characters who can be referred to a basic model. The greater the intellectual demands the reader puts on a text, the harder the author must work to refine or modify the rules defining the game— or even to transform it into its exact opposite. Indeed, he has to parody it, if the reader wishes not merely to reflect along with the author, but to laugh into the bargain.

Among the various generic systems available in the Roman literature of the first century B.C., erotic elegy lent itself in multiple ways to the game of recognition I have just briefly described, using the detective novel as my example. Let us begin by mentioning what was most important here. First, the functioning of texts in this genre—poems composed in elegiac couplets, in which a young Roman *poeta* (poet) recounts his experiences as the *amator* (lover) of a *puella* (young woman)—is based on an odd and yet easily comprehensible set of rules governing the way the *poeta/amator* is to conduct himself with his *puella*. I shall briefly describe these rules below. Second, the generic system stands in a fixed relation to the contemporary reader's everyday world, which is both reflected in the erotic world and simultaneously wrenched out of joint there. We shall see how this happens in the next chapter, when we turn to the historical conditions of production of Ovid's works.

The basic form of the elegiac system is most easily deduced from the opening two books of the collections of elegies by Sextus Propertius (c. 50–15 B.C.) and Albius Tibullus (c. 50–18/17 B.C.). It was presumably first worked out by Cornelius Gallus (c. 69/68–26 B.C.), whose elegies have not survived, a few fragments aside. All three of these poets let the elegiac speaker speak in their name, so that it seems as if we are reading autobiographical confessions. But the stereotyped structures and themes of the poems and collections are by themselves enough to suggest what modern critics rightly take to be beyond question: the experiences of the *poeta/amator* are, no less than the figure of the *puella*—Lycoris in Gallus, Cynthia in Propertius, Delia or Nemesis in Tibullus—figments of the poetic imagination. It follows that the elegiac speaker cannot be identified with the author of the elegies. Indeed, everything seems decidedly artificial here. For, in the relationship between *poeta/amator* and *puella,* virtually irreconcilable opposites clash: the unwavering devotion of a morally upright, poetically talented, young upper-class Roman stands over against the infidelity of a hetaera from the class of freedwomen. Though cultivated and pretty as a picture, the hetaera shows a marked interest in money, jewelry, and the like and is happy to let one of the young man's rich rivals attend to her material wants.

Such a relationship can be sustained only if the *poeta/amator* submits unconditionally to the *puella*'s will on the one hand, and, on the other, consistently cuts himself off from society, which does not approve of such devotion to a woman on the part of a man, the more so as the woman is his social inferior. The man's submission resembles a slave's to his *domina* (mistress) and is for that reason known as *servitium amoris* (erotic servitude). It can manifest itself in the *poeta/amator*'s decision to remain lying on the *dura puella*'s (hard-hearted beloved's) threshold until the break of day, while she, for her part, sports in bed with his rival. On the threshold, the young man can give vent to his suffering by singing a *paraklausithyron* (Greek for a plaint sung at someone's door). For the Romans of Ovid's time, then, "elegy" meant primarily a poem of lament (as it still does today). It is usually in vain that the *poeta/amator* recites his lament before the closed door of his faithless beloved. Indeed, the futility of such erotic courting is a standard generic feature of erotic elegy.

The basic reason for the elegiac lover's isolation from society is the fact that he firmly rejects what the Roman upper class considered to be the ideal life for a young man. Members of the Roman equestrian and senatorial classes typically pursued a political and/or military career and single-mindedly increased their fortunes by engaging in commerce and/or exploiting and aggrandizing their landed estates. The Romans called such activity *negotium* (business; the literal sense is roughly "not doing-nothing"). But the slave of a *puella* does just the opposite: he lives exclusively for love, which is, for the aristocratic Roman, a species of *otium* (doing-nothing). Yet the elegiac lover resolutely and confidently assumes his choice to pursue this kind of life. For he is a soldier in the field of love, meaning that he has chosen to devote himself to *militia amoris* (erotic military service); as a *pauper amator* (impoverished lover), he renounces worldly wealth with all the passion of a moral philosopher.

The elegiac lover takes particular pride in excluding people associated with *negotium* not only from his life, but also from his poetry—in other words, in refusing to compose epics celebrating dramatic affairs of state, wars, or the acquisition of power and wealth. Standing with both feet firmly planted in the poetic tradition founded by Callimachus (see p. 5), he repeatedly and emphatically declares that "major" poetry is not what he is about: his love and his *puella* are his only themes. And this truculent insistence that he has opted to produce "minor" poetry—one speaks in this connection of an attitude of *recusatio* (refusal)—can even profit the *poeta/amator.* For he can accomplish two things by composing erotic elegies: first, the *puella,* if his art appeals to her, may at least briefly bestow her favors on him—although long-term success is out of the question even for "the poetry of courtship" (Stroh 1971); second, both *poeta/amator* and *puella* can win everlasting fame.

In his very first poetic work, the collection of elegies entitled *Amores* (Experiences of love), which bears an outward resemblance to the works of Propertius and Tibullus, Ovid begins to vary and parody the elegiac system of his predecessors, ultimately carrying it to the point of absurdity. Yet even in the other poems that are composed in elegiac couplets but, coming after the *Amores,* no longer consist of a young man's reports on his erotic experiences—the *Epistulae Heroidum* (Letters by mythical women), *Ars amatoria* (Art of love), and *Remedia amoris* (Love therapy)—the set of generic rules just evoked still hovers constantly in the background. Indeed, this holds even for the *Metamorphoses,* which are in hexameter, and for all the other varieties of elegiac poem that Ovid wrote: both the *Fasti* (Festival calendar) and also the poems of exile, the *Tristia* (Elegiac laments) and *Epistulae ex Ponto* (Letters from the Black Sea).

Since we will often have occasion to notice, in our discussions of individual works, the consummate skill with which Ovid modifies the elegiac system, we can for the moment content ourselves with briefly adducing three significant examples. The first involves a text displaying (it seems) purely literary polyphony. Among the *Epistulae* written in the name of various mythical women separated from their husbands or lovers, there is one (Letter 3) in which Briseis, well known as a captive in Homer's *Iliad,* upbraids Achilles, with whom she had been living, for consenting to hand her over to Agamemnon; she begs him to revive their love relationship. In transposing the epic material this story is based on to the realm of elegy, Ovid begins by having the man and woman exchange their wonted roles: he puts the love plaint in the woman's mouth and, adopting her viewpoint, presents the man as a hard-hearted lover. This technique of throwing the system out of joint is often used in the *Epistulae,* as we shall see. In this instance, moreover, Ovid takes a common elegiac metaphor at face value: Briseis is, after all, a slave, and thus in a state of *servitium amoris* in a very literal sense.

The poems in which the elegiac speaker bewails his banishment to Tomis on the Black Sea coast also grow out of a situation defined by interlocking personal roles: here, those of exile and emperor. Again and again, the exile entreats the emperor to let him, if he cannot return to Rome, at least move to a more pleasant place of banishment than the Black Sea coast, which (according to the exile) is almost permanently beset by icy cold and barbarian hordes. On a first reading of this poetry of exile, one does not immediately perceive that what is involved here too is a variation on the traditional elegiac distribution of roles, because the theme turns one's expectations in another direction. But as the borrowings from the language and conceptual world of Propertius, Tibullus, and Ovid's *Amores* begin to pile up, one gradually begins to see that the complaining lover of elegy has here become the man driven to despair by banishment. The exile too is lying on a hard "threshold"; he too cannot hope to enjoy what is waiting behind the "door," in the sense that he too finds his lot a hard one and is denied access to a better existence. Here the polyphony of the text expands to encompass the political realm, so to speak, inasmuch as it is now Augustus who is assigned the role of *dura puella.*

For our third example, which again involves erotic wordplay, let us tarry with the elegiac poet lying at his *puella*'s door. In many passages of elegiac poetry, the ambiguity of Latin words makes it eminently possible to construe—this is already the case in Propertius and Tibullus—an "entry" into the house of the *puella* as an "entry" into her body, which is what the lover is really after (Fruhstorfer 1986). This obviously applies to *Amores* 1.9, where the speaker sets up analogies between the activities of soldier and lover by taking the metaphor of *militia amoris* at face value. Consider, for instance, this metaphor: "ille graves urbes, hic durae limen amicae/obsidet; hic portas frangit, at ille fores"; "The one besieges cities it is hard to capture, the other the threshold/of his hard-hearted beloved; the one breaks down gates, the other doors [*fores*]" (19–20). Here the innocent may attend to nothing more than the empirical situation: the lover finds himself before the door or else forces it open (although the obscene meaning of *foris*/door is attested). But, five lines later, when "violence" is evoked again, the erotic connotation simply sweeps the literal meaning aside, and, with it, the pathos of "pure" love generally associated with elegiac discourse in Propertius and Tibullus: "nempe maritorum somnis utuntur amantes,/et sua sopitis hostibus arma movent"; "Lovers of course take advantage of the sleep of husbands/and set their arms [*arma*] into action while the enemy sleeps" (25–26). Indeed, in view of these examples of Ovid's playful treatment of texts and contexts to generate multiple associations, one might well wonder whether the poet, as he produced his voluminous oeuvre, always managed to avoid the pitfall of spoiling this sort of humor by working the game's stereotypical elements to death. It is true that, from ancient times down to our own day, he has often been criticized for a tendency to use and abuse certain basic elements, ranging from puns to full-length narrative structures. But Ovid's critics have failed to consider that the constant modification of linguistic and literary paradigms, as in the transformations of the elegiac system just examined, not only afforded readers an opportunity to engage in a mental exercise and test their wits in a game of recognition; it was also, and above all, intended systematically to develop possibilities for literary expression that Ovid's predecessors among the poets of antiquity exploited only rarely, if at all.

In the last section of this chapter, accordingly, I shall show that Ovid repeatedly broke new literary ground with his technique of metamorphosing the genre of the erotic elegy. I shall also show that, in so doing, he came close to certain varieties of the genre that holds by far the most important place in the literary spectrum of our day: the novel. That is, I shall sketch, in an introductory overview of Ovid's oeuvre, what will become abundantly clear when we look at individual poems: namely, that Ovid also exploited the procedure of playfully transforming motifs and structures to create poetic genres which offered him diverse ways of telling a "story."

"Before You Can Turn Around, Your Novel's Complete!"

Even in antiquity, as I said, readers criticized Ovid for treating certain themes too often and always at excessive length and thus for serving up too much of a good thing. Or, as Quintilian (c. 35–100) puts it in his *Institutio oratoria* (10.1.88), Ovid is *nimium amator ingenii sui* (rather too fond of his own talent). Many of Ovid's later critics have echoed this criticism, finding confirmation for it from the standpoint of Romantic literary theory. For the Romantics, the fact that a poet borrows his themes from other authors and constantly adapts them to his own ends demonstrates a lack of poetic originality. That Ovid actually elaborated on many of the themes he borrowed was considered particularly unpoetic. The critics failed to see that, in the process, something was created which could very well be called original (assuming that originality is what one is seeking in the first place).

To show how Ovid creates something new by adapting and simultaneously developing a theme, let us take an example: the poem *Amores* 3.7, in which the elegiacally enamored speaker bewails the fact that he was impotent at a love tryst. Many scholars have waxed indignant over the fact that the poet devotes a full eighty-four lines to this theme, which the Hellenistic poet Philodemus of Gadara dispatches in a six-line epigram (*Anthologia Graeca* 11.30) and Tibullus in only two lines of an elegy (1.5.39–40). Doubtless, this indignation has something to do with the fact that "one," or rather *men* (classicists were until recently almost exclusively of the male sex) considered the subject distasteful—indeed, taboo. But even in other, less "outrageous" instances in which Ovid richly embellishes a set theme, the critics have as a rule been unwilling to see this "excess," not as an artistic failing, but for what it manifestly is in *Amores* 3.7: a poetic technique deliberately put to work for purposes of literary innovation, a technique that Ovid pursues in intertextual dialogue with his predecessors. For what we have in this poem is not merely, as with Philodemus or Tibullus, the kind of retrospective reflection that was a standard form of discourse in epigrammatic or elegiac love poetry. Ovid gives us something more: he intertwines the speaker's chronologically unfolding lament with the chronology of his recollections of each particular act in his unsuccessful love-making with the *puella*.

Thus we not only hear a reflective monologue, but also experience "in dramatized form," step by step, in a sort of flashback—and here Ovid draws on all his immense talent for vividly recreating action—the incident that triggered the lover's lament: the first signs of his physical failing, the *puella*'s diligent but unsuccessful efforts to remedy matters, and the early termination of a scene that was highly embarrassing for both participants. And we also witness a sequel to the action during the monologue itself: the thing that was so immobile when the speaker was with the *puella* now begins to stir, getting a good dressing-down right in the middle of the monologue for its poor sense of timing. Thus what we have here is not only a poem, but also an exciting first-person verse narrative. Indeed, because *Amores* 3.7 takes its place in a sequence of elegies in which the speaker reconstitutes his erotic experiences in chronological order, what we have, in fact, is one episode of a first-person novel in verse.

For, after its fashion, Ovid's first work, the *Amores*, is indeed an erotic novel. True, there is nothing original about the fact that Ovid arranges the poems of the individual books to tell an ongoing story. For the principle of fictive chronology—as we may call it to distinguish it from the real order of composition, with which it does not necessarily coincide—is typical of Roman verse collections (and probably also of their Hellenistic forerunners, which have not survived): besides Ovid's immediate predecessors Propertius and Tibullus, for example, Catullus and Horace also use the device. But there is no little difference between Ovid's *Amores* and the "erotic novels" by the two older elegists. In Propertius and Tibullus, it is the elegiac system in its basic form that shapes the speaker's discourse; the *poeta/amator* reflects on his relationship to the *puella* far more often than he actually tells us how it is coming along. Erotic love is here consistently presented in its specifically elegiac manifestation alone, that is, as an experience of *servitium amoris* (erotic servitude) and socially alienated *otium* (inactivity). And as both states are to be understood more as metaphors than empirical realities, it is often well nigh impossible to identify either the situation in which the speaker of the individual poems finds himself or the concrete occasion for his lament. Many a reader, for example, has addled his brains trying to determine just where the speaker is in Tibullus' Elegy 1.2.

In the *Amores,* in contrast, the speaker's erotic experiences are not exclusively elegiac. His "experiences of love"—this is doubtless the most accurate translation of the title *Amores* (Gauly 1990, 33ff.)—are also, and above all, such that both ancient and modern readers can imagine them actually taking place. Thus they offer greater possibilities for identification than Propertius' or Tibullus' *amores*. And, first and foremost, they are always presented so graphically that, as *Amores* 3.7 shows, the borderline between elegy and epic is crossed in certain passages. The poetic technique at work here has already been nicely described by the "Merry Andrew" in the "Prelude in the Theater" of Goethe's *Faust,* Part 1:

> Well, use the wondrous inspirations, pray,
> And set about the poetic business straight away,
> Approach it as you would a love affair:
> You meet, you feel the spell, and linger there,
> And by and by you think yourself enchanted;
> At first you thrive; then obstacles are planted;
> You walk on air, then fall to bittersweet:
> Before you can turn around, your novel's complete!

(Wayne 1949, 34, translation modified)

A "romance" (German *Roman*), in the twofold sense of "romantic adventure" and "narrative of romantic adventures," is precisely what the *Amores* offers from the very first poems of the sequence presented here. Similarly, the fusion of "poetic business" and actually experienced erotic adventures marks the elegiac speaker's twofold role as *poeta* and *amator.*

Amores is, then, a novel in poems. It has a modern fictional equivalent in the epistolary novel, such as *The Sorrows of Young Werther.* One point of resemblance resides in the fact that ancient elegy is a poetic form in which, usually, someone is addressed, as in a letter. In Ovid's first collection of poems from exile, the *Tristia* (Elegiac laments), there is a gradual transition from elegy to letter over the course of the five books in which the poems are arranged. But, with this arrangement, Ovid creates something very much like an "epistolary novel." The exile who bemoans his bitter fate frequently associates his elegiac lament with reports on all he has endured since the day he took his forced leave of Rome. The upshot is a chronological first-person narrative about the narrator's journey to his place of banishment, his first experiences in exile, and his efforts to adapt to his new situation. As his exile wears on, he even goes through a metamorphosis that makes a provincial out of him; he forgets more and more of his Latin (such, at any rate, is his claim). Because he also offers us detailed descriptions of the place and the people, his "epistolary novel" is a fictional travelogue as well. For the moment, we do not need to ask whether what we have here is really something akin to a fictional first-person narrative, and not—as one might suppose—an elegiac autobiography. In either case, the poem bears a resemblance to the modern epistolary novel and, more particularly, to an ancient prototype of the epistolary novel that had already emerged in the Greek literature of the Hellenistic period.

Even more like the modern epistolary novel than the *Tristia* are the three pairs of letters found at the end of our editions of the *Epistulae Heroidum* (Letters to and from mythical women). For not only are the authors of these letters fictional characters—in one, for example, the legendary swimmer Leander writes to his Hero (Letter 18)—but we also have a "real" correspondence, however brief, in all three cases: Leander's letter is immediately followed by Hero's answer (Letter 19). In contrast, the fifteen letters preceding the paired letters, by fourteen mythical women and the poet Sappho, all go unanswered. As we shall see, these fifteen individual letters probably first appeared in three books of elegies in the order in which they have come down to us. Thus they comprised a triptych, like the *Amores,* which is also divided into three books. But here there is no running plot line, as there is in the "Experiences of Love." For, from poem to poem, the myth cycles under-lying *Epistulae* 1 to 14 change.

There is an important difference between the elegiacally enamored speaker of the *Amores* and the female authors of the individual letters of the *Epistulae.* The *poeta/amator* goes through a process of development and (as will appear in a moment) is, indeed, "transformed," like the exile in the *Tristia.* The laments of the women in love, in contrast, are occasioned precisely by their refusal to consent to a change in their love lives. They wish to see the men they love, separated from them when they write their letters, come back and love them just as they did before the separation. That, however—as the reader, in any event, knows—will never happen, at least not the way they want it to. The author of the let-ters that make up the *Epistulae ex Ponto* (Letters from the Black Sea) is in a similar predicament. But while these elegies of exile also follow a rough chronological scheme, they do not narrate successive episodes of a developing story as straightforwardly as the "epistolary novel" *Tristia.* Indeed, the exile here finds himself in a situation that holds out scant prospect for change, at least for as long as he remains in this particular place of banishment.

Among the verse collections in Ovid's oeuvre, then, we find, along-side those structured in a way that invites comparison with the epistolary novel, others that are not so structured. Where there *is* "plot" develop-ment, it is essentially determined by metamorphoses. The exile of the *Tristia* changes from a Roman into a Getan. The speaker of the *Amores* is transformed first from an epic poet into an elegiac poet and lover (that, at any rate, is what he claims to be in 1.3), then into a would-be Don Juan, and finally into the caricature of an elegiac lover, only to go back to being an author of "major" poetry—who, however, now writes tragedies.

In Ovid's remaining works, which do not consist of elegiac poems arranged in series, we again find both novelistic structures and the "principle of metamorphosis." With the composition of the *Ars amatoria* (Art of love) and the *Remedia amoris* (Love therapy), the adaptation of the elegiac system initially proceeded as follows: to show his readers, both male and female, how to avoid suffering the way elegiac lovers do, Ovid slipped into the new role of a professor of love who speaks in the first person and provides systematic instruction in all the arts and branches of knowledge touching on erotic love. Through a process of generic transformation initiated in the *Amores*—and, in a certain sense, the *Epistulae Heroidum* 1–15 as well, since the speakers in that work are women—an elegiac subgenre, the didactic erotic poem, gradually begins to emerge. An additional metamorphosis comes about within each of the two new works. However, it is not the speaker who undergoes it, as in the *Amores*, but his male and female students, and, in their wake, Ovid's men and women readers: in the *Ars*, people with little or no experience of love are changed into consummate lovers, while, in the *Remedia*, the love-sick are cured.

This brings us back to the kinship between Ovid's work and certain species of the modern novel. Admittedly, the *Ars* and the *Remedia* are didactic poems, not narratives. But since a "hero" in love and a "heroine" in love figure in them alongside the professor/poetic speaker—namely, the male and female student or the male and female reader—we can certainly speak of a novelistic theme, at least if we are thinking of fiction, in which it is hardly unusual to find the reader doubling as a character who takes part in the action. Besides, the two poetic manuals have a decidedly "metamorphic" bent.

The theme of transformation is announced in the very title of the major work written immediately after *Ars/Remedia:* the *Metamorphoses*. Ovid, who here treats of mythological transformations, has metamorphosed himself into a "proper" narrator and replaced elegiac with epic meter, although, as we shall see, he has by no means abandoned elegiac themes. At first one hesitates to draw parallels between this poem and the novel. But it may in any case be said that the *Metamorphoses*, regarded from a strictly formal point of view, is probably the most mature narrative work of classical antiquity. Here one encounters such a multiplicity of narrative techniques worked out in the finest detail that no one in search of descriptive models to help provide an adequate account of this text (which I can only do in bare outline in this book) can avoid comparing it to the modern novel. And, after all, the *Metamorphoses* too has a plot line: the ongoing account of the transformations the world has witnessed from the creation of the universe out of chaos down to the Augustan age.

Finally, there is the *Fasti* (Festival calendar). This is yet another didactic poem in elegiac couplets in which traditional elegiac themes again come to the fore. But, this time, the subject of the lesson is the unfolding sequence of the Roman year. What changes here, then, is the seasons. Their succession constitutes the "plot," which in a certain sense again includes the reader, for whom each of the Roman festivals is explained and simultaneously brought to life. But while the professor of love can invoke his (erotic) empirical experience to set himself apart from the reader, the speaker who undertakes to explain the calendar has only a layman's knowledge of his subject. As in the *Metamorphoses,* the utilization of various narrative devices plays a significant role in this work too. Why the "story" of the constant changes of the calendar year should suddenly break off at the end of the first half of the process of transformation is, in the present context, not our concern.

What I have tried to emphasize in the last section of this chapter is that metamorphosis is an important principle in Ovid's works. So far we have been mainly concerned with the phenomenon of generic metamorphosis. It has doubtless become clear by now that Ovid, starting out from the "grammar" of the generic system of "erotic elegy," which his readers knew well, developed new variants of the system—indeed, new genres—that bring to mind certain types of the modern novel. Metamorphosis is not only, however, a salient feature of Ovid's poetic technique; it also contributes significantly to the image that the poet conveys through his descriptions of character and milieu, as I have already at least begun to show. But I cannot go into that in detail before discussing the individual works.

Let me, however, point out at this early stage that change was probably the very thing people did *not* regard as typical of the formative events of the period in which these poems were composed. For one thing, the policies pursued by the first Roman emperor were intended precisely to preserve or revive the most venerable religious, moral, and (so he claimed, at any rate) political traditions. For another, by way of its official discursive and iconographic self-representation, his government encouraged Romans to believe that, with his era, a Golden Age had dawned on earth and that the future could bring nothing better. Hence the question that we shall take up in the next chapter: what information has come down to us about the kind of life Ovid, the poet of changes, led in an era shaped by a ruler who held no brief for the "principle of metamorphosis"?

Approaches to the Poet: Historical and Literary Sources of Ovid's Vita

Playing with His Life

One often reads that Ovid is the Roman poet about whom by far the most is known. But this "knowledge" is based almost exclusively on statements made by the first-person speaker of his work. Two further sources add little more. The indications of the titles in the manuscripts give the poet's full name, Publius Ovidius Naso. (In the poems themselves, one always finds the poet's cognomen, Naso, the only one of his names that fits the meter.) The rhetorician Seneca the Elder (c. 55 B.C.–40 A.D.), who met Ovid when he was studying rhetoric as a young man, says in his *Controversiae,* more than half a century later, that Ovid had a penchant for oratory that stood him in good stead in his subsequent creative work. But Seneca's "memoirs" are of dubious historical value. For, before sitting down to write them, Seneca had come to know the poet's celebrated oeuvre and was manifestly projecting his opinion of it back onto his account of Ovid's early exercises in declamation, of which he even gives us a sampling (*Contr.* 2.2.8). We have here an instance of the practice of drawing inferences about the past from the present that is a hallmark of ancient biography. The child is father to the man, as Seneca knew—because he knew the man.

But is the information that Ovid himself gives us in the first person singular any more reliable? True, most of it does come from a text that is usually referred to as "autobiographical," the poem *Tristia* 4.10. But we saw in Chapter 1 that whenever Ovid says "I" in a work, he has already assumed a role descended from the fictive "I" of erotic elegy. The exile who speaks in the first person must likewise be primarily regarded as

21

incarnating such a role. Using what is considered to be an autobiographical passage from the poem *Ex Ponto* 2.10, Gareth Williams (1994, 42ff.) has shown that there is a certain kinship between this role and that of the speaker of the *Amores*. We shall briefly discuss this passage in our turn.

The exile addresses his elegiac letter to a friend, the poet Macer, whom he had already addressed in the erotic elegy *Amores* 2.18. Here as there, Ovid confronts the "major" and "minor" genres in the person of the epic poet on the one hand and the speaker of the elegies on the other. Thus, following Callimachus, he works a variation on the theme of the *recusatio* (see p. 12). In *Ex Ponto* 2.10, the same theme appears in conjunction with a reminiscence about a voyage the speaker undertook with his friend at some unspecified time in the past. Their journey begins with a tour of "Asia Minor's splendid cities" under Macer's lead. Then, still under Macer's lead, they head for Sicily, where they visit Aetna with its flame, spat out by the Giant lying beneath it. As they travel across the island, they pass by Lake Palicus on their way from Henna to rivers associated with the mythical names of Anapus, Cyane, Alpheus, and Arethusa. The poem even mentions two means of transportation: "seu rate caeruleas picta sulcavimus undas,/esseda nos agili sive tulere rota"; "Whether we furrowed the blue waves in a painted ship,/Or whether a carriage [*esseda*] carried us with swift wheel" (33–34). The voyage is eventful; but, on closer inspection, it turns out that it is also— or perhaps only?—literary. For the fact that Macer serves as guide in the cities of Asia Minor (and thus probably in Troy as well) and does so again on the journey to Sicily, where the travelers reach their first port of call, fire-spitting Aetna, indicates that the world of the *Iliad* and the *Aeneid* (whose hero also travels to Sicily and Aetna) and the epic battles of the Giants are being assigned to the epic poet's domain. As to the way stations on their route across the island—the poet describes them in four lines, as he does Macer's literary realm (21–24/25–28), and mentions them again, in the same order, in the story of the Rape of Proserpina in Book 5 of the *Metamorphoses* (359ff.)—they fall under Ovid's poetic jurisdiction. What holds for the itinerary holds for the means of transportation as well. Not only is travel by ship and coach one of the Augustan poets' favorite metaphors for the author's and reader's progress through a work, but, in particular, the means of transportation used here—both named in the same couplet, each in a line—stand for "major" and "minor" poetry. We find another version of the "painted" ship which "furrows" the blue waves in hexameter in Virgil's *Aeneid* (5.158 or 5.663, for instance); *esseda* is also the name given to the kind of vehicle that carries Cynthia to Tibur in Propertius (2.32.5) and that is supposed to bring the *puella* to Sulmo in *Amores* 2.16.49.

Who can say if Ovid's literary voyage actually took place, and, if so, when? It is of course possible that everything really happened as depicted here. But the intertextuality of Ovid's poem plainly matters more to the poet than its autobiographical content, which he could, after all, have decided to simplify and make more precise. In any event, it is going too far to try to date the journey—which is, naturally, put down to Ovid's youth—and then describe its importance in the poet's *vita* this way: "He came home with a treasure-chest of carefully preserved memories, drawing on them to sustain the marvelous vividness of his verse" (Kraus 1968, 69).

This example admonishes us to exercise extreme caution in evaluating the "autobiographical" references of a poet who plays not only with literary and other contexts, but "with his life" as well. Moreover, Ovid and other ancient writers repeatedly drop remarks to the effect that the world of a poem's speaker can diverge from his author's. The oldest extant passage of the sort is in Catullus: he explains to the two addressees of *Carmen* 16 that they should not conclude from the obscenity of his poems that he himself is immoral. Similar statements occur in several passages in Ovid's work (*Amores* 3.15.4; *Tristia* 1.9.59–60; 2.353–356; 4.10.68; *Ex Ponto* 2.7.47–50). This suggests that we have to scrutinize the purportedly autobiographical indications in the poem *Tristia* 4 very closely indeed before deciding which may be treated as historical facts and which give us reason to believe that the poet has subjected them to literary stylization.

Let us first extract and assemble, from *Tristia* 4.10 and other texts by Ovid, the biographical material whose historical reality no one has cause to doubt. The poet was born to an old family of landed aristocrats on 20 March 43 B.C. in Sulmo, a city some ninety miles from Rome that was the capital of the Paeligni, an Italian tribe. In Rome, he belonged to the second order of the upper class, the *ordo equester* (knighthood). He was trained in the law by eminent rhetoricians, together with a brother exactly one year his senior who died as a young man. That he could have embarked on a senatorial career after completing his education strongly suggests that he was a man of means. In any case, he was wealthy enough to renounce a political and military career at about the age of twenty; by that age, he had already held minor posts in the Roman administration (it is no longer possible to determine precisely which) and was on the verge of attaining the lowest senatorial rank, that of quaestor. Living in the capital without material wants, in constant contact with colleagues and the reading public, he could now devote himself entirely to poetry. It was probably in the fall of 8 A.D., after he had lost his parents, married for the third time, and had a daughter who herself had two children by two marriages, that the Emperor Augustus banished him for life to Tomis, a town in Dobrogea on the Black Sea coast. His banishment took the comparatively mild form of a *relegatio* (relegation), which meant that he was not deprived of his civil rights or property. After publishing several works of poetry—obviously, he could still publish—he probably died in exile, never amnestied by Augustus or his successor Tiberius, despite the appeals for clemency that run through his work. He may have died shortly after finishing Book 4 of *Letters from the Black Sea,* which contains datable references to 15/16. If so, his death can be put around 17/18.

This is meager—so meager that it can no more serve as the basis for a biographical interpretation of Ovid's work, were that our object, than can our biographical data about other Roman poets. But what of the remaining affirmations in *Tristia* 4.10? In my deliberately guarded historical evaluation of the elegy, the statement that, for example, Ovid's father often dismissed the boy's early attempts at poetry as "profitless art" (21–22) must be put down to free embellishment of the "autobiography." The same applies to the first public reading of poems from the *Amores* by their roughly eighteen-year-old author (57–58). But what evidence is there to support this view? Above all: how is one to regard what the exile says in this poem and the other elegies of exile about his life in Tomis? Do they too have only limited historical value? Is the same true of the hints about the reasons for his exile thrown out in a number of the poems about his banishment?

Let us begin with *Tristia* 4.10. Form and content of this meticulously composed elegy turn on pointed, carefully crafted antitheses, of which the dichotomies "carefree youth in Rome/hard old age in exile" and "political career/poetic muse" are the two most important. Ovid has expressed this in structural terms by laying out his "autobiography" on the pattern of Roman prose biographies. This traditional tripartite scheme, which first appears in Cornelius Nepos' *Life of Atticus* (c. 100–25 B.C.) and then recurs regularly in the biographies of the emperors by Suetonius (c. 70–after 121), takes the following form: the first part, not overly long, essentially chronicles the future emperor's life down to his assumption of office; the second, forming a broad middle section, treats, under separate rubrics, the emperor's different virtues (and/or vices) and deeds; the third, which is, again, shorter and basically chronological, recounts the emperor's last years.

In Ovid, the first part is forty lines long; it runs down to the passage in which the exile, after giving us a chronological report on the first twenty years of his life, declares that he acceded to the Muses' demand that he live a life of leisure (*otia*) rather than seeking office as a senator. In other words, he here describes his version of "taking office." The somewhat longer middle section of the poem (41–90) contains two subsections of almost exactly the same length in which, under separate rubrics, we are given further information about the exile's life. In ll. 41–64, he lists the Roman poets famous in his youth, some of whom he knew personally, tacking himself onto the end of the list as its youngest member. In ll. 65–90, he tells us first about his three wives, daughter, and two grandchildren and then about the death of his parents. Finally, the third part of the poem (91–132), roughly as long as the first, is about his "last years" in the sense that the poet, portraying himself as a graying exile, proffers a chronological sketch of the hardships he has so far endured in banishment and then proudly affirms that his muse, a source of constant comfort, has already assured him the kind of fame usually accorded a man only after his death (121–122).

Thus the banished poet presents himself as, on the one hand, a man who has suffered constantly since he left Rome—as we shall soon briefly see, the picture is doubtless overdrawn—and, on the other, as an aging poet who has already achieved immortality. It seems to me plain enough that this stylized self-representation, which is manifestly what matters most to Ovid in *Tristia* 4.10, has also colored the self-portrait of the artist as a young poet. For, at opposite poles from the old man in exile, that boyish writer is the very type of the elegist brimming with youth and vigor. As such, he draws a sharp dividing line, to begin with, between himself and the world of *negotium* represented by his father and brother. In ll. 17–20, his brother's hopes to acquire the "weapons of the forum" are contrasted with the banished author's early poetic bent; the statement about his father follows. Of course, the youthful elegist who proceeds to give public readings of his first love poems must be made to seem as young as possible, since he serves as a foil for the long-suffering gray-haired poet. Only if we fail to appreciate the intended antithesis will we take the exile's affirmation that he had "trimmed his beard but two or three times" when this reading took place (58) so literally that we fix the date of the event as 25 B.C. and identify that as the year in which Ovid began working on the *Amores*. This text is too profoundly shaped by Ovid's playful treatment of the elegiac system for us to exploit it as a database for the historical reconstruction of a vita.

But let us turn from Ovid's youth to his life in exile and the reasons for his banishment. Of course, in both collections of elegies written in Tomis, those of the banished poet's laments which revolve around his absence from Rome have a basis in reality: it undoubtedly was a blow for the real individual Ovid to be cut off from his family, the metropolis with its many cultural advantages, his circle of friends, and the audiences who attended his readings. But what he tells us about the suffering he endured because of an all-but-perpetual icy winter, the proximity of barbarians of the most primitive sort, and the constant threat to which his town was exposed by mounted hordes letting fly with poisoned arrows stands in flagrant contradiction to the persuasive conclusions reached in modern studies of the ancient Black Sea region (most recently Claassen 1990). These studies indicate that present-day Dobrogea was a major grain-producing region, which by itself proves that it cannot have been almost permanently covered by snow and ice. Moreover, as a city that had been founded by Greek colonizers and that boasted a *gymnasion,* a kind of center for cultural activities, Tomis could hardly have been as barbaric a place as the exile never wearies of making it out to be.

The descriptions of the place and the people in Ovid's elegies of exile are thus demonstrably not based on personal observation. Rather, they derive from literary sources such as the equally fictional account of the Scythians in Virgil's *Georgics* (3.349ff.), of which we sometimes hear verbal echoes in, for example, the elegy *Tristia* 3.10. It follows that Ovid's desire to create a polyphonous text has again shaped what he says, so that we should take the world painted in the poems of exile for a poetic world, not an accurate reflection of the real one Ovid was banished to. Indeed, as our discussion of the texts will show, a variation on the generic system of erotic elegy underpins even this "narrative" of an elegiac speaker's experiences.

Of course, nothing requires us to go to the same lengths as some of Ovid's recent critics, who take the story of the poet's banishment to Tomis for pure invention. They can, it is true, marshal the compelling argument that all the ancient texts by authors other than Ovid himself which mention Ovid's exile are plainly influenced by his *Tristia* and *Epistulae ex Ponto,* so that the poet is our only first-hand witness to his *relegatio.* But there are more convincing counterarguments. For example, we might note that, if the theme of the poor banished poet had been a fiction, Ovid could hardly have held his readers' interest with it through nine books of verse containing a total of 6,726 lines. Again, it is conceivable that Augustus was not vexed by a literary game in which, over the course of two or three books, a banished poet's sufferings are laid at his door; had such a game gone on any longer, however, it would surely have galled the emperor, and not without reason.

We may, then, safely assume that Ovid lived in Tomis from about 9 to 18 A.D. But we do not know *how* he lived there. Unfortunately, we also cannot say—this brings us to the second problem posed by his banishment—*why* he had to live there. In the role of the poet making his elegiac lament, he names two reasons for his *relegatio* (going into the greatest detail in *Tristia* 2): to begin with, he committed an indiscretion (*error*) that deeply offended the emperor; second, he was punished for writing the *Ars amatoria,* which, as Augustus saw it, offered lessons in adultery. Even if we assume that the *Ars* really was the second count in the indictment—as we by no means must, since Ovid may have fabricated the charge because, as we shall see (pp. 180f.), he thought he could convincingly refute it—this count would doubtless have weighed less heavily than the first. For, when the banishment order was issued, eight years had elapsed since publication of the *Art of Love.* Moreover, as far as the *error* is concerned, the exile frequently gives us to understand that if he revealed what it was, he would vex the emperor all over again. Naturally people have, since the beginning of the modern era, striven mightily to penetrate the secret of the *error.* Yet although this has given rise to "a whole industry devoted to cracking the mystery," as Gareth Williams nicely puts it (1994, 174), no one has come up with a truly convincing solution down to the present day, and chances are that no one ever will.

What we *can* assess fairly well is the political climate that prevailed around 8 A.D. and might have inclined the emperor to chastise the poet so severely for his *error.* I shall consider the question below. First, however, I need to discuss, within the narrower framework of my account of Ovid's vita, the order in which his works were published. Since it is easier to understand the context here if one knows something about the conditions governing the dissemination of literary texts in Rome about the time of Christ's birth, we shall first discuss that.

From Little Wax Tablets to the Royal Codex

Anybody wishing to form a reasonably accurate picture of what communication between an author and his public was like in antiquity—here too there are very few genuinely historical sources, so that a great deal remains vague—must begin by largely forgetting modern conceptions of the book trade. For while we usually come to know a novel, for example, by reading a published edition of the text, but only rarely by hearing it read aloud and even more rarely by going to a reading by the author, literature in antiquity was primarily written for the ear. Before becoming accessible in book form, a literary work would be read aloud, first by the author himself, but also, both before and after publication, by readers expressly trained for the task. These *lectores,* freedmen or slaves, would ply their art to entertain, say, a rich gentleman, the gentleman and his guests, or, in some cases, a large audience ıeater. And even if a Roman of Ovid's day wanted to read a book in ɪɪɪ ɔ ᴜʌn company, he generally read it out loud.

It seems probable that the phase during which a new work circulated before being published in written form lasted for quite some time. For one of the reasons an author recited his most recent production was to test out the reaction of his public; this would help him decide whether the text should be turned over to a copyist or not, and, if so, whether it ought to be revised first. Initially, the audience at a reading would be very small indeed; but, as the number of those who came to recitations steadily increased, these could eventually attain the dimensions of a public event. The first auditors would be close friends of the writer's; they might be followed by the larger group that we today call a literary circle. But this expression should be employed with caution, because such a group would probably have coincided, in most cases, with the one formed by a patron and his clients. Here the political, legal, and economic interests of those who sought protection and support from a particularly wealthy, influential patrician outweighed the need to encourage a new literary trend by forming a circle that would promote it by word of mouth.

Thus the "circle of Maecenas," which Virgil, Horace, and Propertius are usually said to have belonged to, or the "circle of Messalla," generally supposed to have included Tibullus and Ovid, is not comparable to the literary salons of the nineteenth century. It is, moreover, uncertain whether Ovid really "belonged to" such a "circle" at all, since he was doubtless wealthy enough to manage without one. We do learn in the *Epistulae ex Ponto* that the poet was on close terms with the family of Marcus Valerius Messalla Corvinus and that Messalla was the first to "impel" him to "render" his poems "up to fame" (2.3.75–78). But Ovid was most likely simply a good friend of the patrician's and of his two sons, Messalinus and Cotta. In general, it would seem that he was eager to see his new works move beyond the elite circle of those closest to him as quickly as possible, so that they could be heard by a broad public. One indication of this is the fact that, in striking contrast to other Augustans we know of, Ovid dedicated none of the works that he himself was able to publish in Rome to anyone; moreover, he directly addressed friends in individual poems only in his first work, the *Amores*—and in just three poems at that (1.9; 2.10; 2.18). Again, the fact that Ovid's first public reading is expressly mentioned in the "autobiography" (*Tristia* 4.10.57–58) tends to suggest that he was at pains to reach a wide audience.

However Ovid himself may have gone about reciting a newly composed work, one notices at every turn in his poetry, as in that of the other Augustans as well, that it depends on effects which would have had greater impact in a recitation by the author than on a silent reading. To gain some sense of this, one has only to imagine Ovid himself reciting the conclusion to, say, *Amores* 1.5. Here the speaker—in a public reading, this would have been the flesh-and-blood author standing before his audience—offers a graphic description of the physical charms of Corinna, whom he undressed during a midday tryst. The description starts with her shoulders and works its way down to her legs. The speaker goes on to tell us that, after observing her beauty, he pressed her to him again and again; then, abruptly, he brings the poem to a conclusion with these words: "cetera quis nescit? Lassi requievimus ambo./proveniant medii sic mihi saepe dies"; "What happened afterwards?—who does not know? Exhausted, we both rested./May midday often be like that for me" (25–26). There is no overestimating the stir that must have agitated the togas on the auditors' benches!

In Rome, the audience at an authorial reading would probably have been relatively small when it was recruited from the senatorial and equestrian ranks alone; but audiences could also include members of the other classes living in the capital. However, if the writer wanted to reach an unlimited number of interested listeners in Rome and beyond, he had to prepare and release a final, written version of his work for distribution in book form after the "trial period" of oral publication had come to an end. Now, at last, what he had begun by drafting on his *tabella* (or *codicillus*), a little wax-covered wooden tablet, could set out on its journey for the whole Latin-speaking world. The immediate condition for this was that various people copy the manuscript once it had been given the writer's imprimatur: these would have been friends, copyists working for public libraries—under Augustus, there were three such book collections in Rome—and people in the employ of book dealers. All the copies thus produced might in their turn serve as a basis for further copies; this applied even to the ones held by the book dealers, to whom private persons could dispatch their copyists.

What thus found its way into the reader's hands was not, of course, a book he could leaf through or comfortably read, but a papyrus roll that had to be laboriously scrolled off a rod. And what he found on the papyrus was not always elegant calligraphy, but, often, a rather rough scrawl that would in any event have been hard to decipher because, in this period, there were no upper- and lower-case letters, punctuation marks, spaces between words, or other such devices to facilitate the reader's task. No wonder, then, that those who could afford it—and people who owned literary works were as a rule well off—left the business of reading (aloud) to a *lector*. In any event, this kind of book did not accommodate "reading around" in a work or "opening it here or there." That books took this form may also have had something to do with the fact that what was written on a roll "steadily progressed," constituting a "plot" in the case of literary texts, even when what the roll contained was poems strung out one after the next. Of course, what we find "unrolling" in the extant books of ancient poetry is not always a purposefully unfolding story line; often the individual texts are linked only in a loose conceptual sequence. Yet it always *is* a sequence, somehow; and, as we saw in the preliminary overview in the previous chapter, Ovid visibly made a conscious effort to camp most of his books of poetry on something like a "story."

The surviving manuscripts of Ovid's works are not papyrus rolls; they have all come down to us in that form of the book which, after gaining wider and wider currency from the days of the early Empire on, ultimately replaced the papyrus roll altogether: namely, the codex, ancestor of the modern book. With one exception, a fragment of a fifth-century manuscript of the *Epistulae ex Ponto* (today in Wolfenbüttel, Aug. 4° 13.11), all the Ovidian manuscripts we have are medieval codices. They are, moreover, plentiful. The texts of those dating from the ninth to the thirteenth centuries—for instance, the Paris Codex Regius (Royal codex) of the *Amores, Ars,* and *Remedia* (Parisinus Latinus 6311)—doubtless hew most closely to the wording of the ancient manuscripts. But even these texts are not free of doubtful readings and, in some cases, hopelessly corrupt passages that confront us with major problems, especially in the *Epistulae Heroidum,* Books 5 and 6 of the *Fasti,* and the *Tristia.* Students of ancient literature must resign themselves to the fact that the most trustworthy copy, the last in a long series, may be so corrupt in places that even the most astute textual emendation cannot recover what the author wrote centuries earlier. Critics of Ovid, in particular, would do well to confess what the textual editor Robin Nisbet once put this way: "I could not emend Ovid, because he is too clever." But the bulk of the surviving texts are reliable enough to make meaningful interpretation possible.

In the course of the first millennium after Ovid's death, a number of texts that the codices incorrectly attribute to the poet crept into the Ovidian corpus. Most of this pseudo-Ovidiana is, to be sure, easy to spot, if only because the language it is composed in is plainly not that which was written in Augustus' day, but medieval Latin. It is harder to decide for or against the authenticity of poems that the codices identify as Ovid's when these seem to have been written in roughly the same period as the indubitably authentic work, while displaying suspicious deviations in language and content.

Three texts ought not to be regarded as Ovid's, for the arguments of the philologists who have branded them pseudo-Ovidiana are more persuasive than the arguments for their authenticity: (1) The *Consolatio ad Liviam* (Poem of consolation for Livia), an elegy nearly five hundred lines long, in which the author tries to comfort Livia, Augustus' wife, for the premature death of her son Drusus, killed in an accident in 9 B.C.; (2) the elegy *Nux* (The walnut tree), a 182-line poem in which a walnut tree standing by the side of the road complains that passers-by can throw stones at it with impunity—a text one can read as an allegory for Ovid's plight in exile; and (3) the *Halieutica* (On fish and fishing), a very fragmentary text (it contains only 134 hexameter lines) that is hard to emend in places. The one intact passage of this didactic poem begins with a comparison between the means of self-preservation available to fish and land-dwelling animals and breaks off in the middle of a long ichthyological catalog. Pliny the Elder (23/24–79) was already of the opinion that the *Halieutica* had been composed by Ovid during his exile; many recent critics convinced of the poem's authenticity have imagined the banished author—who, they felt sure, must often have been bored (who knows?)—perched on the cliffs of Tomis, watching the fishermen and hauling out his own hook and line now and again. But there is nothing to add to John Richmond's (1981, 2746–2759) well-argued demonstration that the poem is spurious.

There are, however, many other works by Ovid whose authenticity is *not* open to question. It is therefore about time that I make my voice heard—if none too loudly—on the question of how to date these works, a problem that has long fueled heated controversy.

Much Ado about the Chronology of Ovid's Works

Ovid prefaces the *Amores,* from which (as the elegy *Tristia* 4.10 tells us) he recited in public when he was only eighteen, that is, around 25 B.C., with the following epigram:

> Qui modo Nasonis fueramus quinque libelli,
>   tres sumus; hoc illi praetulit auctor opus.
> ut iam nulla tibi nos sit legisse voluptas,
>   at levior demptis poena duobus erit.

> We who were only recently five little books by Naso
> are now three; the author preferred this work to that.
> Since reading us is no fun for you anyway,
> with two of us removed the punishment will at least be lighter.

Unanimity reigns among Ovid's critics about the meaning of these words: Ovid here gives us to understand that the text before us is the "second edition" of the *Amores,* which comprised five books when first published but has now been cut down to three. There is, however, no consensus on the approximate date of publication of the lost "first edition," for attempts to reconstruct it have not yielded conclusive results. Poem 1.14 can probably be dated around 15 B.C. on the basis of its allusion to captured Sygambri, members of a Germanic tribe; if we assign it to the "first edition," then that edition saw the light around 15 B.C. If not, then the first edition appeared sometime between 25 and 15 B.C.

The "second edition," that is, the extant *Amores,* is usually dated around the year of Christ's birth. For there is a topical allusion in the *Ars amatoria* which indicates that that work appeared not long after the first half of the year 1 B.C., and the majority view is that the *Ars* is mentioned in *Amores* 2.18. This elegy, which rings a playful change on the *recusatio* motif (see p. 12), begins with a passage in which the speaker tells the epic poet Macer his reasons for continuing to write minor poetry, unlike Macer himself. His (repeated) attempts to leave his *puella* have failed, he says. So has his effort to switch to writing "major" poetry, which he describes as follows:

> sceptra tamen sumpsi curaque Tragoedia nostra
>   crevit, et huic operi quamlibet aptus eram.
> risit Amor pallamque meam pictosque cothurnos
>   sceptraque privata tam cito sumpta manu;
> hinc quoque me dominae numen dedixit iniquae,
>   deque cothurnato vate triumphat Amor.
> quod licet, aut artes teneri profitemur Amoris
>   (ei mihi, praeceptis urgeor ipse meis!),
> aut quod Penelopes verbis reddatur Ulixi
>   scribimus et lacrimas, Phylli relicta, tuas.

> I grasped the scepter nonetheless, and out of my efforts there grew
> a tragedy, and for this work I was really not at all unsuited.
> Cupid laughed at my cloak and colorful buskins
> and the scepter that I, a private citizen, had so lightly taken up.
> From here too the divine power of my unsympathetic mistress drew me away,
> and Cupid triumphs over the great poet with his buskins.
> Here is what I can do: I can either tell of tender Cupid's arts
> (Woe is me, I am being led into narrow straits by my own precepts!)
> or write about what is reported to Odysseus in Penelope's words,
> and about your tears, abandoned Phyllis.

(13–22)

The last distich contains an allusion to *Epistulae Heroidum* 1 and 2. There follow allusions to *Epistulae* 5, 11, 6, 10, 4, 7, and 15 and then a short report on the answers that one Sabinus has composed to six of these letters (1, 4, 7, 2, 6, and 15). In closing, the speaker says he suspects that Macer too would gladly go over to the elegiac "camp."

Thus the speaker has also not managed to "desert" to the "major" genre of tragedy. He continues to do what is permitted: to profess "Cupid's arts" (*artes Amoris*) and compose letters by mythical women. It is the words *artes Amoris* and *praecepta* (precepts) in ll. 19–20 which most critics take as an allusion to the *Ars amatoria*. I, however, believe that the distich describes, with epigrammatic brevity, the situation the elegiacally enamored speaker finds himself in at the point he has reached in the unfolding "love story"—it is not over yet!—by Elegy 2.18. I shall substantiate this thesis in my discussion of the *Amores* in the next chapter (see p. 57).

If my interpretation is right, then what is being referred to here is the work in progress, the *Amores,* not the *Ars.* But then it follows that the extant text of the *Amores* antedates the *Ars,* in which that collection of elegies is also mentioned along with the *Epistulae Heroidum* (3.343–346). This, in turn, casts doubt on the claim that the surviving version of the *Amores* represents the "second edition" of a work previously released in a "first edition." For what might the hypothetical unabridged edition of the extant collection of elegies, with its carefully conceived narrative structure, have looked like? Was it too an elegiac love story containing, simply, additional episodes? If so, for whom was the condensed version produced? For readers in a rush? But, on that assumption, the second distich in the epigram would have to be taken literally, not understood as it is very obviously meant to be—ironically.

I consider the two lines in which the reader is told that the three-book version represents less "punishment" than the one in five books to be a witty allusion to Callimachus' famous dictum to the effect that a "big book" is "a big evil" (see p. 5). The new *poeta doctus* who is publishing his first book of verse wants to make it clear from the outset that this is his way of "enrolling" in the Alexandrian literary tradition. And he does so by carving out of a great mass of early drafts—there is absolutely no need to take literally even the "five books" it is supposed to have luxuriated into!—a work that conforms to the standards set by an authority on art, Callimachus. In the "test phase," that is, during his public readings from the as yet unpublished *Amores,* Ovid had perhaps left the impression that he was already *nimium amator ingenii sui* (see p. 15). Now he can assure the critical reader that it isn't so. Therein lies the ironic point of the epigram.

Ultimately, the discussion that scholars pursued for decades about the chronology of Ovid's early works was much ado about nothing. Now, at any rate, the matter does not seem at all complicated. Around 15 B.C.,

Ovid published the *Amores,* after reciting erotic elegies before various audiences for some time. But he did not deem all the elegies he had been reciting worthy of publication. Before releasing the work, his first publication, he had already begun to compose epistolary elegies "by" mythical women and brought some of them before the public in poetry readings; the new variant of the genre clearly created such a stir that Sabinus immediately penned the letters of response cited in *Amores* 2.18. Ovid proceeded to publish the written version of the heroines' individual letters sometime between 15 and 1 B.C. By then, there existed a total of fifteen such elegies, very probably divided into three books containing five elegies each (see p. 77). The *Ars amatoria* and the *Remedia amoris* followed; as Gaius Caesar's Parthian expedition is mentioned in both works, they must have been released not long after the first half of the year 1 B.C., and, at all events, before the prince's death early in 4 A.D. Publication of *Epistulae* 16–21, that is, of the paired letters, in one, two, or three books (see p. 86), must have come later, since they exhibit linguistic and metric affinities with the *Metamorphoses* and the poetry of exile.

But what of the tragedy mentioned in *Amores* 2.18? The description offered there of the speaker's attempt to compose a work of "major" poetry is preceded, in 1.1, by the confession that he had wanted to write an epic in the style of Virgil's *Aeneid* but was prevented from doing so by Cupid, who scoffed at the idea just as he would later scoff at the speaker's plan to write a tragedy. The poet then began to compose an epic about the battle of the gods and the Giants; the *puella* prevented him from finishing it (2.1). Since commentators on both passages interpret them not as autobiographical confessions on Ovid's part, but as variations on the *recusatio* motif, the tragedy scene may be read the same way. Here the poem anticipates a metamorphosis that occurs at the end of the *Amores:* the poet is turned into a tragedian after all. And it is precisely this metamorphosis which the speaker of 3.1 promises the personification of tragedy, after she and the personification of elegy have had an argument about which of them he rightfully belongs to.

In a word, all of this may simply represent a further variation on the *recusatio* motif. The choice of tragedy as the "major" genre which the elegist goes over to in the end may be conditioned by the fact that Ovid could hardly have opted for (masculine) epic in the compelling scene with the women who personify the "major" and "minor" genres of tragedy and elegy. However, Quintilian and Tacitus offer direct, and Seneca the Elder indirect testimony (for these passages, see Stroh 1969) that Ovid composed a *Medea;* two lines from it are even cited for us. Did Ovid really write such a tragedy? He does not mention a *Medea* in the *Amores;* moreover, in exile, he declares that he "never wrote anything for the theater" (*Tristia* 5.7.27–28). But the exile does make the following statement in *Tristia* 2, the letter to Augustus, to show the emperor just how serious a poet he can be:

> sex ego Fastorum scripsi totidemque libellos,
>   cumque suo finem mense libellus habet,
> idque tuo nuper scriptum sub nomine, Caesar,
>   et tibi sacratum sors mea rupit opus;
> et dedimus tragicis sceptrum regale tyrannis,
>   quaeque gravis debet verba cothurnus habet;
> coeptaque sunt nobis, quamvis manus ultima coeptis
>   defuit, in facies corpora versa novas.

> Six books of *Fasti*, and again as many, have I written;
> and each book-roll ends with its appointed month;
> this work too, above which I recently wrote your name, Caesar [Augustus],
> and which is dedicated to you, has my fate interrupted;
> and I have given the tragic buskins a work about kings,
> and the solemn buskin has the language he must;
> and I have sung—although the work begun lacked the crowning
> touch—of bodies metamorphosed into new forms.

(549–556)

Does this mean that Ovid wrote a play after all? But the title *Medea* goes conspicuously unmentioned here. Moreover, the distich 553–554 is not very elegant, if only because of the repetition of the word "buskin" (attempts have been made to emend it); again, this distich separates the *Fasti* from the *Metamorphoses*—ll. 555–556 refer to the second of these two works—both of which are said to be incomplete. Might someone have inserted this distich here on the assumption that the speaker of the *Amores* who describes his transformation into a tragedian was in fact Ovid describing himself? And could it be that he or some other anonymous writer who felt a need to supply the tragedian with a tragedy published a *Medea* in Ovid's name, and that the Elder Seneca, Quintilian, and Tacitus took this play to be authentic, just as Pliny the Elder failed to recognize that the *Halieutica* was pseudo-Ovidiana? This didactic poem, the *Consolatio ad Liviam,* and the *Nux* show that, even in the early Empire, there were poets who could produce very faithful imitations of Ovid. And even if the *Medea* is spurious, the choice of theme was a clever one, for it was one Ovid often treated—on two occasions, at length (*Epistulae Heroidum* 12; *Metamorphoses* 7.1–403).

We can, of course, only speculate here. But, in the middle of the generic transformation which Ovid very methodically pursued from the

Amores through the *Epistulae* to the *Ars* and the *Remedia,* the intrusion of a work of "major" poetry strikes one as altogether incongruous. Earlier critics claimed to detect a process of artistic maturation here, but this was the wish fulfillment typical of biographical interpretation, which failed to understand how deliberately the *poeta doctus* had organized his life's work around the elegiac system. It was, again, Quintilian who had blazed the way for these philologists of an earlier day; he felt called upon to remark that "Ovid's *Medea* seems to me to show how much the man could have achieved if he had only chosen to rein in his talent rather than give in to it" (*Institutio* 10.1.98). Precisely because, on the evidence of this statement, the tragedy stood out sharply from the rest of Ovid's work, I cannot really believe in *Medea*'s authenticity. But even if the play *was* written by Ovid, it has been lost, so that I may perhaps be forgiven for devoting as little time to its pitiful remains as I do to all the other fragments of Ovid's lost works that antiquarian erudition has dutifully collected and published.

Back to the texts that have come down to us. Ovid had to break off work on the *Fasti* and the *Metamorphoses*—so the exile affirms, at any rate, in the passage of the letter to Augustus cited a moment ago—when his punishment befell him. But, once again, there is no need to assume that he is transmitting a piece of exact biographical information here. For the poet is speaking in the role of a victim of caprice bent on depicting his punishment as excessive for the benefit of the man responsible for it. Precisely this idea—that a poet's ability to work was curtailed by his banishment—constitutes the theme of several poems of exile. But then what is the historical reality at the core of Ovid's statement about the way the *Fasti* and the *Metamorphoses* came to be written?

In two other passages in the *Tristia* (1.7.13–30; 3.14.19–24), the exile tells us how far his work on the *Metamorphoses* had progressed when his banishment order was issued. Before leaving Rome, he says, he threw the work into the fire; yet it was not destroyed. For copies had already been made of a version that was still lacking the finishing touch. This claim too may represent an attempt by Ovid to present himself as a poet cramped by the authorities. And his sole aim in telling the story of this auto-da-fé may be to remind the reader of Virgil's desire to burn the *Aeneid* just before his death. As to the statement that the *Metamorphoses* required further polishing, it might be intended to redouble readers' admiration for a text they would have to regard as unfinished when it is in fact a consummate work of art—at least in the version we have. If so, we should put the date of publication of the *Metamorphoses* around 8 A.D.

But we must now add, in order to round out the discussion in the second part of this chapter, that an author in Ovid's day would sometimes, before releasing a manuscript for distribution in written form, ask his closest friends to look it over and propose final revisions. If the exile is referring to one such version of the *Metamorphoses,* then Ovid may well have completed the work only in exile. This would also explain why passages in a number of the myths recounted in the poem—that of Icarus and Daedalus, for instance (8.183–259)—can be construed as allusions to the exiled writer's plight (Sharrock 1994b, 171–173).

There is a short passage in the *Fasti* in which the commentator on the calendar alludes quite directly to his fate as exile (4.81–84). It follows that that poem, or at least the surviving version of it, was in fact still unfinished around 8 A.D. Nevertheless, there appears to be a contradiction between, on the one hand, the banished poet's above-mentioned affirmations about the history of its composition and, on the other, what the text of our manuscripts reveals on this score. To begin with, the fact that we have only the books about the months from January to June flies in the face of the declaration, "six books of *Fasti,* and again as many, have I written [*scripsi*]." Could *scripsi* mean something like "I have conceived and planned out?" At any rate, our discussion of the work will show that Ovid may, after all, have deliberately brought it to an end after finishing the first six books.

But what are we to make of the exile's claim that he dedicated the *Fasti* to Augustus? In the extant text, the commentator on the calendar addresses himself at the beginning of Book 1 to Germanicus, the emperor's adopted grandson, turning to the emperor himself only in the proem to Book 2. There is a consensus among Ovid scholars around the following solution to the problem: around 8 A.D., Ovid is supposed to have completed the first six books in a version that began with the proem which now opens Book 2. After calling a provisional halt to work on the rest of the poem, he set about revising the text he had in hand after Augustus' death in 14 A.D., taking the new political situation into account. But because he died some three years later, so the argument runs, we now possess "a second edition" of Book 1 alone.

It is not only because the poet now dedicates this book to Germanicus that it is thought to be a second edition: one could, after all, meet this argument with the objection that Augustus and his life's work come in for frequent praise in the *Fasti,* and that Germanicus, a member of the emperor's family, thus merely "sits" in the "antechamber" of the poem's real addressee. It would follow that Ovid did not move the proem to the emperor from the beginning of Book 1 to the beginning of Book 2, something it is difficult to imagine him doing in any case. But the principal argument for the "second edition" theory, and one much harder to refute, is that a number of political allusions in Book 1 may well be built on the presumption that Augustus is dead, whereas he is definitely treated as still alive from Book 2 on. Here I would simply like to point out, very cautiously, that these are just allusions, and that, whenever allusions refer to current events, we risk misinterpreting them because the fragmentary historical record has led us astray. A second source of possible misunderstanding is that someone who merely *alludes* to politics wishes to express himself as obscurely as he can, a technique that would certainly have recommended itself to a banished writer. Fortunately, we can give this problem a wide berth. For, as we shall see in discussing the version we have of the *Fasti,* Book 1, it is integrated as tightly as possible into the structure of the extant work, which obviously constitutes a self-contained whole. I can, then, forgo all discussion of the history of its composition.

It is not particularly difficult to date the *Tristia* and the *Epistulae ex Ponto,* because here many of the references to the times are less ambiguous. Since, as will appear, the five books of the *Tristia* present themselves in their entirety as an "epistolary novel," the corpus was most likely published as a whole; the publication date was sometime after 12 A.D., the latest year alluded to in the poem. Ovid published Books 1–3 of the *Epistulae ex Ponto* in 13 at the earliest; they too represent a unified whole. If it was the poet himself who put together Book 4—if, that is, the elegies it contains were not collected posthumously, which is conceivable, as I shall show—then that book may have begun circulating in written form before Ovid's death in 17/18.

Before I summarize my thoughts—which are admittedly not *always* uncomplicated—on the chronology of Ovid's works, I should like to say a word about two of his works that I have so far deliberately left aside. One, an elegiac didactic poem that has come down to us in fragmentary form (100 lines), bears the title *Medicamina faciei femineae* (Cosmetics for the female face). This work, composed shortly before the *Ars amatoria,* in which it is mentioned, contains in its proem (*Medicamina* 3.205–206) a passage on the cultural significance of feminine beauty care that was expanded in a celebrated section of the *Ars* (3.101ff.; we will come to it in due course). There follow instructions on how to make cosmetics; these break off in the middle of the fifth recipe. The other work, a poetic curse, is, like its (lost) model by Callimachus, entitled *Ibis,* after the Egyptian stork. In this elegy of 644 lines, the bird's name masks the identity of the man being cursed. The only very recently exiled poet vents his hatred for a personal adversary in Rome by calling an interminable catalog of gruesome punishments down on his head. The exquisite tortures in question are among those undergone by both historical and mythical men and women. The special twist here stems from the fact that the exempla have been encoded, sometimes beyond recognition.

With their unusually massive outlay of erudition, both poems stand out so sharply from the rest of Ovid's oeuvre that one might be tempted to treat them too as spurious. But what strikes us today as altogether too artificial may in fact have been a special treat for readers of the day, given that both works emphatically situate themselves in Alexandrian traditions. The *poeta doctus* here so unrestrainedly advertises himself as, precisely, *doctus,* that one must have a huge stock of cultural knowledge at one's fingertips to appreciate his art properly. Acquiring it would cost us too much effort; I trust that the reader will not take it amiss if I leave my comments on both poems at that.

Let me now sum up my thoughts on the problem of the chronology of Ovid's works. Before being exiled (around 8 A.D.), the poet published the *Amores* (c. 15 B.C.), *Epistulae Heroidum* 1–15 (between 15 and 1 B.C.), *Medicamina faciei femineae* (before 1 B.C.), *Ars amatoria* and *Remedia amoris* (between 1 B.C. and 4 A.D.), and *Medea* (if that tragedy was his), as well as, perhaps, the *Epistulae Heroidum* 16–21 and, in provisional versions, the *Metamorphoses* and *Fasti* 1–6. In exile, he published the *Tristia* (after 12 A.D.), *Epistulae ex Ponto* 1–3 (c. 13/14), 4 (c. 17/18), *Ibis,* and the extant version of *Fasti* 1–6; he may also have published the *Epistulae Heroidum* 16–21 and the extant version of the *Metamorphoses.*

Now that we have some sense of the chronology of Ovid's works, let us cast a quick glance, before concluding this chapter on the historical conditions of his creative activity, at the Roman political events that formed the backdrop for his writing.

The Augustan Backdrop

The period in Roman history that coincides with Ovid's lifetime may be broken down into five stages. The final phase of the civil wars ran from 43 to 31 B.C.; it culminated in the Battle of Actium, on 2 September 31, at which Antony was defeated by Octavian, the future Emperor Augustus. The gradual transition from Republic to monarchy took place between 31 and 17 B.C.; it was as a monarchy that the Roman state saw the period of its first flowering, which extended from the great Secular Games of 30 May–3 June 17 to the premature death of Gaius Caesar, Augustus' designated successor, on 21 February 4. In contrast to these years of prosperity, the period extending from the adoption of Tiberius on 26 June 4 and his designation as "crown prince" to Augustus' death on 19 August 14 was wracked by crises in imperial domestic and foreign policy. The following years, down to Ovid's death (17/18), were those of the first phase of Tiberius' rule. In our discussion of these five periods, we may run the first and the second together, since Ovid was still only a child in 31 B.C. Furthermore, between 43 and 31 B.C., the conditions presiding over the literary production of those of Ovid's predecessors who wrote elegy were more or less identical to those that obtained in the period 31 to 17 B.C. We shall begin by examining them.

A sociohistorical interpretation of the poetry shaped by the elegiac system in the period down to 18 B.C. (see pp. 10ff.) probably does well to treat it as an expression, couched in coded literary terms, of Gallus', Propertius', and Tibullus' reaction to the political situation of the Roman upper class of their day, when the regime based on aristocratic senatorial rule was being reorganized as an autocracy. This matters a great deal to us here. Plainly, we are dealing with a poetic form of protest against a social development that, beginning in the early fifties, fundamentally altered a young patrician's chances of pursuing a political career.

Let us pass the main features of this process in quick review. If young nobles in Rome had heretofore enjoyed a certain equality of opportunity and a real prospect of having a say in the government of the Roman state as they advanced from office to office, now all hope of political success came increasingly to depend on the arbitrary decisions of a few great *imperatores* (military commanders). During the civil wars, it was above all the two most powerful men in the First and Second Triumvirates—Pompey and Caesar in the first case, Antony and Octavian in the second—who decided who would be named to magistracies or posts of military command and what their prorogatives would be. In pursuit of their policies, they resorted to unscrupulous and illegal methods such as corruption, electoral fraud, favoritism, and violence in the form of murder or terror exercised by armed bands. After the Battle of Actium, these conditions largely disappeared, but now Octavian-Augustus, as the politician who emerged victorious from the power struggle, proceeded to legalize, step by step, what had long since existed in practice: control by one man, who now styled himself *princeps* (first in rank), over the distribution of political and military offices and the attendant prerogatives.

Something else had changed in the last years of the civil wars: the attitude of the imperatores and their countless followers toward the code of public and private morality that the Roman patricians had, at least officially, zealously upheld since Rome's beginnings. Time and again, virtues such as soldierly steadfastness, the defense of aristocratic honor and dignity (*dignitas*), and fidelity—to one's wife, for example—were openly and quite unceremoniously cast aside. The elegiac poets felt that this was a sign of moral decline. By way of protest, they provocatively replaced the old system of virtues with their own elegiac "value system."

Thus, in a "world out of joint," service to one's *puella* (*militia amoris*) was put on a par with a military career. Again, a noble Roman who would otherwise have maintained conjugal fidelity (*fides*) until the day he died, bartered away his dignity by abjectly catering to the caprices of a mistress from the class of freedwomen (*servitium amoris*)—and not just any freedwoman, but one who led the life of a hetaera.

Thus, as late as the middle of the twenties of the first century B.C., Propertius and Tibullus withdrew, in a way we would today call escapist, to a countercultural "make love, not war" world. Their retreat had clear parallels in those of the two other great Roman poets of the period of literary history that stretches from 43 to 17 B.C., notwithstanding these poets' receptive attitude toward the policies of the victor in the civil wars. For Virgil's works are set in the fictive realms of his Arcadian shepherds (the *Bucolics*), a rural Golden Age (the *Georgics*), or the mythical heroic deeds performed by the Romans' first ancestors (the *Aeneid*). Similarly, in the verse collections that Horace published before 20 B.C., two of the main themes are the internalization of Roman virtues and flight to the morally pure atmosphere of the "poetic landscape"—even, in one case, the Blessed Isles in distant seas (*Epode* 16).

However, in 17 and the years immediately following, ethically motivated disaffection from the state gave way, in Horace and Propertius (Virgil and Tibullus were already dead) to enthusiastic endorsement of what Augustus had made of Rome since 31. The lyric poet Horace composed the ceremonial hymn for the Secular Games (17); in his fourth book of odes (c. 13), he hailed, in particular, the peace that had been secured by the successful military campaigns of Augustus and his stepsons Drusus and Tiberius, as well as the promulgation of the laws on morality. By including in his fourth book of elegies (c. 16) legendary explanations, patterned after Callimachus' *Aitia,* of still current Roman cults, the elegiac poet Propertius served notice that he appreciated the emperor's systematic effort to renew these religious institutions. Augustus had, indeed, accomplished a great deal, both at home and abroad, in the fifteen years in which he solidified his one-man rule. To be sure, the Republic and, with it, the patriciate's right to have its say in determining state policy had been lost for good. But the fact that the civil wars had been brought to an end, the border regions pacified, the organs of government subjected to a masterly administrative reorganization, the temples rebuilt, and Rome beautified through a program of urban construction had begun to bear fruit. Unprecedented peace and prosperity had convinced a majority of the members of the upper class to become, first and foremost, private citizens willing to help govern the world empire in strict compliance with the princeps' bidding.

The erotic poems that Ovid published between 17 B.C. and 4 A.D. were very much in keeping with this new state of mind. For they were tailored to fit the reading needs of aristocratic private citizens who, for one thing, had made their peace with the new state, and, for another, did not want the poetry they read to be forever reminding them, directly or indirectly, of deplorable moral conditions or even of Augustus' achievements. Thus they must have welcomed the fact that Ovid's elegiac erotics were not set in a realm of unrealistic countercultural protest, but rather, as we shall see, played a game with the literary tradition that was very nicely attuned to the world of readers' actual experience. Similarly, the reading public must have found it congenial that, in the wake of this turn away from escapism and back toward the Rome of their day, Augustus' world continued to make its presence felt only in the form of a resplendent backdrop—the elegant metropolis which the princeps, by erecting new public buildings, temples, columned halls, and statues, had invested with a splendor never before seen in the capital. In the *Ars amatoria,* the professor of love glorifies this real Rome, gilded over by the "power of images" (Zanker 1987), while simultaneously rejecting flight to the myth of ancient Rome:

simplicitas rudis ante fuit; nunc aurea Roma est
　　et domiti magnas possidet orbis opes.
aspice quae nunc sunt Capitolia, quaeque fuerunt:
　　alterius dices illa fuisse Iovis.
Curia consilio nunc est dignissima tanto,
　　de stipula Tatio regna tenente fuit.
quae nunc sub Phoebo ducibusque Palatia fulgent,
　　quid nisi araturis pascua bubus erant?
prisca iuvent alios, ego me nunc denique natum
　　gratulor: haec aetas moribus apta meis.

Earlier, a peasant simplicity reigned; now Rome is golden
and possesses the mighty riches of the subjugated world.
Behold what it is now, the Capitol, and what it once was:
you will say it used to belong to some other Jupiter!
The Curia is now truly worthy of so eminent an assembly of councilors
　　[the Senate];
it was built of straw when Tatius was king.
the Palatine, now shining in the radiance of Phoebus and the commanders
　　[the commanders' statues],
—what was it save a pasture for oxen who pulled the plow?
Let others delight in what is old; I consider myself fortunate to have been born
now; this age suits my temperament.

(3.113–122)

Of course, Augustus' splendid edifices also serve, in Ovid's erotic elegies, as "pick-up spots" for amorous Romans who do not hesitate to cheat on their present spouse. And that seems rather hard to square with Augustus' effort to regulate even the love lives of the upper class in the framework of his reorganization of the state. In 18 B.C., that is, not long before Ovid's first poem saw the light, Augustus had enacted his laws on marriage; a special court dealt violators heavy sentences, up to and including banishment. Of these laws, the *lex Iulia de adulteriis* prohibited *adulterium* (adultery) for married freewomen and made it a crime for a man to seduce a married woman or an unmarried Roman freewoman (whether she was a virgin or a widow). The *lex Iulia de maritandis ordinibus* sought to motivate those of senatorial and equestrian rank to marry and father children by promising them certain privileges if they did. That Ovid did not quite bring the erotic world of his early poems into line with these laws may have elicited, at most, a disapproving frown or even a secret smirk from Augustus in the period from 17 B.C. to 4 A.D., when the Empire was flourishing under the princeps' rule. But the situation seems to have changed in the crisis years 4–14.

This period of Augustus' rule was, to begin with, marked by a number of political problems—indeed, catastrophes—that occurred both in the Roman Empire and beyond its borders. In Rome itself, the populace was feeling the effects of grain shortages, exorbitant taxes, a heavy debt burden, and conflagrations. In the provinces, peace had again been jeopardized by revolts in Pannonia and Dalmatia, and, later, in Germany as well; the Romans sustained several costly defeats, notably in the famous Battle of Teutoburg Forest in 9 A.D. Augustus was, one suspects, even more deeply shaken by the conflicts that kept flaring up between him and other members of his family than by such political setbacks. Virtually all this domestic strife was rooted in the princeps' repeatedly frustrated efforts to find a successor to his liking, efforts which had begun to go awry well before 4 A.D. But even when he adopted Tiberius, who was to become the next emperor, on 26 June of that year, the emperor's family continued to be wracked by scandal. Thus, in 7 and 8 A.D., Augustus banished Agrippa Postumus and Julia, the children of his daughter Julia, who had herself been exiled in 2 B.C. The reason was probably that they had links to opposition groups.

Augustus' contemporaries, whose experience of all these events was influenced by the "power of images" and their reading of Virgil's *Aeneid*, must have been bewildered to see precisely this ruler so stubbornly dogged by misfortune. For they were encouraged to think of the Augustan period as the return of a Golden Age that would never end. Indeed, the princeps' policies had, officially, always been conducted under the banner of a "renewal" of old practices and traditions—first and fore-most, the institutions and values of the old Republic. (Of course, this was hardly the reality of the matter.) We can see how important it was to Augustus to cultivate an image of himself as a statesman of restoration in, for example, the fact that this image survives even in the record of his achievements (*Res Gestae*) which he ordered published in stone and bronze when he was seventy-six, and which we can still read today on the tablets known as the *Monumentum Ancyranum*.

It may therefore be assumed that a Roman poet, above all after the first Principate plunged into crisis, was well advised to bring the content of his work into conformity with the Augustan glad tidings of the return of the Golden Age and the restoration of the old Republic. At first sight, it appears that Ovid really did make concessions of this order in the poems he began to work on between approximately 4 and 8 A.D., the *Metamorphoses* and the *Fasti*. For, in the great hexameter work, world his-tory peaks in Augustus' reign, while the narrator begs the gods to post-pone the emperor's elevation to their ranks, to be expected after his death, for as long as possible (15.861–870). And the commentator on the calendar frequently dwells at great length on the religious festivals that commemorate the achievements of the imperial family, while giving us very graphic versions of the myths of Rome's origins.

When we inspect the two works more closely, however, we see—as has already been suggested a number of times here—that the world of Ovid's erotic elegies remains a living presence at every turn. Moreover, the elegiac world so powerfully asserts its dominion over that of the gods and Roman religion that even they often seem to be ultimately nothing but welcome occasions for witty, playful transformations of the elegiac system. After all, it is not the principle of preserving what is old that characterizes human existence as presented in the *Metamorphoses* and the *Fasti*. Rather, it is the principle of change. Thus a much dis-cussed passage in the *Metamorphoses* (15.420–452) makes it seem at least conceivable that, just as the once mighty cities of Troy, Sparta, Mycenae, Athens, and Thebes were fated to disappear, so Rome too will not live forever. Again, in the *Fasti*—to cite a facetious example this time—a vet-eran of Caesar's legions who is regaling the narrator with a rapturous ac-count of the battle fought at Thapsus on 6 April 46 B.C. suddenly sees his conversation with his interlocutor cut short by a downpour (4.377–386). That is how unresplendent the glorious 6th of April turns out to be on this occasion!

We do not know whether, and, if so, to what extent Augustus was aware that even the *Metamorphoses* and the *Fasti* did not necessarily square with the ideological foundations of his policies, or, at any rate, could seem not to. If he *was* aware of this, then it is likely that he would have reacted with greater irritation to Ovid's poetic productions after 4 A.D. than before and that even the works which the poet had published in the prosperous years of his reign would now have appeared to him in a different light.

Is it mere coincidence, then, that Ovid was (probably) banished the same year as the emperor's granddaughter Julia? Julia was, as the official explanation of her sentence had it, punished for her loose sexual mores, that is, for violating the *lex Iulia de adulteriis*. I have already said that it is idle to speculate about this, because the poet divulges too little about the reason for his banishment. It is just as futile to try to determine why neither Augustus nor his successor Tiberius showed the poet clemency or why Ovid pays his addresses to Germanicus, Tiberius' adoptive son, with such striking frequency in the works he wrote in Tomis. We must content ourselves with noting that two major preoccupations of Ovid's work, playful treatment of elegiac erotics and the idea that the power of metamorphosis sweeps all before it, must have been a source of irritation for the emperor and his family. But whether the fact that the poet often sounded these themes sufficed to earn him banishment to the end of his days without hope of recall is a question that will doubtless remain forever shrouded in mystery—like almost everything else that the individual Ovid encountered on his path in life, from the moment the young Roman poet composed his first erotic elegy to the year the exile published his last laments. Thus, if we are to get to know Ovid, there is nothing for it but to consider the various roles he plays in his works. Let us now proceed to make our way through these works one by one.

Erotic Novel and Elegiac Poetics: The *Amores*

The first-person "narrator" and "hero" of the "novel" that unfolds before the mind's eye when Ovid's collection of elegies *Amores* [Experiences of love] is read straight through plays a double role: he functions simultaneously as elegiac poet and elegiac lover. We shall therefore call him the *poeta/amator.* The term may seem a bit clumsy, but it will serve the useful purpose of constantly reminding us, as we examine each of the elegies in turn, that these poems sustain not only an erotic plot but also a reflection on poetics that is pursued throughout, directly and indirectly. Together, these two levels of enunciation generate a field of tension. As *amator,* the hero increasingly loses control over his relationship to his beloved *puella* (young woman) as the "plot of the novel" develops; in the end, he bemoans her repeated infidelities and yet is unable to break with her. As *poeta,* on the other hand, he keeps a firm grip on his elegiac work, and, in the end, has it in his power to opt for another genre.

Book 1: "Womanufacture" and What It Leads To

The brief description of the *Amores* just given will already have awakened a suspicion that is confirmed as soon as one reads the two programmatic poems placed at the head of Book 1. For these two poems present the first-person narrator's experiences of love not as a poetic transposition of the personal experiences of the real author Ovid, but as a highly artificial literary construct. The first thing to be constructed is the elegiac *poeta*'s role:

Arma gravi numero violentaque bella parabam
  edere, materia conventiente modis.
par erat inferior versus; risisse Cupido
  dicitur atque unum surripuisse pedem.

Weapons in weighty rhythms and violent wars was I making ready
to sing, and the matter suited the measure.
The first line was as long as the second. Then Cupid laughed,
they say, and stealthily stole a foot.

(1.1–4)

The speaker, that is, was getting ready to write an epic when the god of
love changed his second hexameter line into pentameter by stealing a
foot, thus transforming the first couplet into an elegiac distich and the
speaker himself into a writer of erotic elegies. As to the role of elegiac
amator, a second metamorphosis confers it upon the speaker, who tells
us that when he protested against the first change, pointing out that he
was not at all in love, Cupid fixed that too by letting fly at him with an
arrow. After a sleepless night brings his new predicament home to him,
the *poeta/amator* confesses in the second elegy that he is in the process of
turning into Cupid's willing slave. He says to the god of love: "en ego,
confiteor, tua sum nova praeda, Cupido;/porrigimus victas ad tua iura
manus"; "Look here! I confess; I am your new victim, Cupid,/I hold out
my vanquished hands, to act in obedience to your laws" (19–20). And
he falls in with the procession of captives marching ahead of the victor's
triumphal chariot.

   What happens in the next three elegies (3–5) reflects a three-step sequence of events that unfolds with clockwork precision on a precon-
structed plan. A declaration the *poeta/amator* makes to an unnamed
puella represents the beginning of the action: he intimates that he will remain faithful to her for years on end, as behooves a true elegiac lover—
indeed, that he will serve her like a slave and, as elegiac poet, make the
two of them world famous (3). The equivalent of the middle part of the
action consists in a longer elegy (4) in which the *poeta/amator* describes
his efforts to resolve a problem: because the *puella* still belongs to another, he gives her systematic instruction in how to act at a banquet that
both he and the couple will attend, teaching her how she can deceive her
current partner by secretly entering into relation with her new *amator*
and how, for the latter's sake, she can limit herself to performing "the
minimally required service" for her present partner that night. The finale is constituted by the success that follows the profession of love (3)
and lessons on love (4): the *poeta/amator* reports that the *puella* joined

him in bed during an afternoon siesta (5). For readers, this happy ending comes complete with its crowning touch, for they at last learn the *puella*'s name—Corinna—and are rewarded with a detailed description of the beauty of her naked body:

> quos umeros, quales vidi tetigique lacertos!
> forma papillarum quam fuit apta premi!
> quam castigato planus sub pectore venter!
> Quantum et quale latus! quam iuvenale femur!

> What shoulders, what arms did I see and touch!
> The form of her breasts, how well-suited for clasping!
> How flat her belly beneath the firm bosom,
> how long and lovely her hips, how youthful her thighs!

(5.19–22)

What the speaker relates in Elegies 3–5 exactly corresponds to the tripartite scheme of action in a Greek erotic novel such as Longus' *Daphnis and Chloe:* budding erotic relationship/obstacles (e.g., separation)/ lovers' reunion. But, in Ovid's elegiac erotic novel, we get another forty-five episodes that culminate in the very opposite of a lovers' reunion. The reason is that the two operations which assure the *poeta/amator* temporary success also create the essential conditions for a series of failures later in the story. These conditions boil down to the fact that the *poeta/amator,* himself insincere when he makes his declaration of love (3), professes a doctrine of love that encourages the *puella* to be insincere in her turn (4).

The *poeta/amator* does not directly reveal the hypocrisy of his profession of elegiac love (3), but he does make the reader aware of it—for example, by likening the fame that his poetry will win for the *puella* to the fame of three mythic women, Io, Leda, and Europa. But all three are seduced by that notorious Don Juan Jupiter after he has undergone a change of form (3.21–24): this by itself justifies the suspicion that the *poeta/amator* too aspires to become a Don Juan, his profession of monogamous love for Corinna notwithstanding. And he does at least try to do so from the beginning of Book 2 on. Similarly, when we read the instructions the *poeta/amator* gives the *puella* on how to hoodwink her current lover (4), we cannot help but think that they will later backfire on her new one, although he profits from his teachings for the time being. As Elegy 2.5 will show, these fears are well founded.

Anyone who tries to piece together a first impression of Corinna from the lesson in erotics (1.4) and the report on the subsequent erotic adventure (1.5) will quickly realize that the process of literary construction carried out in Elegies 1–5 reaches its acme in the characterization of the *puella*. For this woman strikes us not as the *poeta/amator*'s real-life beloved but as the product of a mechanical compilation of his fantasies. In particular, the passage just cited, in which he describes the beauty of each part of her nude body, starting at the top and working down—but beginning with her shoulders rather than her face (5.19–22)— demonstrates in exemplary fashion that Corinna is not the poetic reflection of a woman who actually lived in the Rome of Ovid's day. Rather, she owes her existence to what Alison Sharrock and Maria Wyke have very aptly called "womanufacture."

If, with this in mind, we examine the words used to describe Corinna in 1.5 and the rest of the *Amores* with an eye to the full range of their possible meanings, then the impression that she is a literary construct, already conveyed at the level of the erotic "novel," is confirmed at the text's "metapoetical" level as well. For, in connection with the *puella,* Ovid often makes use of terms that also occur in Roman texts on poetics—especially words used to describe minor poetic genres. Here is a small example: "ut stetit ante oculos posito velamine nostros,/in toto nusquam corpore menda fuit"; "As she stood before my eyes unclothed,/nowhere on her whole body [*corpus*] was there a blemish [*menda*]" (1.5.17–8). Not only the *amator,* but also the *poeta* is much concerned that there be nothing to "emend" (see p. 30) on any *corpus* he has to do with. In the case of the *poeta,* what is involved is the corpus of his elegies, for Callimachean tradition stipulates that he should file and polish his texts with the utmost care. Thus, when Corinna, the product of "womanufacture"—she is often referred to as, simply, the *puella*—is mentioned in "polyphonous" lines like those just cited, the reader is being invited to associate her with *poesis* (Greek for "poetry," from *poiein,* "to make"). We have, then, two matching pairs of terms, *poeta/amator* and *poesis/amata*. We need now to consider the way Ovid treats this constellation in the *Amores* and the implications that that has for the development of both the erotic novel and elegiac poetics.

Let us first survey the rest of the erotic novel. Critically important here is the extremely subtle adaptation of a theme that occurs throughout world literature, one modern readers are most likely to be familiar with from the Frankenstein narratives: the theme of the creature that, manufactured and brought to life by a human being, eventually turns on its creator. For Corinna, the product of poetic "womanufacture," is likewise the "work" of her lover in the sense that he has, in 1.4, given her systematic instruction in how to deceive a man. In the course of the erotic novel, she repeatedly deceives the *poeta/amator;* in 2.5, she even deliberately applies to the *poeta/amator* himself his lesson on how to fool her partner at the banquet. Thus, in her way, this "creature" too "strikes back."

The *puella*'s infidelities are already a theme in the remaining elegies in Book 1 (6–15), which we have yet to discuss. But it is never explicitly said that she deceives the *poeta/amator.* These elegies take him through yet another phase of their relationship, which unfolds in a context colored by his remark at the end of 1.5 (26) that he hopes he will often have trysts with the *puella* like the one described here. This phase is divided into two narrative sequences; like the opening sequence in Book 1 (1–5), each is made up of five poems (6–10/11–15). The structure of Books 2 and 3 of the *Amores* is also based on such pentads; Ovid would again use the pentad as the organizing structure of several of his later poems.

The narrative sequence that runs from Elegy 6 to Elegy 10 opens with the description of a situation diametrically opposed to the event depicted in Poem 5: seeing that his beloved's door has been closed on him, the *poeta/amator* strikes up a *paraklausithyron* (see p. 11), but to no avail (6). Why does she refuse to let him in? And what reason does he have for striking her later, as Poem 7 tells us he does? He does not say, but Poem 8 confirms the reasonable suspicion that he has a rival. Here the *poeta/amator,* who has eavesdropped on a conversation between his beloved and an old bawd, reports that he heard the old woman telling his *puella* how she should go about seducing a rich man enamored of her and how she should handle him afterward. True, in the next poem (9) the *poeta/amator* makes his friend Atticus a boastful speech in which he compares a lover's strenuous life to a soldier's (see p. 12). But this is obviously nothing but a braggart soldier's (Latin: *miles gloriosus*) attempt to flee reality. For now, as we learn in Poem 10, the *puella* has suddenly taken a very keen interest in receiving presents, as she could have learned to do only from consorting with a rich man.

Accordingly, the *poeta/amator,* who is for his part poor, suddenly realizes that his *puella*'s beauty is flawed after all and informs her that he no longer finds her physical appearance altogether bewitching. Thus, at the end of the second narrative sequence, the state he has been in since Cupid let fly with his arrow seems to have changed once again (10.11: *mutatus*). In fact, it has not: the third narrative sequence in Book 1 opens with a renewed attempt on his part to couple with his *puella.* He asks her in writing for permission to go see her in the middle of the night (11). The response is negative (12), but the very next lines we read come from the mouth of a *poeta/amator* who, early in the morning, is lying in bed in the *puella*'s arms (13). To be sure, his next appearance on the scene revives our suspicions that his beloved is interested in another man. For she has used so much dye on her hair that it has fallen out. Yet the dressing-down that the *poeta/amator* gives her (14) betrays no jealousy; indeed, he seems rather to be crowing. The crowing grows even louder when, in the epilogue to Book 1 (15), he prophesies that he will be rendered as immortal by his poetry as an imposing series of Greek and Roman poets he makes a point of listing by name.

It will already have become apparent that we learn about the course of the erotic novel in Book 1 principally from long speeches that the *poeta/amator* makes the *puella* and others. Here he pursues the systematic education of the *puella* that he initiated in Elegy 4, attempts to impose his will on her, or simply talks big. No doubt about it: the *Amores'* elegiac lover is an incorrigible braggart, and it is precisely this character trait that, as was already suggested, will trip him up later. For the moment, however, his bombast does him no real harm. For he almost always manages to accomplish absolutely . . . nothing at all. Indeed, this is a hallmark of the *poeta/amator* (as of other figures in Ovid's later work): massive outlays of eloquence yield no tangible result. This is of course quite funny every time; it is especially so in Elegy 13. There the *poeta/amator,* lying in the *puella*'s arms, makes a lengthy argument intended to convince Aurora, the goddess of the dawn, to postpone daybreak. Here is his considerably more succinct report on her response: "iurgia finieram scires audisse: rubebat,/nec tamen assueto tardius orta dies"; "I had stopped my scolding; one might think she had heard it: she turned red./But day began no later than usual" (47–48). Until very recently, biographical interpretations of Ovid's poetry judged the excesses of "his" rhetoric irritating. But once one has distinguished the speaker of the *Amores* and Ovid's other works from the author, it is easy to see that the verbiage calculated to produce a rhetorical effect, for which Quintilian had already taken Ovid to task (see p. 15), is not an end in itself in his writing. This is not *Ovid's* style, but his characters'. For Ovid, rhetoric is a means to an end: he can produce comic effects by setting a torrent of words over against a divergent reality. More: he can, in flatly satirical fashion, expose those who make such tremendous efforts to sound eloquent. He often utilizes this technique in the *Amores* to make the protagonist of the erotic novel look like a fool.

Thus anyone who centers his reading of the *Amores,* Book 1 on how the *poeta/amator* behaves in his relationship with the *puella* will simply laugh. He will laugh even harder if he attends to Ovid's handling of the elegiac system. For instance, the *paraklausithyron* (6) is not addressed to the door, as it generally is elsewhere, but to the slave who guards it; that is, the slave of love appeals to the solidarity of the other *servus!* Similarly, the idea that a suitor can pine away during a long courtship is wittily taken at face value: thus the slave doorkeeper need only grant the suppliant a narrow passage (3–4). And what is the ultimate reason for the lament at the door? The fact that time is slipping by. Whence a kind of refrain that is sounded five times in succession, tagged, each time, onto a group of four couplets: "tempora noctis eunt; excute poste seram"; "The hours of the night are passing by; quick, draw the bolt from the doorpost!" The *paraklausithyron*, which is, according to literary tradition, a languishing plea spoken by a lover who has been locked out by his *domina* (mistress), is here recited as if it were a tedious grammar exercise.

No question about it, this is very funny. But readers of the *Amores* who take due account of what the *poeta/amator* has to say about the poetics of the elegy—something much harder to appreciate than his comic predicament—will also realize that Ovid is at pains to make the reader reflect deeply on the nature and potential of elegiac poetry. This concern stands out not only in the programmatic elegies at the beginning and end of each of the three books (1.1/1.15; 2.1/2.18; 3.1/3.15), which explicitly discuss the art of poetry; it is also—indeed, especially—noticeable between the lines of all the poems in the collection. To be sure, one needs to have a certain familiarity with the appropriate terminology in order to grasp what the *poeta/amator* is obliquely saying in such passages.

Let us take an example. Whenever the *puella*'s hair is mentioned in Book 1 of the *Amores,* it is treated as something more than a mere erotic stimulant. Of course, its erotic role in a stringently closed society like that of ancient Rome was particularly important, as one can easily imagine if, for the sake of comparison, one considers the function of the shawl women wear over their heads in the East. However, in Ovid, an elegant coiffure also emblematizes minor poetry in the Alexandrian tradition. In the very first elegy in Book 1, the *poeta* declares, before Cupid changes him into an *amator,* that he has no *materia* (theme) for his elegies, that is, "neither a boy nor a *puella* with long, elegantly done-up hair" (20). He acquires such a *puella* as *materia* shortly thereafter (3.19). Subsequently, her hair is mentioned again and again—until it falls out because she uses too much dye on it. At that point, the *poeta/amator* praises what she has ruined in these terms:

. . . erant tenues et quos ornare timeres,
   vela colorati qualia Seres habent,
vel pede quod gracili deducit aranea filum,
   cum leve deserta sub trabe nectit opus.

. . . it was fine [*tenues*], and one would have hesitated to do them up,
like the cloths the dark-skinned Seres wear,
or the thread the spider draws out [*deducit*] with graceful foot [*gracili pede*],
when she weaves her delicate work [*leve opus*] beneath the secluded beam.

(14.5–8)

Someone unaware of the context might well imagine that what the *poeta/amator* has in mind is the artificially refined lines of a work of minor poetry. In any event, the terms I have drawn attention to in this passage recur very frequently in Roman literary theory.

In 1.14, then, we hear, besides the voice of an *amator* who gets very worked up about his beloved's overly enthusiastic hair care, the voice of a *poeta* who is for his part reflecting on the art of poetry. In this role, however, he is not a ridiculous plaything at the mercy of his "material," the *puella*, but rather has that material completely under control: for he is here discussing a rule he himself strictly observes, namely, that excessive color does not become poetry in the Callimachean tradition. Similarly, in a scene that occurs earlier in the erotic novel, in which we hear him rebuking himself for having lifted his hand against the *puella* (7), he is more than just the silly figure he cuts as a bathetic, raging *amator.* People have always found it quite amusing that the *poeta/amator,* who ruins the *puella*'s hairdo (among other things) when he hits her, abruptly concludes his exaggerated declarations of remorse with this very workaday remark: "neue mei sceleris tam tristia signa supersint,/pone recompositas in statione comas"/"And now, lest such sad signs of my crime remain,/do your hair up again and put it back in the right form" (67–68). This too is doubtless very funny. But something else is involved here: namely, the ancients' metapoetical discussion of the *poeta furens* (raging poet), a type who wildly churns out verse on a correspondingly low aesthetic level. Horace gives him a section all to himself in his celebrated *Ars poetica* (Art of poetry) (453ff.). If we bear that passage in mind as we read Elegy 7 (Morrison 1992), then we will perceive, in the *amator*'s concluding remark, the *poeta*'s conclusion as well. He means to say, roughly, this: "Now that I have shown that I can write like a *poeta furens* when I want to, I will again impose the ordered forms of Alexandrian poetics on my work."

As we can see, the relation of tension between metapoetical reflections and the entertaining presentation of the *poeta/amator*'s first experiences with the *puella* makes itself felt as early as the first book of the *Amores*. But what is barely recognizable here emerges all the more forcefully from the beginning of Book 2 on: the *poeta/amator*'s attempt to invent new forms of elegiac love and, side by side with it, his effort to invent new forms of elegiac poetry.

Book 2: Don Juan as Poet and Lover

The middle section of the elegiac erotic novel consists of twenty episodes that tell the story of the protagonist's attempted infidelity as *amator* and as *poeta*. In most manuscripts, there are only nineteen elegies in Book 2 of the *Amores,* but this is because two elegies have obviously been run together in Elegy 9, which in fact ends with line 24; the passage 9.25–54 is Elegy 10, the eleventh elegy is the twelfth, and so on. Book 2 is, like Book 1 (and Book 3), divided into pentads. Thus the continuing plot of the erotic novel is presented to us, as I shall now show, in four narrative subsections, each comprising five poems.

Elegy 1 is, at the thematic level, closely related to the first elegy in Book 1, since the speaker is again prevented from composing an epic here; in the present instance, the epic was to have been about Jupiter's struggle with the Giants. Now, however, it is not Cupid who interferes, but the *puella;* she closes her door on the *poeta/amator* and so incites him to woo her with elegies again. But anyone who concludes from this that the *puella* is still, as in Book 1, the sole object of the *amator*'s erotic desires will find she has missed her guess as soon as she comes to the paired Elegies 2 and 3. Here the *poeta/amator* has just met another *puella;* he bids the eunuch guarding her not to stand in the way of a relationship between him and the *puella,* who lives with another man. Naturally, the rhetoric he mobilizes again falls short of its goal. But, nothing daunted, the *poeta/amator* declares in the programmatic fourth elegy that he is incurably polygamous. As proof, he inventories, like Leporello in the famous "Catalog Aria" in Mozart's *Don Giovanni,* the peculiar charms of all the many different female types he finds attractive. Here is an extract from the text:

> molliter incedit: motu capit; altera dura est:
>   at poterit tacto mollior esse viro.
> huic, quia dulce canit flectitque facillima vocem,
>   oscula cantanti rapta dedisse velim;
> haec querulas habili percurrit pollice chordas:
>   tam doctas quis non possit amare manus?
> illa placet gestu numerosaque bracchia ducit
>   et tenerum molli torquet ab arte latus:
> ut taceam de me, qui causa tangor ab omni,
>   illic Hippolytum pone, Priapus erit.
> tu, quia tam longa es, veteres heroidas aequas
>   et potes in toto multa iacere toro;
> haec habilis brevitate sua est: corrumpor utraque;
>   conveniunt voto longa brevisqie meo.
> Non est culta: subit quid cultae accedere possit;
>   ornata est: dotes exhibet ipsa suas.

One walks softly: the way she moves wins me; another is hard,
but can become softer if a man touches her.
Because this one sings sweetly and modulates her voice with the greatest ease,
I would like to steal kisses from her as she sings.
This one flits with a nimble thumb over plaintive strings:
Such skillful hands—who can resist loving them?
That one pleases with the posture she adopts when she dances and
    rhythmically moves her arms
and twists her tender hips with supple skill.
To say nothing of myself, I who am sensitive to every charm:
Station Hippolytus there and he'll turn into a Priapus!
You, because you are so big, resemble the heroines of ancient times,
you are tall enough to take up all the space in the bed;
this one is easy to hold in one's arms because she is short: both
    knock me out,
they answer to my desires, the tall one and the short one.
One is not well groomed; I imagine what she would gain if she were
    well groomed;
Another is bejeweled; she makes the best of herself.

(23–38)

A regular Don Juan, then? For the moment, only because he talks big, as we have already said. And before his words can give way to deeds, the first narrative sequence comes to an end with an elegy (5) in which the *poeta/amator* vividly describes how the *puella*, following the instructions he gave her in 1.4, is unfaithful to him before his very eyes. Thus what we only surmised all through Book 1 has now plainly happened; this in itself indicates that Elegy 2.5 marks the end of one line of action.

Elegy 6 takes up a subject unlike anything that has preceded: the death of Corinna's parrot. Is the *poeta/amator*'s tear-jerking obituary for the *puella*'s darling pet his way of making a fresh start at courting her favors? The text offers no straightforward answers as to the function the passage has in the book as a whole. We shall come back to this question later.

The pair of poems comprised of Elegies 7 and 8 tends rather to create the impression that "Don Juan" is on the move again. For now it is time for a little hanky-panky with Corinna's slave. But only with a slave, after all: anyone who gives that circumstance due weight will conclude that the *poeta/amator*, a man of equestrian rank, no less (1.3.8), is at best a would-be Don Juan (the more so as he obviously has to resort to blackmail to induce even the slave to keep going to bed with him). No wonder, then, that the *poeta/amator* tells Cupid in Elegy 9a (9) that he would like to quit his service. Have things really come to such a pass? No; for he does not give up yet, but, in a second speech addressed to the god of love (9b or 10), takes everything back. For the night is not just for sleeping (39–40 [15–16]). But what else *is* it for? Prospects are no rosier at the end of the second narrative sequence than they were at the end of the first. The only new development is that the windy rhetoric now takes the form of a pair of speeches of the "pros-and-cons" sort.

The rhetoric is even windier in Elegy 10 (11), in which the *poeta/amator* tells his friend Graecinus that he is now in love with two *puellae* at the same time. He no doubt *is* in love. But so what? At all events, the conclusion to the poem is sheer wishful thinking:

> . . . mihi contingat Veneris languescere motu,
>   cum moriar, medium solvar et inter opus;
> atque aliquis nostro lacrimans in funere dicat
>   "conveniens vitae mors fuit ista tuae."

> . . . may it be my lot to expire amidst the movements of Venus,
> and, when I die, I want to disappear in the heat of action.
> And at my funeral, let someone or the other say, weeping,
> "Your death was in keeping with your life."

> (35–38)

Thus the *poeta/amator* hopes to breathe his last in the midst of the sexual act; but, in the context of Elegy 10 (11), that seems like little more than a wild erotic dream. On the other hand, it is a stubborn fact that Corinna is planning a sea voyage and thus, probably, another little infidelity. For when the *poeta/amator* speaks of "treacherous paths" (8: *fallacesque vias*) in Elegy 11 (12), the one in which he discusses Corinna's travel plans, it is not only fickle waves that come to mind. Moreover, he strikes us as remarkably devoted here. First, making a show of his concern, he tries to impress upon Corinna that it would be safer for her not to take the trip. Then he promises her that, if she sets out after all, he will welcome her warmly on her return and blindly believe everything she tells him about her journey. When, in the sharpest imaginable contrast to this attitude, akin to *servitium amoris* (erotic servitude), he strikes the pose of a triumphant war hero in Elegy 12 (13), boastfully declaring that he is now holding the *puella* in his arms—what a triumph!—one is on the whole inclined to take his word for it. But why this excessive bravado? It is strongly reminiscent of the braggart's flight from reality in 1.9.

And, in fact, the pair of poems (13/14 or 14/15) that rounds off the third narrative sequence affords us a glimpse of a bitter reality that had never before found its way into the world of elegy: Corinna has had an abortion. The *poeta/amator* would like to think that he is the one who has gotten her pregnant, but he cannot be sure (13.5–6), and his two rhetorically dexterous commentaries on the painful situation, which consist, in part, in giving the *puella* new lessons, again show that he is a man who likes to work his jaws. Not only has his plan to become a Don Juan already foundered; in the next two elegies, the *poeta/amator* is separated from the *puella* and badly misses her. In Elegy 15 (16), he sends her a ring to say this in his stead—how gladly would he go to her himself in the guise (that is, transformed yet again) of a ring! In Elegy 16 (17), we even find him outside Rome, on his estate in Sulmo; from there, he requests that the *puella* come see him, and we again see him in the state of *servitium amoris* in the next two poems. He expressly acknowledges that he is a slave of love in Elegy 17 (18), declaring at the end of the elegy that he will sing of no one but Corinna in his books of verse. And he reports at the beginning of Elegy 18 (19) that he has repeatedly attempted to break with the *puella* but that her tender caresses have kept him bound to her and elegy.

In Poem 18 (19), which we have already mentioned in connection with the chronology of Ovid's works (see p. 32), the *poeta/amator* even lets the *puella* dissuade him from writing a tragedy. The only freedom left him amounts to a choice between two elegiac subgenres. One of his options is "to profess tender Cupid's arts" (19), though that has a disadvantage (20): "ei mihi, praeceptis urgeor ipse meis!"; "Woe is me, I am being led into a sorry pass by own teachings!" We may simply take this for an allusion to the fact, recounted in 2.5, that the *puella,* following the instructions he himself gave her in 1.4, was unfaithful to him before his very eyes and that their relationship went into crisis soon after. Thus one of the two ways of continuing to write elegy consists in pursuing the *Amores.* The other would involve composing elegiac letters from mythical women (21–26). It is evident that nine such letters already exist; but, for the moment, the poet continues the *Amores,* as is shown by the fact that there is one more poem in Book 2 (19 or 20), followed by another whole book.

Thus the *poeta/amator* presents himself in Elegy 18 (19) as a "Don Juan" of poetry as well. First he mentions his attempt to jilt elegy by writing a tragedy, and then he reports on his activity as the author of the *Epistulae Heroidum.* This represents an "infidelity" within the realm of the elegiac insofar as the elegiac speaker in the *Epistulae Heroidum* is not the *poeta/amator.* If we now look back, from this vantage point, on the course the elegiac romantic novel has so far taken in Book 2, we can see that the *poeta/amator*'s desire to commit "infidelities" in the realm of elegy has already been evoked, at least indirectly. For, in Elegy 4, the

"Catalog Aria," the various female types are described in such a way that one can also read this passage as a metaphorical description of the variability of the rhythms, stylistic devices, and themes of elegiac poetry, as Alison Keith has noticed (1994/95). This appears with particular clarity in the above-quoted lines from the poem, in which, among other things, various musically gifted *puellae* are described in metapoetical terms.

Elegy 6, the *poeta/amator*'s lament on the death of Corinna's parrot, can also be construed metapoetically. To do so, we need first to notice its connection with the preceding elegy, in which we learn how the *puella* is unfaithful to the *poeta/amator* before his very eyes. Here is how he reacts:

> sicut erant (et erant culti) laniare capillos
>   et fuit in teneras impetus ire genas;
> ut faciem vidi, fortes cecidere lacerti:
>   defensa est armis nostra puella suis.
> qui modo saevus eram, supplex ultroque rogavi
>   oscula ne nobis deteriora daret.

> Just as it was (and it was elegant), I felt the urge
> to tear her hair and go for her tender cheeks.
> When I saw her face, my strong arms sank:
> By her own weapons was my beloved protected.
> I who had been wild but a moment ago begged her on my knees and
>   of my own volition
> to give me kisses no less sweet.

(5.45–50)

This report on what is decidedly "unmanly" behavior might pave the way for, say, a monologue by a *poeta/amator* who has doubts about his own virility, like the one we are in fact served up later in 3.7. Is it far-fetched, then, to take the dead parrot in Elegy 6—given that birds have from ancient times to the present been pressed into service as phallic symbols—for a representation of the *poeta/amator*'s flaccid penis? Probably not, the more so as a major pre-text for our elegy, Catullus' lament on the death of Lesbia's sparrow (*Carmen* 3), should probably also be interpreted along these lines, among others.

It is more important, however—this is obviously the main concern of Elegy 2.6—to remind the reader of the *poeta/amator*'s whole personality by way of a description of the parrot's nature. He and the bird have in common not only a knack for imitation (23–24), a "mouth quick to learn" (62), garrulousness (26–29), a simple way of life (31–32), and a love of peace (25–26); there is also the fact that the parrot says *Corinna, vale*

(Corinna, farewell) (48). Who, in the present state of his relationship to the *puella,* has more reason to utter these words than the one who quotes them? For, as *amator,* he has been deeply disappointed by the *puella.* But the *puella* also stands, as we have seen, for *poesis* (poetry). It follows that we can also read this *vale* as if the *poeta* had addressed it to poetry.

As I have already said, the *poeta/amator* does not bid farewell to elegy as such in the "erotic novel." It is true that he tries to; yet he succeeds in switching neither to epic (2.1) nor to tragedy (2.18 [19]). But we should now consider the fact that Corinna, as *poesis,* stands mainly for the type of elegy in which a *poeta* and first-person speaker presents himself as an *amator* who faithfully serves a single *puella*—in other words, love elegy in the tradition of Gallus, Propertius, and Tibullus. In that perspective, the "farewell!" addressed to Corinna certainly does have major implications for the poems that follow Elegy 2.6 in the *Amores.* For it is one of the first in a long series of elegies that work major variations on "classical" themes and thus unmistakably identify the *poeta/amator* as a "Don Juan" in the elegiac realm. It seems to me significant that Elegy 18 (19)—in which the *poeta/amator* explicitly says that, besides the *Amores,* he is in the process of composing elegies of another sort, the *Epistulae*—should be directly followed by an elegy, still in Book 2, whose themes diverge quite sharply from those to which the first two books in the verse collections by Propertius and Tibullus had accustomed readers.

With this elegy (19 or 20), the *poeta/amator* again appears as a Don Juan in the realm of love. And he attempts great things. He challenges the partner of a woman he has recently fallen in love with to square off with him in a titillating game: he wants his rival to offer him keen competition, because he doesn't find easy erotic success at all exciting. Similarly, the *poeta/amator* requests that the new *puella* often turn him down:

> tu quoque, quae nostros rapuisti nuper ocellos,
> saepe time insidias, saepe rogata nega,
> et sine me ante tuos proiectum in limine postes
> longa pruinosa frigora nocte pati.
> sic mihi durat amor longosque adolescit in annos:
> hoc iuvat, haec animi sunt alimenta mei.

> You too, you who have recently bewitched my eyes,
> fear traps often, say no often to my entreaties
> and let me, sprawled on the threshold before your door,
> suffer long hours of cold in the frosty night.
> Thus love endures for me and grows through long years;
> this causes me deep joy, this nourishes my feelings.

(19–24)

Here the *poeta/amator* again appears as a big-mouth and a professor of love. But, just as he is capping his lesson with an aphorism, he drops a remark which betrays that he continues, after all, to sense the danger that he might repeat a blunder he once made with Corinna: "si qua volet regnare diu, deludat amantem./(ei mihi, ne monitis torquear ipse meis!)"; "If a woman wants to be mistress of the situation for a long time, let her pursue her game with her lover/(Woe is me! may my own advice not come to torture me!)" (33–34). Things do not, then, look very good for our Don Juan. To be sure, he speaks in 2.19 (20) as if he were already involved in a proper relationship with a new *puella,* but his boastful pose does not make what he says seem very credible. As elegiac *poeta,* on the other hand, he *is* plainly unfaithful in this poem. For the elegiac system is here thrown out of joint—is, indeed, pushed to the point of absurdity. The *poeta/amator* in Propertius and Tibullus complains bitterly when the *puella* and his rival make life hard for him; he has already done so in Ovid as well and will do so again, for example in 3.8. In 2.19 (20), however, the speaker energetically urges the *puella* and his rival to make his life more difficult. Thus he takes as great a distance as possible from the rules that govern the "classic" love elegy. At the same time, he prefigures Book 3, in which he will again engage in this kind of "infidelity," while also trying his hand at very different elegiac forms.

Book 3: Farewell to Two Mistresses

Book 3 returns to the subject of the *poeta/amator*'s infidelity in the very first elegy, which, although it is a programmatic poem, does not treat of infidelity at the metapoetical level alone. For the personification of elegy introduced here is, as it were, Corinna's twin sister. Indeed, she is identical to Corinna. Like the *puella,* she is provocatively attractive (7–10)—for instance, she too wears a robe so thin it is transparent (1.5.13/3.1.9)—and, again like Corinna, she is the reason for the *poeta/amator*'s dissolute life (15–22; 49–60). As the *puella* had done in 2.1 and 2.18 (19), the beautiful Lady *Elegia* here manages to dissuade the man who has hitherto been her admirer from switching to a "major" genre for the space of another book—though for the last time—and this despite the fact that Lady *Tragoedia* in person also bids for his favors. Thus the *poeta/amator* can again do in 3.2 what he first did in 2.2: try his luck as a Don Juan.

We do not hear another word about his previous venture in this line, described in 2.19 (20). This too weighs against chalking it up as a genuine success with someone besides Corinna. The same holds for the adventure with another *puella* that he recounts in 3.2. There, while watching a chariot race at the circus, he pulls out all the stops of the art of seduction; to be sure, this yields nothing more than a new torrent of words. But something else *is* new here, for what is said allows one to visualize the accompanying scene much more vividly than do similar passages earlier in the *Amores:* we are a step away from *Ben Hur* on the silver screen. This is partly due to the fact that the *poeta/amator* occasionally interrupts his exhortations to the *puella* to say something to other spectators (21–24; 73–74). Turning to them (not the reader, as is suggested by the misleading punctuation of some modern editions), he announces, after winding up his long seduction speech: "risit et argutis quiddam promisit ocellis"; "She has laughed and promised something with eloquent eyes" (83). Then he says to the new *puella,* by way of conclusion (84): "hoc satis est, alio cetera redde loco"; "That is enough. Give me the rest somewhere else."

Will she? It seems rather improbable after this show, and the text says nothing to that effect. On the other hand, Elegy 3 does rather unambiguously suggest that the *puella* to whom the *poeta/amator* has declared his love back in 1.3 has betrayed him again, for, in 3.3, he accuses her of breaking her oath to him (even if he was not honest with her either in 1.3). True, he counters her infidelity in 3.4 with a new brazen appeal to yet another *puella*'s partner: as it is futile for the man to keep her under surveillance, he says, given that her virtue will be safe only if she wants it to be, he should be nice to her "friends" from the start and even go carousing with them. Thus we again find the *poeta/amator* blustering and dispensing lessons in love. But then—in 3.5—he has a dream which an augur interprets to mean that the *puella* will leave him for other men: he dreams that a very beautiful cow leaves her own bull to join others.

The dream narrative in 3.5 stands in the sharpest possible contrast to the account of the rendezvous with Corinna in 1.5, as is further emphasized by the words that open each poem: "it was midday" in 1.5 is linked to, but also contrasts with "it was night" here. In fact, when one compares all fifteen elegies in Book 3 with all fifteen in Book 1 (something I cannot do in detail here), one discovers, at every turn, thematic affinities between the poems designated by the same number. This in itself suggests that the critics who consider 3.5 to be pseudo-Ovidiana are wrong. Furthermore, this elegy rounds off the first pentad in Book 1 and thus has an important function both on the metapoetical level and with respect to the further course of the erotic novel.

Let us take the erotic novel first. For one thing, in the poems following 3.5, the *poeta/amator*'s dream becomes reality: four different elegies show us that Corinna definitively belongs to his rival (8, 11, 12, 14). For another, matters have now come to such a pass that he can neither hope to have a "normal" elegiac relationship with the *puella* nor count on her to betray her new partner: in a long speech in Elegy 6, he reproaches— in vain, needless to say—a swelling mountain stream for overflowing its banks and closing off the way that leads to the *domina* (2). In Elegy 7, which we have already discussed (see p. 15), the *poeta/amator* bewails the fact that an attempted infidelity came to naught because he was impotent; in Elegy 8, he complains that the *domina* (5) is consorting with a nouveau-riche officer. As in the sequence 2.5/6, after being directly confronted with the existence of a rival, the *poeta/amator* intones a funeral dirge (9). This time, however, it is not just a parrot that has died, but rather Tibullus, one of his three Roman predecessors in the genre of elegy. When read with an eye to what they say about poetry, these lines quite clearly foreshadow the "death" of the genre in the author's current literary production; that death will be announced at the end of Book 3. In any event, the source of his inspiration has momentarily dried up: Elegy 10 informs us that the *puella* must abstain from all sexual activity during the festival of Ceres, which happens to be in progress. The *poeta/amator* can do nothing but point out to the goddess, in a highly characteristic little tirade, that, back in the days when she was enamored of Iasius, she would not have been at all happy about forgoing love as he now has to. Be that as it may, the situation at the end of the second pentad can be summed up in a phrase: "sex off limits"!

Some editors have divided Elegy 11 into two elegies (in part so that there will still be fifteen poems in Book 3 after they have eliminated Elegy 5). One is certainly reminded of 2.9a/b (9/10) when, in 3.11, the *poeta/amator* claims that he has gotten over his love for the *puella*, only to impose a new stint of *servitium amoris* (erotic servitude) upon himself in the latter half of the same elegy. But, in 2.9a, the *poeta/amator* addresses his renunciation of love to Cupid, and we have no reason to think that he will retract it anytime soon. In contrast, the special charm of 3. "11a" (11.1–32) lies precisely in the fact that we *do* expect him to go back on what he says: in all the negative remarks he makes about the *puella* to justify his decision to break with her, it is more than evident that he finds the memories associated with this woman's "abominable acts" as sweet as they are painful. This seems to me to stand out especially clearly in the lines in which he says,

> quando ego non fixus lateri patienter adhaesi,
>   ipse tuus custos, ipse vir, ipse comes?
> scilicet et populo per me comitata placebas:
>   causa fuit multis noster amoris amor.

When have I not, full of patience, clung tightly to your side,
myself your guard, myself your partner, myself your companion?
Yes, of course—you pleased people too when I was with you,
our love prompted many to love.

(17–20)

This speech is evidently a monologue; it is not addressed to an "accused" whom we are to imagine as actually on hand. The *puella*'s lover therefore finds it easy to talk tough for as long as he is conjuring up his negative experiences with her. But as soon as he imagines himself requesting that, in future, she spare him her caresses and the sort of words that go with them (31–32), the memory of those words and caresses also comes flooding back. No wonder that, at this point, our so obviously wavering hero immediately crumples and that the recollection of the *puella*'s beauty administers the coup de grâce.

"Find yourself another" (28): we can only conclude that he never meant it. In any case, there have long been *many* others, for in Elegy 12 we hear the *poeta/amator* complaining that, because he has publicly praised Corinna in his verse, he has, like a pimp, brought troops of admirers swarming round her. Then, in Elegy 13, we again find him far from the *puella;* he has accompanied his wife—so, suddenly he has a wife to think of, although we had not even been told of her existence earlier!—to a festival in her native region of Faliscus in honor of none other than . . . Juno, patron goddess of marriage. Finally, in Elegy 14, he makes a very curious kind of attempt to come to terms with the *puella*'s inconstancy: he asks her to tell him nothing at all about her escapades. If she grants that request, he says, she can pursue her adventures in bed with another man to her heart's content:

> illic nec tunicam tibi sit posuisse pudori
> nec femori impositum sustinuisse femur;
> illic purpureis condatur lingua labellis,
> inque modos Venerem mille figuret amor;
> illic nec voces nec verba iuvantia cessent,
> spondaque lasciva mobilitate tremat.

> There it should cause you shame neither to take off your tunic,
> nor press thigh tightly to thigh;
> there the tongue should bury itself in purple lips
> and desire find expression in a thousand ways;
> there neither sounds nor encouraging words should be lacking,
> and the bedstead should be rocked by lusty movements.

(21–26)

This, of all passages, is the only one in the whole of the *Amores* in which the *poeta/amator* describes lovemaking—in a speech intended as a warning for his unfaithful beloved. Thus we again find him giving her lessons on love—the similarity to the *Ars amatoria* leaps to the eye (see p. 105). But the *puella* is to apply these lessons when she is being unfaithful to him! As if that were not enough, the *poeta/amator* goes so far as to say that, should he ever catch his beloved flagrante delicto, she should deny even what he has seen with his own eyes!

Just one poem follows this episode of the elegiac erotic novel; it serves as epilogue to both the book and the work as a whole (15). "Find yourself another poet," the *poeta/amator* here tells Venus (15.1); he declares in the same breath that he is about to go over to Bacchus' genre, which presumably means tragedy. (Thus it is perhaps true after all that the poet wrote a tragedy, notwithstanding the echo of the tongue-in-cheek "find yourself another" in 11.28—true, at least, within the fiction of the *Amores*.)

So much, then, for our overview of the third and final part of the erotic novel. A theme crucial to its development in Books 1 and 2 appears in Book 3 as well: the idea that the *poeta/amator* is hoist by his own petard, that is, his own teachings. When, in Elegy 11, he complains about the furtive signals of young men at the *convivia* (banquets) he attends with the *puella* (23–24), we recall that, in Elegy 4, he cynically advised the partner of another *puella* to attend *convivia* along with the woman's "friends" (47–48). But this motif is now submerged by the theme that, from Elegy 5 on, dominates the erotic novel in Book 3: the idea that the *poeta/amator*'s whole sex life has ended in failure. Thus, at the close of the book, he can bid elegy farewell without having to take formal leave of the *puella* whose praises he once sang in elegies. For she has long since left him de facto, just as the cow left her bull in his dream.

But it follows that, once the *poeta/amator* has dreamed that dream, he really has no further reason to write elegies about the *puella*. Indeed, several of the poems in Book 3 that come after Elegy 5, like, in a certain sense, Elegy 5 itself, belong to a different subgenre or else anticipate certain themes of Ovid's later poems, above all the *Metamorphoses* and the *Fasti*. A dream like that recounted in 3.5 could easily be imagined in either of those works. In 3.6, branding a mountain stream an "enemy of love," the *poeta/amator* invokes any number of rivers (25–82) that, he reproachfully tells the stream, took on human form to make love to *puellae;* he lingers over the story of the river god Anio's rape of Rhea Silvia, the mother of Romulus and Remus. The catalog of rivers and the myth could equally well have taken their place in the two major works; the same holds for the legend of Ceres' affair with Iasius, which the *poeta/amator* recounts for her in 3.10 to buttress the argument that the "ban on love" is unjust. In 3.12, having "prostituted" Corinna by publishing his elegies, he rattles off a long catalog of mythical metamorphoses to prove that readers have not credited first-person narratives about *puellae* by other poets who tell similar tales; why then have his rivals chosen to believe that Corinna really exists? Lastly, in 3.13, the description of the festival in honor of Juno even includes an *aition* (explanatory legend) of the sort we might expect to find in the *Fasti* or the last two books of the *Metamorphoses*.

Thus, as *poeta,* the speaker of the *Amores* undergoes a metamorphosis in the course of the work itself: starting out as a writer of elegies centered on a *puella,* he is transformed into a writer of other kinds of elegiac poems. The *amator*'s final metamorphosis unfolds in parallel with this one. On the one hand, he appears as the caricature of a *servus amoris* (slave of love); but, on the other, he finds himself more alienated from the now irrevocably polygamous *puella* than ever before. This stage of his transformation is reached, at the latest, by the last pentad in Book 3: regression toward *servitium amoris* at the mere thought of the *puella*'s beauty (11); plaints about unexpectedly finding himself acting as her "pimp" (12); an excursion with his wife that may leave us wondering about the reasons for the concomitant separation from the *puella* (13); and a readiness to tolerate all the *puella*'s infidelities, on condition that she conceal or deny everything (14). Set over against the conclusions of elegiac romantic novels by Propertius or Tibullus, this reads very much like a distortion bordering on the grotesque. At all events, the *amator* has now definitely lost control over his relationship to the *puella.*

But, as *poeta,* he definitely remains the master of his fate. For, from one end of the book to the other, he single-mindedly prepares to part company with elegy. His experiments with different variants of the genre prime the reader for this; so does a series of statements on poetics which, again, must be made out between the lines. These metapoetical pronouncements are typically generated, as they were earlier, by the ambiguity of words that apply to both *puella* and *poesis* (poetry). This is especially easy to see in Elegy 12, about the *poeta/amator* who puts the *puella* on public offer by publishing *poesis.* But what is the implication for poetics when, in Elegy 14, the *poeta/amator* requests that the *puella* consistently conceal her erotic adventures? Is *poesis* too being asked to conceal what it is "up to," that is, to hide its message, which should at best be comprehensible only after decoding?

It certainly seems clear that the request the *poeta/amator* makes of the *puella* hardly provides a solid basis for pursuing a relationship with her.

For, if she granted it, his beloved would have her own erotic novel, one that would exclude the *poeta/amator,* who would not be able to "read" it. But then it would no longer be possible to equate the *puella* with *poesis.* Again, *poesis* certainly did emit hidden messages down to Elegy 3.14, but precisely *not* at the level of the erotic novel; such messages concerned rather, say, poetics (and, at least conceivably, politics, which we shall come to shortly). If *poesis* too were now entirely encoded, so that even the reader could not understand the (hypothetical) rest of the erotic novel without a special effort, then the *Amores* would look very different from this point on. It follows that, with 3.14, the poem in the form it has hitherto taken has in every sense come to an end. The *poeta/amator* can bid farewell to elegy in 3.15 and turn to tragedy instead.

Indeed, one of the special virtues of the *poeta/amator*'s contribution to elegy resides in the fact that his way of narrating the erotic novel makes it both easy to follow and lifelike at the same time. In any case, modern readers, although they find the concerns of antiquity particularly remote from their own, seem to appreciate this, since the *Amores* enjoys a certain popularity today. That gives me my cue for a transition to the last section of the present chapter, in which I shall attempt a general assessment of Ovid's first work from a modern standpoint, but also, as far as possible, from an Augustan one as well.

Amor, Roma, and the Moral of the Novel

Is there "a moral" to the tale of the *Amores*—that is, an idea, message, intended effect, or whatever else one may wish to call it? If so, it surely does not have just one, the one right message your senior high teacher is looking for when he asks, "What is the poet trying to tell us?" That such an approach can yield answers which are eminently suspect ideologically has been demonstrated often enough by the official "guardians" of the heritage of antiquity over the course of the last century. That is not the least of the ways in which philologists have brought the literature entrusted to their care into disrepute with many of their contemporaries. Let us see, then, what one can offer by way of an interpretation of the *Amores* as a whole when one approaches the poem with all due caution.

What can probably be ruled out when it comes to this text—although one can of course not be absolutely certain—is a moral in the narrow sense. Doubtless, it is possible to interpret in a "moralistic," even a *decidedly* "moralistic" sense, the little fable about a young man who is in love with a beautiful lady and tumbles into the slough of deceit and deception he himself has created. But in Ovid, for one thing, the hilarity provoked by the description of the fiascoes and sorry predicaments that the *poeta/amator* repeatedly maneuvers himself into with his braggadocio and his pedantic little lectures easily drowns out the message, which it perhaps trails in its wake, that "he gets what he has coming to him." For another thing, thanks to the superposition of two levels of textual meaning, the direct and indirect statements on poetics relativize the "plot of the story," indeed, undermine it. Thus it turns out that a poem which, on a superficial reading, seems to be a would-be Don Juan's catalog of female conquests is simultaneously, on closer inspection, a catalog of metrical and stylistic devices and an inventory of elegiac themes (2.4).

Probably none but Ovid's highly educated contemporaries could appreciate the highly artificial game that the poet here plays with textual "polyphony," in the wake of the Alexandrians, the poets of Catullus' generation, and the elegists of the intervening period. They alone would have been amused to see how Ovid was already playing with and parodying the elegiac system in the *Amores,* if not carrying it to the point of absurdity. It would have led us too far afield if I had tried to show how often the *Amores* offers us clever take-offs on poems by, say, Propertius, down to their very wording; this is done so wittily as to leave us with the impression that the main aim of Ovid's three books of elegies is to parody the first three books of elegies by his predecessor (Morgan 1977). We are pointed in this direction from the moment we begin reading the *Amores.* For there is no mistaking the fact that Ovid's *poeta/amator,* who is rather mechanically made to fall in love when Cupid steals a foot from him and pierces him with an arrow, and who does not even mention Corinna's name until he reaches the fifth poem in the collection, stands in comic contrast with the *poeta/amator* of Propertius' elegies: the sight of his Cynthia's eyes suffices to kindle the passion of Propertius' *poeta/amator,* and her name is the very first word that crosses his lips.

Yet parodying the works of his predecessors was doubtless not an end unto itself for Ovid, if only because the poetry of Catullus, Propertius, and Tibullus did not offer him a sufficiently juicy target, *pace* many contemporary critics. The verse of the three Roman poets may well approximate Romantic conceptions of love poetry rather closely, in contrast to Ovid's; but such conceptions by no means tally with those poets' conception of themselves or with the idea that cultivated readers of their own day—including Ovid—were likely to have had of them. For they too were *poetae docti* in the Callimachean tradition and they too produced comic effects by parodying still other authors. Catullus', Propertius', or Tibullus' manner of writing poetry is therefore not different enough from Ovid's to enable him to create new literary art by parodying their work.

It seems rather more plausible that a central concern of the author of the *Amores,* as an elegist writing when Augustan Rome had reached the height of its glory, was to cast an ironic light on the late Republican social criticism of his predecessors. For Propertius and Tibullus most probably used the elegiac system to confront the discourse typical of the ruling class of their times with the countercultural universe of those who advocated "making love, not war" (see p. 41). Ovid, in contrast, no longer taps elegiac "values" for purposes of indirect political protest; he takes them literally, with feigned naïveté, or else arranges for the *poeta/amator* to honor them in the breach, by, for example, owning up to his promiscuity. Yet elaborating this specifically Roman variant of a witty literary game in the Alexandrian tradition was probably also not Ovid's main aim in the *Amores.* Playful treatment of the texts of earlier elegiac poets merely provided him a springboard for something that obviously mattered more to him: the transformation of a genre—that is, working up new literary forms out of what his predecessors' had already achieved.

In all likelihood, then, Ovid's chief interest lay in literary innovation. Specifically—as the "erotic novel" contained in the *Amores* shows—his aim was probably to develop the techniques that Callimachus' successors had already put to work to tell stories in verse. And in that endeavor, in turn, he was doubtless more interested in the aesthetics of form, ways of handling thematic material, and metapoetical reflections than in conveying a philosophically or socially relevant message. Yet the majority of his contemporaries can hardly have judged his intentions aright. On the contrary, Quintilian's remarks, quoted above (pp. 15 and 35), give us reason to suspect that Ovid's works were partially misunderstood because, for example, the opinions and acts of his poetic persona were identified as his own. When those who conflated poet and persona were supporters of the Augustan policy of restoration, the consequence, which no doubt made itself felt very soon after the first elegies later collected in the *Amores* became known, was surely disgruntlement over "Ovid's" attitude toward sex.

At any rate, one can construe several passages in the *Amores* as mockery of Augustus, whether the voice one hears is Ovid's or the *poeta/amator*'s. By way of example, we might cite a number of poems that can be taken to refer, as Wilfried Stroh (1979a) has shown, to the *lex Iulia de adulteriis* (see p. 43). Consider 3.14. One can, if one wishes, see in the speaker of the elegy a caricature of a Roman husband cuckolded again and again by his wife. On this reading, the woman's husband would be requesting that she scrupulously conceal her infidelities both because he wants to spare her a trial for adultery and because he himself wants neither the scandal that such a trial would bring nor the separation from his wife likely to ensue if she were found guilty. It is quite possible that Ovid had such an interpretation of the poem in mind, although this can of course no more be proven than any other interpretation can be. However, whether that is really "what the poet is trying to tell us" does not matter at all. It is enough to know that Ovid's contemporaries could read mockery of the marriage laws into his text and that Ovid therefore ran the risk, from the moment the *Amores* was published, of getting his first bad marks from Augustus' followers or even from Augustus himself.

Indeed, it must have been the poet's free-and-easy attitude toward the world of eros that shocked rather than amused conservative Romans. The senatorial caste had long regarded AMOR, a palindrome of ROMA, as a force within the state that had to be domesticated and brought into line with the strict moral standards of a patriarchal society. Thus the many contemporary observers who were not even willing to tolerate erotic love as a condition for biological reproduction must have been horrified by the fact that the *Amores* could treat of subjects such as an act of intercourse that "exhausted" both the man and the woman (5.25), the sight of naked female beauty, or merely the sophisticated flirting practiced by the upper classes in their salons. Certain Romans in Augustus' day were probably also offended by the fact that the thought processes and behavior of the species *homo amator*—intimate matters, after all— were scrutinized with such utter lack of inhibition in the *Amores*, and, what is more, presented with a rare flair for description.

But that is precisely what makes Ovid's collection of elegies seem so modern to today's readers. Our impression that it closely reflects our own concerns is not just due to the fact that it can be compared to the erotic literature of our day and judged quite as "liberal," "tolerant," and morally "humane." For what makes many poems in the *Amores* particularly appealing for our permissive societies of the turn of the twenty-first century is doubtless Ovid's sexual psychology. Let us once again consider the man who, in 3.14, is betrayed time and again by his partner, and the solution to his problem as he works it out in the course of that elegy. Undeniably, the kind of mutual understanding that he calls for is scarcely practicable even in our callous world of business and electronic technology, because it is rooted in secretiveness and self-deception. As a psychological model, however, the *poeta/amator*'s idea can hold its own alongside—indeed, stands up well in comparison with—all the theories that sexologists have recently put forward, sometimes rather fancifully, as to the best ways of achieving the ideal sexual relationship.

Thus 3.14 and many more of the poems found in the *Amores* offer modern readers, in particular, characters and situations they can identify with. Indeed, Ovid himself declares that his male and female readers would discover a reflection of their own experiences in the "experiences of love" (that is doubtless what the title *Amores* means) narrated by his elegiac alter ego. For, at one point, the *poeta/amator* makes the following programmatic announcement:

> me legat in sponsi facie non frigida virgo
>   et rudis ignoto tactus amore puer.
> atque aliquis iuvenum, quo nunc ego, saucius arcu
>   agnoscat flammae conscia signa suae
> miratus diu "quo" dicat "ab indice doctus
>   composuit casus iste poeta meos?"

> I should be read by the young girl whom the sight of her betrothed
>   does not leave cold,
> And the inexperienced boy touched by love, which he has not
>   known before.
> And any young man who has been wounded by the bow that I have
>   now been wounded by
> should recognize the signs testifying to the fervor of his love,
> and long wonder, and say: "What informant has supplied the poet
> the information he needed to describe my own case there?"

(2.1.5–10)

In our day too, even the reader who from the outset forgoes any attempt to appreciate Ovid's little textual games, asking for nothing more than what is promised in these verses, will be given entire satisfaction. That the description of the speaker's erotic experiences recalls similar descriptions in novels is surely a good part of the reason.

Elegiac Love versus Mythical Reality: The *Epistulae Heroidum* and the Paired Letters

Ovid's second collection of poems, the *Epistulae Heroidum* (Letters by heroines, that is, by mythical women), contains fifteen elegies cast in the form of letters. In Book 3 of the *Amores,* the poet gave us our first glimpse of a budding generic transformation; now, in the new elegiac corpus, he no longer speaks as a *poeta/amator,* but adopts an elegiacally enamored woman's role. In each of the fifteen *Epistulae,* he embodies a different *amatrix;* in the last, the letter by Sappho, he even takes a part symmetrically opposite to the one he played in the *Amores,* becoming a *poetria/amatrix.* Thus the role-playing in the *Epistulae Heroidum* would seem to represent the direct continuation of a generic development that began to come into view in the *Amores.* It does not matter much whether the metamorphosis from elegist to tragic poet that the first-person narrator of the Elegy *Amores* 3.15 informs us he has undergone belongs to the fictional world of the poetic text alone (see pp. 33–36 and 59) or is to be read autobiographically—whether, that is, Ovid really did turn briefly to tragedy after publishing the *Amores.* For it may be inferred from the poem *Amores* 2.18 that he composed nine epistolary elegies before releasing the collection known as the *Amores* in the form in which we have it (see p. 64). And that is reason enough to suppose that there is a particularly close relationship between the basic poetic scheme of the first and second collections of elegies.

That Ovid is the author of the letters contained in the codices but not mentioned in *Amores* 2.18 (Letters 3, 8, 9, and 12–14) is as little to be doubted, in my view, as is his authorship of the Letter "by Sappho" (15). Those who contend that these seven elegies are pseudo-Ovidiana do not convincingly substantiate their thesis: the case they make against these poems' authenticity, which has to do with the content of Elegies 3, 8, 9, and 12–15, is based partly on aesthetic prejudice, partly on the fact that they have not given due consideration to recent analyses of the narrative and thematic structure of Ovid's work. The linguistic arguments they offer are by themselves insufficient to make their point. We know too little about what could and could not be said in the Latin of the Augustan age to exclude texts from Ovid's corpus simply because they contain a few expressions unusual for him. The same holds for the paired letters, that is, the letters included in editions of the *Epistulae Heroidum* as Elegies 16–21, although the authenticity of these poems, most likely written some time after Letters 1–15, has also been questioned.

The first-person speakers of the fifteen *Epistulae Heroidum*, which we shall consider first, play a double role, like the speaker of the *Amores*. On the one hand, the women who write these letters present themselves as *puellae* who love the men they address in accordance with the elegiac system (see pp. 10ff.), thus identifying themselves as belonging to the unreal world it represents. On the other hand, they are part of the "reality" of a story that was simply a given for Ovid. In Letters 1–14, this story is constituted by Greco-Roman mythology; in Letter 15, by the set of legends associated with Sappho. Since two antithetical modes of life clash here—the elegiac mode and the one that is "real" for the female speakers of these letters—tensions arise in Ovid's second collection of elegies too. Friedrich Spoth was the first to offer a comprehensive demonstration of this, in a book (1992b) to which my account is deeply indebted.

Penelope as Exemplar

Let us take the first *Epistula* to illustrate this relation of tension between elegiac love and mythical reality. Penelope here writes to her husband Odysseus not long before they are reunited. It seems as if she were altogether predestined for the role of an elegiac speaker—at least at first glance. For, from what we know of her from Homer's *Odyssey*, which is unquestionably Ovid's major pre-text, she shows herself to be more fully committed than any other mythical heroine to one of the central "values" of the elegiac system: readiness to accept an eternal alliance (*foedus aeternum*) with her partner founded on her unwavering fidelity (*fides*) to him. Thus, as far as Penelope is concerned, the condition that prompts her letter is a twenty years' wait for her husband, absent as a result of his participation in the Trojan War and his subsequent wanderings. From the very first lines of the introduction to her letter, his wife shows that she has felt and lived "elegiacally" throughout the long years of their separation:

Hanc tua Penelope lento tibi mittit, Ulixe.
  Nil mihi rescribas tu tamen; ipse veni!
Troia iacet, certe Danais invisa puellis—
  vix Priamus tanti totaque Troia fuit!
O utinam tum, cum Lacedaemona classe petebat,
  obrutus insanis esset adulter aquis!
Non ego deserto iacuissem frigida lecto,
  non quererer tardos ire relicta dies
nec mihi quaerenti spatiosam faller noctem
  lassaret viduas pendula tela manus.

This letter is being sent to you, the dilatory one, by your
  Penelope, Odysseus.
It is not necessary that you write back to me;—come yourself!
Troy, to be sure, has fallen, hated by Greek women [*puellis*].
Priam and all of Troy were hardly worth so much!
O, would that, in the days when he hastened toward Sparta with
  his fleet,
the adulterer [Paris] had been sent to the bottom of the raging sea!
Then would I not have lain, cold, in the lonely bed,
and would not—forlorn—complain that the days pass slowly,
and, as I seek to beguile the long night, the hanging web
would not weary my widowed hands.

(1–10)

As the lament of an elegiac speaker complaining that she cannot be with the one she loves, this passage displays an unmistakable affinity with the *paraklausithyron* (see p. 11). Admittedly, here it is a *puella* (3) who seeks "to beguile the long night." But it is all the more appropriate that Penelope should find herself—as the *puella* usually does in a *paraklausithyron*—not in front of the door, but behind it. And it is equally appropriate that, as she waits there, she should while away the time of her separation from Odysseus doing just what an elegiac *amator* would want her to be doing: weaving (cf. Propertius 1.3.41; 3.6.16).

Yet the elegiac speaker in *Epistula* 1 is not separated from the person to whom she addresses her lament by a mere door, and for the space of a mere night. A vast ocean is lying between Penelope and Odysseus and has been for twenty years. That is the situation in the myth, which, even if it is fiction for the reader, is bitter reality for Penelope. If we now compare this reality with the "concrete situation" that elegiac love creates, we see how remote from reality such erotic love is. The exalted desire for a *foedus aeternum* ignores the limits imposed by time, for it is proffered as the ideal of a countercultural philosophy of life. But anyone who, like Penelope, has lived through "only" twenty years of this "eternity" knows how much frustration and loneliness so long a time span can bring. She will also have learned that the *foedus aeternum* brings a significant "metamorphosis" with it, one the elegiac *poeta/amator,* dreaming dreams that transcend time, never pauses to consider. Penelope sums up this metamorphosis in a pointed remark at the end of her letter: "Certe ego, quae fueram te discedente puella,/protinus ut venias, facta videbor anus"; "It is certain that I, a young woman [*puella*] when you left,/have become, even if you come immediately, an old woman [*anus*] in your eyes" (115–116).

Penelope has been lauded by countless poets as the personification of marital fidelity. She herself tells us what the harsh reality of serving as a shining example is like: plainly, it causes her nothing but heartbreak. This way of presenting the celebrated monument of *fides* has a touch of "remember that you must die" (*memento mori*) about it—indeed, a touch of satire that is underpinned by this admonition. To that extent, what Ovid's *Epistula* 1 has to say is profound and deserves to be taken seriously. But this serious statement is made possible by an underlying literary game that consists in taking the escapist philosophy of the elegiac system at face value and in confronting this unrealistic ideal with the reality of a mythical life-story. The tension that breeds has a comic effect, and it is of course no accident that such comedy is related to the kind Ovid creates in the *Amores* through his playful treatment of the elegiac system.

For example, as in the *Amores,* so here too we have a playful variation on the elegist's demand—reducible to the formula "make love, not war"—that *militia amoris* be preferred to real military service. Penelope too rejects military service, which, in the guise of the battle for Troy, has robbed her of her husband and constantly exposed him to the risk of death during the first ten years of his absence. Whenever she mentions Troy in the first part of her three-part letter, in which she recapitulates the history of the war as she sees it, the city is cast as her very personal enemy. No wonder, then, that the destruction of Troy, in Penelope's description of it, seems like a special favor shown her by heaven: "Sed bene consuluit casto deus aequus amori:/Versa est in cineres sospite Troia viro"; "But a god who is just when he beholds chaste love served me well:/Troy has been reduced to dust, and my husband still lives" (23–24). Nonetheless, ten years after the event, Odysseus has still not come back to her. Hence she has to temper her statement about her intimate enemy after all: "diruta sunt aliis, uni mihi Pergama restant"; "it was destroyed for others; Troy still stands for me alone" (51). War continues to stand in love's way. That is all the elegiac lover has eyes for when she passes her subjective judgment on the significance of a contemporary event that was, be it recalled, a politically and economically crucial affair of state.

The absurdity pointed in the line just quoted is already quite funny. But the comedy is even more pronounced in the second of the letter's three parts. Here Penelope takes up the theme of "Odysseus' wanderings" (57–80). As she knows very little about them and so fears all sorts of things—especially her husband's erotic entanglements (76)—she expresses a wish that he engage in real *militia* after all:

Utilius starent etiam nunc moenia Phoebi;
  irascor votis heu levis ipsa meis!
Scirem ubi pugnares et tantum bella timerem
  et mea cum multis iuncta querela foret.

It would be more useful if the walls of Phoebus [one of the gods who built
  Troy] still stood—
ah! how inconstant I am, my own wishes anger me!
Then I would know where you are fighting [*pugnares*] and would only fear wars
and my lament would be joined with many others.

(67–70)

This is outright betrayal of the elegiac system! But it should be noted that *pugnare* [to fight] also has erotic connotations, something the speaker of this elegy "knows" quite as well as the speaker of the *Amores* (see p. 14). With that in mind, one can indeed understand why Penelope would prefer to have to worry about Odysseus' engagements on the battlefield rather than his homeward voyage, especially as it is common knowledge that her fears about the wanderer's engagements in other women's beds are only too justified.

One sees how wittily and resourcefully Ovid, pursuing a game begun in the *Amores,* plays with genre and his readers' accumulated knowledge of the literary tradition. In Penelope's letter, he gives us first Homer's *Iliad* and then his *Odyssey* in a new, elegiac perspective. The theme of the hero's wanderings accordingly yields, in the third part of the letter, to an elegiac assessment of the situation prevailing in Ithaca just before Odysseus returns (81–116). But rather than discuss this passage and its comic effects here, I simply refer the reader to the brilliant interpretations of Alessandro Barchiesi (1992) and Friedrich Spoth (1992b). For I need to make a few more general remarks about Penelope as "exemplar."

In this heroine's letter as in all others in the *Heroides* through the fourteenth, the elegiac speaker speaks only as a lover, without reflecting on poetics. Yet Ovid's elegiac poetics constantly peep out between the lines of the *Epistulae Heroidum* too. For example, the Propertian or Ovidian *poeta/amator*'s refusal to write an epic—his *recusatio*—finds its equivalent, in Penelope's letter, in the heroine's opposition to the Trojan War, which is, of course, an epic theme. Again, the speakers of these letters by heroines resemble the *poeta/amator* in that they too let wishful thinking shape their image of the person they love. What is not yet obvious in Letter 1 emerges the more clearly in several other *Epistulae* in the collection. The addressee is not regarded as he is usually portrayed in myth; rather, it is taken for granted that he will comport himself like an elegiac lover. However, this kind of "man-ufacture" can no more attain the desired end than "womanufacture" can.

That elegiac lament, admonition, and courting are usually unavailing and hence futile is shown still more compellingly by the *Heroides* than by the *Amores.* Although Penelope calls on Odysseus to come home in her letter and does in fact see him again soon after writing it, the fact that she writes him is not what brings the hero back to Ithaca. It is rather— this too is something the reader knows from the *Odyssey*—the actions of the gods, favorably inclined toward the wanderer, together with the hero's own resolve. As in the *Amores,* a vast outpouring of elegiac rhetoric proves vain, here and in all the other *Epistulae* (none of which is less than 120 lines long!). And, once again, the reader who attends closely to this process has endless occasion for amusement. He is particularly well placed to laugh in the *Epistulae,* because he has a better overall view of things than the elegiac speaker; thus he realizes, as she does not, how ridiculous an all-too-rigid adherence to the elegiac system can appear when it butts up against concrete reality. For the reader, who is of course familiar with the mythical material Ovid drew on to compose the *Epistulae,* can see that the reality of the situation dooms the outpouring of elegiac eloquence to failure in every instance. Especially funny here is the fact that the unrealistic elegiac system is by its nature tailored to the social conditions of late Republican Rome, whereas the "reality" it fails to measure up to is that of a heroic myth (or the Sappho legend) not infrequently associated with the marvelous.

Needless to say, the gap between the elegiac and "real" worlds in the *Heroides* is not always funny or at least not funny for all readers; today's reading audiences are probably the least inclined to laugh. For the myths underlying these elegiac letters almost always end in tragedy— indeed, often *are* tragedies in the versions Ovid uses. Thus in some cases the situation that gives rise to an *Epistula* is immediately followed, in "reality," by the death of the woman who writes it or the man to whom she is writing. But, in a manner as witty as it is profound, Ovid endlessly twists and parodies elegiac rhetoric even in such poems, or plays on words to undermine it and push it to the point of absurdity. Thus, for readers of his times capable of discerning all the intertextual nuances, the aesthetic pleasure produced by the poet's literary playfulness must have outweighed the tendency toward emotional involvement in the tragic situations in which the letter-writers find themselves. In the following discussion of Letters 2–15, I shall accordingly highlight the tension between elegiac love and mythical reality at work in each.

Letters 1–15: Heroines in Three Pentads

I suspect that Martin Pulbrook (1977) and Wilfried Stroh (1991) are right to assume that *Heroides* 1–15, which are not divided into separate books of poems in the manuscripts, appeared on three different papyrus rolls containing five elegies each when the work was first published sometime between 15 and 1 B.C. This is, at any rate, quite plausible, if only because the three books such a reconstruction yields are each about as long as a book of the *Amores*, a work known to have been divided into three books, and are also, again like the *Amores*, organized in pentads (see p. 50). Thus even the surface structure of the *Epistulae* indicates that it should be regarded as a pendant to the *Amores*. Moreover, thematic and structural patterns both within and across pentads show that Ovid's second collection of elegies is, like the first, a triptych that was composed with scrupulous care throughout.

The *Epistulae* in "Book 1" (1–5) are, unlike those in "Book 2" (6–10) and "Book 3" (11–15), based on just two myth cycles, which, moreover, alternate: Letters 1, 3, and 5 are based on the story of Troy, Letters 2 and 4 on the cycle of myths whose central figure is King Theseus of Athens. The elegies in the "first book" have one thing in common: hope springs eternal in all of them. Thus every one of the heroines who writes a letter is hoping either that her separation from the man she loves will end (1–3 and 5) or that her love-suit will be crowned with success (4), although, in all five cases, the prospects that the women's desires will be fulfilled could hardly be bleaker. According to mythological tradition, only two of them see their wishes come true, and in neither case does the fact that the women write their letters have the slightest influence on the matter. Only one really lives happily ever after—Penelope, the author of *Epistula* 1.

Phyllis, the next heroine in the series, has been waiting four months for Demophoon, the son of Theseus, to come back from a journey and now writes to ask that he return. She and Demophoon fell in love when he arrived in her kingdom, Thrace, after a shipwreck. But Demophoon seems to have broken both his promise to spend only a month in his native city, Athens, and his oath to marry Phyllis. Because we do not know the source for Ovid's treatment of this story, we can only surmise, on the basis of indications in other texts, that the better informed reader of Ovid's day knew that the Demophoon of the legend never did come back and that Phyllis therefore hanged herself. Indeed, she says in her letter that, in her desperation, she is contemplating killing herself that way. But she also envisages death by poison, drowning, or the sword (131ff.). Thus she proffers her lover a whole catalog of suicide methods that lends the concluding passage of her letter an unintentionally comic touch: it reads like a caricature of the kind of bathetic outburst of despair we expect from the *poeta/amator* in Propertius or Tibullus.

While we cannot, in this instance, appreciate Ovid's playful treatment of literary tradition at its full value, we are much better off when it comes to Letter 3, which presupposes, above all, familiarity with Homer's *Iliad*. The author of this letter is Briseis, the slave and beloved of Achilles, one of the Greek warriors fighting before the gates of Troy. Achilles has reluctantly handed Briseis over to Agamemnon, the commander of the Greek army. Convinced that his honor as a hero has been besmirched because he has, as it were, been compelled to give her up for reasons of state, he sulks and fumes and refuses to take part in the battle for Troy. This shows Briseis, who wants to go back to Achilles, a way to make good her wish. For Achilles' refusal to join the fray is costing the Greeks such heavy losses that, hoping for a reconciliation, Agamemnon finally offers, among other things, to give Briseis back to the furious warrior. This gets him nowhere; but now Briseis too tries to convince the hero to stop sulking. In her letter, she connects the request that he take her back with the demand that he again take up arms. But that is not only as "unelegiac" as can be imagined; it is also tantamount—though Briseis, to be sure, does not know it—to inviting Achilles to commit suicide, since it has been prophesied that he will die at Troy. On the other hand, it is more than elegiac that Briseis, a slave, should compose an erotic letter in verse. For, in doing so, she *literally* reduces herself to the state of *servitium amoris,* normally only a metaphor for elegiac lovers (see p. 11).

It is particularly conspicuous here that, for Ovid, one important way of working variations on elegy is to reverse the roles the elegiac system assigns men and women. In *Epistula 4*, Phaedra assumes the *amator's* role in the sense that she uses her letter as "courting poetry" (Stroh 1971). Her objective is to win the love of Hippolytus, the son of her husband Theseus by a first marriage. Indeed, she even poses as a professor of the art of love, thus recalling, among other things, the *poeta/amator* of *Amores* 1.4. He trained his *puella* above all, as we have seen (pp. 47ff.), in the art of deception. Phaedra's *ars amatoria* also initiates her beloved partner into the art of keeping up false pretenses. Here the aim is to disguise an erotic relationship which antiquity considered to be equivalent to incest as a licit relationship between stepmother and stepson: when they embrace, people will actually approve (139–140). Thus they will reap special benefits from the fact that they are living together in the same house. For, as Phaedra says to Hippolytus, "Non tibi per tenebras duri reseranda mariti/ianua, non custos decipiendus erit"; "You will not have to unbolt the hard husband's door/At night, nor be compelled to trick a guard" (141–142).

How convenient! Free home delivery of elegiac love! It is inconceivable that Ovid, who repeatedly and quite as nonchalantly has the speaker of the *Amores* parody the elegiac system, does not mean to make us chuckle here too. These two elegiac lovers have something else in common: their sophistic rhetoric goes wide of the mark. As we know from Euripides' tragedy *Hippolytus,* Phaedra will of course, after her initial love-suit fails, write another letter, to Theseus this time, falsely accusing his son of "daring to lay violent hands on [Theseus'] bed" (885–886)—and then kill herself. Shortly thereafter, Poseidon/Neptune will slay Hippolytus at Theseus' behest. The contemporary Roman reader would have had that too in mind as he read the "first" letter; the tension between it and the "second" is another important feature of Ovid's intertextual game (Casali 1995b).

With the last letter in "Book 1," we come to a myth that occurs near the beginning of the story of Troy: thus the "chronology" of Letters 1, 3, and 5 has run backwards from the eve of Odysseus' return through an incident that occurs not long before Achilles dies to a series of events that follow directly upon Paris' judgment. Among those affected by this last set of events is the nymph Oenone. She had been the beloved of the Trojan king's son before Venus, the goddess whom he had declared to be more beautiful than Juno or Minerva, turned his thoughts to abducting Helen. Oenone writes Paris her letter just after he arrives in Troy with his new love. In an attempt to win him back, she very graphically describes their earlier erotic relationship, which sprang up in the period when Paris was a shepherd on Mount Ida. Oenone presents their liaison as a rural idyll. One is reminded of Tibullus' elegies, in which the speaker links his hopes for *foedus aeternum* (see p. 72) with the *puella* to escapist fantasies of a bucolic existence; he especially wants to be far from the business of war in that rural world. Oenone accordingly portrays her idyll as the alternative to a love bond that will drag Paris into participating in the battle for Troy. We have come full circle. At the beginning of "Book 1," Penelope, sitting in Ithaca, cursed war as an obstacle to love; what she said then now finds confirmation from across the sea.

"Book 2" (6–10) contains only one more letter based on themes from the legend of Troy (8) and the legend of Theseus (10); the remaining three letters are by female characters who appear in the legends of the Argonauts, Aeneas, and Hercules (6, 7, and 9, respectively). In contrast to "Book 1," in which the heroines ply the art of persuasion mainly because they are still hoping that their love will be returned, "Book 2" is dominated by expressions of despair and resignation. I anticipate my discussion of "Book 3" to note that the women who write the letters it contains, Letter 13 excepted, basically recount the fate that has befallen them. Thus the triptych of the *Epistulae* bears a striking resemblance to that of the *Amores*. For in the *Amores* too we find an elegiac speaker who, in Book 1, feels rather confident about his relationship with his beloved, complains about her infidelity and his separation from her in Book 2, and, in Book 3, inserts several, sometimes rather long narrative passages into his elegies.

In the *Epistulae* as in the *Amores* (see p. 61), structural and thematic parallels link the individual books. There is no mistaking the fact that Letters 6–10 form a series which runs parallel to that formed by Letters 1–5. Hypsipyle, who writes *Epistula* 6 to Jason, is in many respects comparable to the Penelope of *Epistula* 1. Her letter is addressed to the leader of the Argonauts; his expedition to Colchis, where the Argonauts go to recover the Golden Fleece, represents the second most important epic subject after the story of Troy. (Ovid's main source here is Apollonius Rhodius' *Argonautica*.) Hypsipyle writes to Jason in her capacity as wife and mother, the same capacity in which Penelope writes to Odysseus, whose sea journey occasionally recalls that of the Argonauts. For Jason had interrupted his expedition to Colchis in Lemnos and lived there with Hypsipyle for three years, promising, when he told her good-bye, to return as her husband. During his absence, she bore him twins. But, at the time the letter is written, he has already returned to his native Thessaly and is lavishing his attentions on Medea of Colchis rather than the letter-writer. That is why Hypsipyle now curses him and his new love; indeed, Hypsipyle's letter tells us more about Medea than about Hypsipyle herself. Later, in "Book 3," Medea too will address an *epistula* (*Epistula* 12) to Jason, thus providing the "sequel" to Letter 6. Ovid, who forged similar links between *Amores* 1.4 and 2.5 and 2.19 (2.20) and 3.4, has now struck out on the path leading to the epistolary novel.

Hypsipyle's despair, expressed in the curse she hurls at Jason at the end of Letter 6, corresponds to Dido's at the beginning of her letter to Aeneas, who, even as she writes, is making preparations for a journey from which he will never return (7). Here the heroine expresses her resignation by comparing her *Epistula* to the song of a dying swan (1–2). As she reveals in the letter's closing lines, the sword she will use to kill herself is already lying in her lap (183ff.). But before she at last resolves to commit suicide, her thoughts swing back and forth between outbursts of despair and arguments intended to make Aeneas change his mind; this vacillation brings *Epistula* 7 closer than any other of the *Epistulae Heroides* to the elegies of Propertius and Tibullus, with their often utterly confusing structure. Indeed, the clash between elegiac wishful thinking and mythical reality is particularly pronounced in this letter. Unlike Virgil's Dido—the *Aeneid* is Ovid's pre-text here—this Dido cannot see, so hopelessly has love clouded her vision, that Aeneas, who was sent her way by a shipwreck, must sail on: he has been charged with a divine mission whose accomplishment will lead to the foundation of Rome. The heroine's elegiac "man-ufacture" casts the man who in the epic is given the epithet *pius* (pious) as a "fickle playboy, [and] his historic mission as aggressive pan-erotic womanizing" (Spoth 1992b, 152). At the end of the present chapter, I will speculate as to whether we can draw conclusions about Ovid's attitude toward Virgil and Augustus from this portrayal of Aeneas. For now, let me note only that Ovid's treatment of Dido is simply comic: he has her, as it were, misinterpret Virgil's *Aeneid!*

As Dido's situation in Letter "2.2" recalls Phyllis' in Letter "1.2"—both queens lament the fact that a lover who "arrived out of the blue" did not remain with them—so the situation of the author of *Epistula* 8 ("2.3"), Hermione, recalls Briseis' ("1.3"). For as Briseis was compelled to pass from Achilles' protection to Agamemnon's, so Helen's daughter has a similar experience with the *sons* of these two warriors. After being legally wedded by her grandfather Tyndareus to Agamemnon's son Orestes, Hermione is abducted by Achilles' son Neoptolemus, because her father Menelaus had betrothed her to him before the gates of Troy. In her letter, therefore, she begs Orestes to press his legal claim, making legalistic arguments and employing the corresponding terminology, something that, at first glance, hardly seems in keeping with elegiac discourse. But what we are reading is an elegy, after all, and the world of this genre has its "laws" like any other. If we further consider that what we have here is an altogether classic elegiac triangle—the *puella* and the rival indoors, the *amator* outside—then it follows that Orestes is "dutybound" to take action: one learns in *Amores* 1.9, for example, that the *amator*'s nightly forays into his rival's house may be likened to the corresponding professional duties of a soldier (see p. 14). One of the special charms of this elegy thus resides in the fact that Hermione recalls Orestes to his duty with the law code under her arm. The elegiac system accordingly becomes a *corpus iuris civilis.*

Deianira, the author of *Epistula* 9 ("2.4"), which she writes to her husband Hercules, has something in common with Phaedra ("1.4"): she too is to blame for the death of the man she loves. Some time before writing her letter, she sends Hercules, who has recently begun cheating on her and is not in the country when she writes, a tunic soaked in the blood of the centaur Nessus. She thinks it is a love potion that will enable her to win back his affections. But as she learns even as she writes, the centaur's blood is in fact poisonous and has eaten away the hero's flesh; in the end, he is driven to seek death by fire. Before learning the news of her husband's agony, for which she herself bears the blame, Deianira has admonished him, in her letter, to hold high his hero's honor: it is, she says, absolutely incompatible with the *servitium amoris* that he has now twice taken upon himself. At the moment it is Iole, captured in the war, who has bent him to the yoke; earlier it was the Lydian queen Omphale, who, Deianira reminds him, even ordered him to don women's clothing and spin wool. Deianira thus reproaches Hercules for acting like an elegiac *amator*. It is plain that readers are "physically" confronted with the consequences of her unintentional act because they are now in a position to recognize a new variation on the love/war antinomy more readily than before: they can say to themselves that a *puella* who enslaves her *amator* is, after all, preferable to a wife who, because she wants her man back and wants him to act the valiant warrior, kills him (see, for a similar interpretation, Casali 1995c).

Ovid scholars have often criticized the poet for having Deianira go on writing to her husband after she learns that he is dying. And they have waxed positively indignant over the fact that Ovid's Ariadne writes a letter to Theseus, *Epistula* 10, after he has stolen away, abandoning her on the uninhabited island of Naxos. But quite apart from the fact that one can only laugh when one begins to wonder how the letter is supposed to reach its destination (although classicists may find this a bit less amusing than others), the paradoxical situation in which the letter-writers find themselves both here and in other *Epistulae* offers a very apt illustration of the ineffectiveness of elegiac discourse. Thus, in Letter 10, the futility of Ariadne's attempt to convince her beloved to return to her is also reflected in her reaction when, before writing her letter, she wakes up and discovers that the bed beside her is empty. In minute detail, Ariadne relates how she searched for Theseus on the shore before catching sight of his ship sailing away; then, she tells us, she tried to capture his attention by shouting, waving wildly in his direction, and, finally, flying a makeshift flag of alarm. Elegiac isolation here appears in the form of a situation akin to Robinson Crusoe's. This is all very compellingly portrayed, and there is no lack of comedy about it, whether open or veiled. For example, Ovid arranges for Ariadne to recall that she cried out after Theseus as he set sail, "Flecte ratem! Numerum non habet illa suum!"; "Turn the ship around! It is still missing one member of its crew!" (36). Particularly when compared with the most important of its pre-texts, Catullus' *Carmen* 64 (132–201), Ariadne's letter appears as a veritable compendium of typically Ovidian textual games. It may be that Ovid wanted "Book 2" of the *Epistulae,* whose first elegy culminates in a curse—as does, incidentally, Ariadne's monologue in Catullus, though not Ovid's *Epistula* 10—to end with as much unintentional humor as possible in the letter-writer's declarations. In any event, Letter "2.5," like Letter "1.5," with which it is also linked by its very vivid description of a natural scene, constitutes an extremely memorable finale. At the same time, with its high proportion of narrative passages, it serves as a bridge to the next book.

Like the third book of the *Amores,* "Book 3" of the *Epistulae,* with its longish narratives, looks ahead to the *Metamorphoses* and the *Fasti.* From a thematic point of view as well, *Letters* 11–15 resemble Ovid's two later works more closely than do *Letters* 1–10, whose thematic resemblance to the *Amores* stems, rather, from the fact that their heroines face problems with which the readers of the Augustan period could easily identify. In the world of *Letters* 11–14, in contrast, sex or crime or both assume forms (as they also do in many of the tales of the *Metamorphoses* or the *Fasti*) that Ovid's contemporaries must have encountered only rarely in their own lives, if ever. Thus Canace (11) bears her brother a child; Medea (12) is on the point of deciding to murder her children; Laodamia (13), whose husband has gone off to war, transfers her affections to a surrogate, a wax doll that bears her husband's features; and Hypermestra (14) has just gone through her wedding night, during which she, like her forty-nine sisters, was supposed to kill the groom. As for Sappho, the author of *Letter* 15, she is a female poet, a rare phenomenon indeed in the Rome of c. 15–1 B.C. What is more, she reports her erotic dreams with a lack of reserve that shocks even modern American critics of Ovid; indeed, she goes so far as to describe an orgasm that she brings on by recalling the caresses she exchanged with the lover who has since left her (134).

We have, then, an extremely varied program ahead of us, lively enough even for those hooked on today's thrillers. This only makes it the more remarkable that Canace is not at all shocked by what she recounts in the letter of farewell she writes her brother Marcareus (11) before committing suicide on her father's orders: the first stirrings of her love for her brother, her pregnancy, an attempted abortion, her labor pains, and parturition (27ff.). She presents these experiences in the mode familiar from elegiac tradition, that of an elegiac speaker recapitulating his first erotic experiences. The incongruity between Canace's lexicon, familiar thanks to Propertius', Tibullus', and Ovid's *Amores*—for instance, Canace compares the lack of experience that left her unprepared for her pregnancy to a raw recruit's (50: *rudis miles*)—and the events it evokes could hardly be greater. Here intertextual play reaches its limits. It is therefore not easy to understand why Ovid critics of an earlier day, such as Ulrich von Wilamowitz-Moellendorf, who felt that the *Heroides* were "unpoetic" because they were wanting in "genuine emotion," exempted this poem, of all texts, from their damning judgment of the work. Indeed, they even confessed that they were deeply moved by it.

In *Epistula* 12, Medea presents herself as an elegiac lover when she describes her experiences with Jason from the moment she fell in love with him in Colchis down to his marriage with the Corinthian princess Crëusa, which has just taken place. Her self-stylization too stands in sharp contrast with mythical reality. For the deeds that Medea has so far done for Jason's sake, which she feels have earned her, the mother of his children, the right to marry him, not his infidelity—these deeds were the acts of a witch and a murderer, and, as such, anything but elegiac. Medea therefore avoids discussing them in any detail, choosing rather to play up the theme, in pleading with Jason to come back to her (183ff.), that her acts were above all meant to win his love. To be sure, should Jason reject her (as he eventually does), she has something far more "unelegiac" up her sleeve than anything she has engaged in before, something which unmasks her elegiac pose once and for all. In the last line of her letter, she hints at her scheme this way: "Nescio quid certe mens mea maius agit"; "My soul is most certainly preparing [*agit*] something greater [*maius*]" (214). She means the murder of her children, but she formulates her hint, as Friedrich Spoth has observed (1992b, 203–204), as a kind of anti-*recusatio,* in other words, "metapoetically": in the elegiac lexicon, a tragedy can be *maius* than what we have read up to this line—for example, a tragedy in which Medea acts (*agit!*) as a child-murderer. Is Ovid alluding to the *Medea* that Seneca the Elder, Quintilian, and Tacitus ascribe to him (see pp. 34–36)? Perhaps.

Laodamia, who has a premonition that her husband Protesilaus, the addressee of her letter (13), will not return from the Trojan campaign—in fact, he will be the first Greek casualty—pens another repudiation of *militia,* in the proper sense of the word, neatly summing up her position in a line that has become famous: "Bella gerant alii: Protesilaus amet!"; "Others may wage war; let Protesilaus love!" (82). But she takes her interpretation of "make love, not war" too far when, defying custom, she demands that her warrior act in a decidedly unwarlike manner. We are once again reminded of the way the elegiac speaker "forms" his partner in the *Amores.* This applies in spades to the aforementioned ersatz activities with the wax doll (151ff.).

Hypermestra, the author of the next Letter (14), was ordered by her father Danaus to replace love with war; as we have already noted, she was supposed to kill her husband Lynceus, the man she writes to, on her wedding night. The style she uses in explaining how it happened that she did not carry out the order is the same circumstantial, elegiac style that Canace and Medea employ in their narratives. Yet the way Hypermestra treated Lynceus was, so to speak, one-sided. She limited herself to a *recusatio* of the violent act: that is, she spared her husband's life and let him get away. It is obvious, however, that she did not do so out of love for him—she does not, in any event, mention love in her letter. And all she asks of Lynceus, now that her father has had her put in chains and condemned her to death, is that he help free her or else kill her and then see to it that she gets a decent burial. What we have here is thus a poem like *Amores* 3.13, an elegy with nothing erotic about it placed just before the end of a collection of erotic elegies. Ovid perhaps wishes to emphasize, by arranging for Hypermestra to compare her tribulations with Io's in an atypically lengthy narrative (85–108), that he is again deviating from the generic norm. He will come back to the myth of this woman changed into a cow in the *Metamorphoses* (1.568ff.).

Epistula 15, Sappho's letter to Phaon, who has left her, should likewise be read as the pendant to a poem found at the end of the *Amores.* With its metapoetical reflections (1–8; 195–206), it functions as an epilogue, like *Amores* 3.15. Sappho, however, is not only a *poetria,* but also an *amatrix.* As in the *Amores,* the two functions stand in a relation of tension, so that there is good reason for comparing the letter with the earlier collection taken as a whole. The comparison brings out striking parallels. Like *Amores* 1.1, the letter opens with a justification for switching from another genre (lyric, in the present instance) to elegy (1–8). Major themes of the first book of the *Amores* appear in the first long subdivision of the letter (9–96): the elegiac speaker's self-presentation (9–20; 27–45; 59–84); a description of the beloved (21–26; 85–96); reminiscences of the shared joys of love (46–50); and an expression of the speaker's fear of rivals (51–56). In the second part of the letter (97–156), Sappho recounts the experiences, dreams, and thoughts she has had since Phaon left her. This parallels Book 2 of the *Amores* in the sense that the plot line of Book 2 runs from the *puella*'s first act of overt infidelity to a moment of crisis in her relationship with the speaker.

The third part of the letter (157–220) begins, like Book 3 of the *Amores,* with a divine epiphany (it is a naiad who appears here). As in the earlier text, the theme is a farewell to love and poetry. But, unlike the *poeta/amator*, what Sappho wants is not to make the transition to a new genre; rather, if she should survive her leap from the Leucadian rock into the sea, thus freeing herself from love's grip, she vows to consecrate her lyre to Apollo and thus give up writing altogether. Of course, at the close of her letter, Sappho once again appeals to Phaon, asking him, despite all, to make a decision for or against her. Thus this *Epistula* ends the same way the mythical women's letters do. But that by no means alters the fact that Sappho's letter ought to be regarded as the real pendant to the *Amores.*

Letters 16–21: A Triptych with an Apparently Happy Ending

We do not know the title of the collection of three paired letters that Ovid published sometime between 1 and 8 A.D., or perhaps only after he was banished. In existing editions, it appears as part of the *Epistulae Heroidum* (or *Heroides*). Yet only half of it consists of letters by women: Letter 16 is addressed by Paris to Helen and Letter 17 is the response to it; the authors of the paired Letters 18 and 19 are Leander and Hero, and 19 and 20 are written by Acontius and Cydippe. At one point, Ovid himself refers to an erotic epistolary elegy by a mythical woman as, simply, an *Epistula* (*Ars amatoria* 3.345). Should we take this to mean that the title of both collections was simply *Epistulae*? If so, we would no longer need to ask if Ovid considered Sappho one of the Heroides. But, apart from the fact that there is no way of solving the problem, people have quite simply acquired the habit of speaking, on the one hand, of the *Epistulae Heroidum*—in part as a way of distinguishing these letters from the *Epistulae ex Ponto*—and, on the other, of the paired letters.

The question as to the written form in which Ovid brought these paired letters before the public poses still another problem. Together, they come to 1,570 lines, a length that would probably have exceeded the limits of a single book-roll. Of course, the possibility that all six *Epistulae* were collected in a single book cannot be ruled out. However, a book of Ovid's usually contains 700–800 lines, which is only about half the total number of lines in the paired letters. Martin Pulbrook (1977) therefore assumes that the letters of the "heroes" made up one book and those of the women they loved another. That too is conceivable. We have seen that the first collection of letters includes a "pair of letters" split in two by the dividing line between two books: the two *Epistulae* addressed to Jason by Hypsipyle ("2.1," i.e., 6) and Medea ("3.2," i.e., 12). Our discussion of the second collection, however, will show that it too constitutes a triptych that one can recognize as such only if one reads the six letters in the order in which they have come down to us in the manuscripts. It is therefore also conceivable that the collection consisted of three short books, each made up of a single pair of letters.

Paris' and Helen's letters (16/17), taken together, comprise a "novella" about the beginnings of an erotic relationship. Paris is a guest in the palace of the Spartan king Menelaus; the king is off on a journey and Paris is alone with the king's wife Helen. Paris now writes her a profession of love, contending that Venus has "given" her to him and substantiating his claim by recounting how he pronounced his famous judgment (39–136; these lines are indubitably authentic, although they appear in only one printed fifteenth-century version of the text). The next section of the letter, the first part of Paris' love-suit (137–284), again recalls the opening of Book 1 of the *Amores*. Proceeding as the *poeta/amator* does there in Elegies 3, 4, and 5, Paris praises Helen's beauty (137–162), introduces himself (163–214), and describes the feelings of jealousy tormenting him; they were hardest to bear, he says, when he found himself with his beloved and her husband at a feast (215–284). Then, in the second part of his letter (285–376), he rebuts every imaginable objection to the idea of his carrying Helen off to Troy.

As we have seen, the elegiac speaker of the *Amores* begins his courtship of his *puella* by making speeches (1.3 and 1.4) in which he basically feigns a willingness to be true to her and incites her to deceive her partner of the moment. Both stratagems are initially successful but ultimately backfire. Paris' courtship of Helen has exactly the same effects, as we know from the story of Troy. However, the principle informing his letter is not deception but self-deception. Paris misinterprets signs he has already seen indicating that his abduction of Helen will lead to the struggle for Troy. If one disregards this self-deception, one can certainly take his arguments seriously, which is why Helen finds it hard to counter them, although she too argues skillfully. Of course, she undoubtedly understands that Paris' hopes that the abduction will not touch off a war are illusory. But she is the one who relies on deception. From one end to the other, her reply to Paris shows that she returns his love; yet she strains to conceal this behind her counterarguments and a facade of virtue. Thus, like the Sappho of *Epistula* 15, Helen too resembles the *poeta/amator* of the *Amores*, even if the resemblance stops at the fact that she too is dishonest.

Leander's and Hero's letters (18–19) grow out of an erotic relationship that has already gone on for some time. The dominant theme here is that of the separation of the two lovers: between them lies the Hellespont, which Leander swims across under cover of darkness, because both lovers have to conceal their relationship from their parents. But, for seven nights running, a storm has made this form of communication with Hero impossible, so that it has to be replaced with an epistolary exchange. A delay (*mora*) has interrupted the progress of the "erotic novel," and both *Epistulae* deal primarily with the question as to whether Leander should put an end to this *mora* betimes by venturing out onto the sea despite the storm. Ultimately he does, drowning in the process, as ancient readers knew from Ovid's (lost) Hellenistic source. If only he had spent the *mora* writing rather than swimming! It is true that, in one of Horace's satires, a friend recommends (among other things) that the poet, who is having trouble writing verse, try a bath in the Tiber as an alternative (2.1.1ff.). But although Leander was merely an *amator* and no *poeta*, he would have been better advised—so we may interpret the story at the metapoetical level—to compose more elegiac letters rather than battling a storm at sea, as one often finds heroes doing in epics. Moreover, Hero and Leander have failed to take to heart the lesson that lovers need to be well versed in the *ars moratoria* taught, as we have seen, in Ovid's *Art of Love* (see p. 9).

The object of Acontius' *Letter* (20), like Paris', is doubtless courtship. Yet Acontius has conducted a "relationship" with his Cydippe—in writing, at any rate—for quite some time. For, in a temple of Diana's, he once rolled an apple inscribed with a few words at the *puella*'s feet; she read aloud what was written on it—a promise, in the name of the goddess, to marry Acontius. On the day she was to marry another man, therefore, she fell ill; another date was set for that marriage, but the same thing happened, and not just once. Acontius now writes her a declaration in which he makes a hair-splitting defense of his "legal claim." As it has before, this kind of rhetoric once again proves ineffective; yet Cydippe, though she is entirely capable of countering Acontius' arguments in her letter (21; lines 13–248 have again come down to us only in a printed fifteenth-century version of the poem), has to bow to a fate rendered inevitable by the oath she swore before the goddess. For the last time in a verse letter, Ovid points a conflict between elegiac discourse and mythic reality.

The poet doubtless put this pair of poems at the very end of the series of letters because his model was here, for the first and only time, an elegiac text—and one found in Callimachus' *Aitia* at that (see p. 6). What is more, he managed to combine this sort of homage to the first great *poeta doctus* with a particularly witty metapoetical game. For the apple bears what is far and away the shortest text in either of the two collections of letters; yet, despite its brevity, this text is much more effective than all the other voluminous elegiac texts they contain. But is that any wonder? "A big book is a big evil."

Furthermore, it is, for a finale, entirely appropriate that the period during which Acontius and Cydippe write to each other exactly coincides with the period immediately preceding a wedding. Hence the structure of the collection of paired letters matches that of the story line of a Greek novel, whose three-step development we have already compared to the sequence *Amores* 1.3–1.4–1.5 (see pp. 47f.). Thus the paired letters 16/17 correspond to the beginning of a romantic relationship; 18/19 to the phase of obstacles and separation; and 20/21 to the events that lead straight to the happy ending. We have seen that the erotic novel contained in the *Amores,* as well as the internal structure of the first two parts of Sappho's letter, bears a resemblance to Parts 1 and 2 of this triptych structure. But whereas Part 3 of both the *Amores* and the letter gives us the very opposite of a happy ending, we find a surprising reversal of the pattern in the third part of the collection of paired letters. Yet if the epistolary novel contained in *Epistulae* 20 and 21 culminates in peace, joy, and domestic bliss, it must be said that the circumstances under which it does are so problematic that the "happy ending" is really nothing of the sort.

Epistulae and Postal Secrets

In the first half of the twentieth century, Latin scholars considered Ovid's erotic epistolary elegies to be very poor poetry indeed. When they began to reconsider in the late 1960s, they directed their attention to the poet's unlimited capacity for depicting the subtlest stirrings of the human heart. If, with this in mind, we approach the *Epistulae* after reading the *Amores,* we will immediately be struck by the fact that the second collection of elegies surpasses the first in the variety of its descriptions of human psychology. This has its explanation above all in the fact that the mythical women (and men) who, in their letters, discuss their relationship to someone they love, repeatedly go beyond the narrow limits of the problematic of romantic relationships and sex to express emotions arising from other experiences of happiness and pain. Thus Hermione's thoughts, for example, range freely from a vivid recollection of the trials and tribulations of life without her legitimate spouse to reminiscences of the solitude she knew as a child as a result of the permanent absence of her parents:

> Parva mea sine matre fui; pater arma ferebat;
>   et duo cum vivant, orba duobus eram.
> Non tibi blanditias primis, mea mater, in annis
>   incerto dictas ore puella tuli.
> Non ego captavi brevibus tua colla lacertis,
>   nec gremio sedi sarcina grata tuo.

> As a little girl, I lived without my mother; my father
>   bore arms,
> and, though both were alive, I was bereft of both.
> I could not, mother, as a little girl in her first years
> say tender words to you, lisped with an uncertain tongue,
> Could not stretch short arms out toward your neck,
> nor sit in your lap as a precious burden.
>
> (8.89–94)

In recent years, readers have rightly praised the psychological insight that Ovid displays here and in countless other passages of the *Epistulae*. It certainly is not going too far to speak, in connection with this kind of descriptive skill, of the "emergence of the literary man of modern times," as Gustav Adolf Seeck puts it (1975, 436). But such an approach tends to concentrate on the opportunities for identification that the speakers of the *Epistulae* offer the reader. There is, admittedly, good reason for this; but it makes it easy to overlook the distance that Ovid's intertextual play puts between speaker and reader.

Yet, in the two passages in Ovid's oeuvre in which the first collection of *Epistulae* is mentioned—*Amores* 2.18.21–34 and *Ars amatoria* 3.345–346—the focus is exclusively on the wit and playful eroticism of the work. In *Amores* 2.18, the *poeta/amator* tells us about a certain Sabinus who has brought back answers to *Epistulae* 1, 4, 7, 2, 6, and 15 from the towns and villages where the addressees of those letters are living. Thus this poet, who probably was a real historical personage, expanded individual letters into pairs of letters in a way the second collection of *Epistulae* has familiarized us with. Both the curious fiction that made Sabinus a messenger boy as well as a glance at the letters to which he chose to have their recipients respond suggest that his poetic vision of things was a comic one. For, as Konrad Heldmann has shown (1994), the *Epistulae Heroidum* do not really leave room for answers. For instance, Penelope expressly tells Odysseus not to write her a letter but simply to come back home (1.1–2). If he did respond, contrary to her express wish, this was itself proof of how lightly he took her fervent plea for his speedy return.

Ovid would hardly have given so large a place to his report on the *Epistulae* written by Sabinus if he had not wanted to suggest that we should regard his *Epistulae* too as products of his sense of humor. It must be added that he mentions Sabinus' letters in the context of a *recusatio* (see p. 34). What is more, in the role of the professor of erotics in the *Ars amatoria* (3.345–346), Ovid advises the *puellae* whom he is coaching in the art of seduction to recite passages from the *Epistulae* with their best art—

presumably when in company. The manifest object of the exercise is to win the attention of a man (Spoth 1992a). But the professor of love could not recommend the epistolary elegies as an effective means to this end unless he believed that their handling of erotic themes was comparable to that of the *Amores,* which he mentions in the same context.

The *Epistulae* too is simply so rich in little literary and erotic games that we cannot *not* read it as a product of the merry muse. The playful character of the work also makes it hard—indeed, impossible—to identify unambiguous authorial intentions behind passages in which one can, if one likes, discern references to Augustan Rome. When, say, Dido's despair over the fact that Aeneas has left her (Letter 7) inclines her to treat the travels he undertakes on his divine mission as Casanova-like bedhopping, one can perhaps argue that Ovid is here hinting at his doubts about Augustus' mission, prefigured as it is by Aeneas'. But the fact remains that the voice we hear is not Ovid's, but Dido's; and it is, before all else, simply amusing to see how wide of the mark this woman is in her interpretation of events that had world-historical significance for contemporary readers. If we find this funny, does it follow that we are making light of what Dido misinterprets and are therefore mocking Virgil's *Aeneid?* We certainly may make fun of both if we wish; but nothing says that we have to. And nothing at all in the text enables us to say where Ovid stands on the matter.

The poet invites his readers to join in a game, leaving as much room for play as possible. The heroines, as we have seen, confuse what seems to be and what really is, because they fail to distinguish elegiac daydreams from reality. Moreover, by insisting that a situation which has come to an irrevocable end be prolonged, many of them blind themselves to a principle whose significance for the world of experience (and for his own literary production!) Ovid emphasizes time and again: the principle that everything is always changing. One can argue that the *Epistulae*'s way of representing this sort of behavior stems from neutral observation of a phenomenon that is human, all-too-human. Or that it is a satiric presentation of the *theatrum mundi* that oscillates between the comic and the serious. Or that it is a description of moral infirmity influenced by popular philosophy. Or that it is anything one likes. It is doubtless fortunate that Ovid has stamped the *Epistulae* "secret" in the sense that he does not even indicate whether there is a right way to read his text—and, if so, what it is.

Love Theory between Appearance and Reality: The *Ars Amatoria* and the *Remedia Amoris*

Common to the *Amores* and *Epistulae Heroidum* is the fact that their speakers have negative experiences of love. We shall now learn from two elegiac poems comprising a four-book series of lessons on love, the *Ars amatoria* and the *Remedia amoris,* that men such as the *poeta/amator* and women such as, say, Phyllis (see *Ars* 3.37–38 or *Remedia* 55–56) can prevent a relationship from breaking up or, should the breakup be inevitable, can easily get over it, if they accept the guidance of the speaker of these two works, the *praeceptor amoris* (professor of love). Two lecture courses are on offer: depending on one's needs, one can take a course on the art of love, which guarantees romantic success, or another on love therapy, which promises a sure way out of unhappy love affairs. The *praeceptor amoris* owes his existence to yet another in a long line of "metamorphoses." In the exordium to the *Ars,* he declares that his knowledge rests on concrete experience (29: *usus*) and, as he pursues his explanations, makes frequent reference to edifying episodes with his *puella,* two of which are manifestly identical to episodes the *poeta/amator* recounts in the *Amores* (compare *Ars* 2.169 or 551–552 with *Amores* 1.7 or 2.5). Obviously, then, the speaker of the first collection of elegies has been made wiser by experience and has, as a result, become a professor of love.

A comparison of the *Ars* and the *Remedia* with other ancient manuals reveals that the *praeceptor amoris* is the product of a *literary* metamorphosis as well. The manuals most closely akin to his are the Greek handbooks on sex (which have been lost, with the exception of a small papyrus fragment); they describe, above all, positions for intercourse—the *Ars* too treats that theme! (3.769–808)—and present themselves as the work of a sexually experienced female slave or prostitute (Parker 1992). Against the background of this tradition, the *praeceptor amoris* also appears as a woman who has been changed into a man. This may be one reason that he so demonstratively and so often poses as a writer of didactic epic, presenting himself as a latter-day Hesiod (*Works and Days*), Lucretius (*The Nature of Things*), or Virgil (*Georgics*). Of course, he does so above all in order to expand the intertextual frame of reference of his erotic didactic poem to include not just elegy, but also didactic poetry. Traditional structural features of this kind of epic—prologues, epilogues, digressions on mythology and the history of civilization—as well as the elevated style and, in particular, the formulaic language of the apostrophes to the students (for instance, "add to this . . ."), are very wittily parodied in the *Ars* and the *Remedia*. These two works thus provide one of many bridges to the poems Ovid would write next, the *Metamorphoses* and the *Fasti*. For the game played here is pursued in them, as we shall see.

Far more important, however, are the literary references that both the *Ars* and the *Remedia* establish by exploiting the conventions of erotic elegy. For the course in *praecepta amoris* (rules of love) has nothing of the systematic structure of a manual about it, but rather follows the chronological scheme of an elegiac erotic novel: like the *poeta/amator* in the *Amores*, the male student the preceptor addresses in Books 1 and 2 of the *Ars* passes through all the successive stages of an erotic relationship. This time, however, he does so not at the level of practical personal experience, but rather in theory, that is, in an ongoing series of lessons on love corresponding to these different stages. The protagonist of the erotic novel constructed in this fashion is no longer the elegiac "I," but rather his male student/reader, or, so to speak, the "elegiac thou." Much the same thing happens with the female student/reader in Book 3 of the *Ars*. As to the *Remedia*, it is an inverted erotic novel: its male and female students/readers undergo the successive stages of a psychotherapy at the theoretical level, immediately before and just after the protagonist is freed from the trammels of an unhappy love affair.

Unlike the erotic novel contained in the *Amores*, however, these novels have happy endings. For they see to it that their main characters attain their respective goals, at least theoretically: in *Ars* 2 and 3, in bed, and in the *Remedia*, in front of the *puella*'s door, which the *amator* now serenely strolls past. But is it possible for students and readers, male or female, to believe that they will really achieve the success they are seeking by putting the *praecepta amoris* into practice? It is, if they think that the felicitous course of an erotic relationship or liberation from an erotic entanglement can be rationally planned and organized. Many readers, however, will draw comparisons with their own concrete experience and conclude that practice fails to confirm certain of the preceptor's theories. For them, a field of tension will spring up between the world of elegiac erotics and the real world as they know it. Does this mean that the second of the two poles of this field of tension, the one represented by myth in the *Epistulae Heroidum,* lies wholly outside the world of the text in the *Ars* and the *Remedia?* We shall see that, in this world as well, love theory is situated somewhere between appearance and reality.

Ars Amatoria, Books 1 and 2: The Art of Deception in Three Easy Lessons

The male student's course in the art of love is divided into three lessons, as the *praeceptor amoris* himself announces in advance. Book 1 offers instruction on where to find a *puella* in Rome (41–262) and how to bed her down (263–770), while Book 2 is about how the *amator* can firmly bind the *puella* to him. The course accordingly begins with an erotically oriented topography of Rome. In a kind of guided tour of the city, the preceptor makes shorter or longer stops in various public buildings and the forum, theater, circus, and arena. He then names the public ceremonies—for instance, victory celebrations—which, like banquets, provide occasions for sighting a *puella.* He concludes with a few comments on two spots women frequent outside Rome.

Already, in this first lesson, there emerges an antithesis crucial to the preceptor's "pedagogical theory." It appears, on his presentation of the matter, when people of an earlier day are compared with those of his own times. Over against the simplicity and coarseness of the mores that once prevailed, he sets the refined civilization he lives in: the kind of erotic activity he teaches is, he says, one facet of that civilization. Accordingly, love is for him essentially based on reason, emotional self-control, and a discriminating aesthetic. Thus he makes sexual commerce between men and women look like a sophisticated parlor game. And Augustus' Rome, with its architectural splendor, provides a welcome backdrop for the picture he draws.

In the first lesson, the preceptor offers a memorable illustration of the contrast he sets up between past and present. It comes in the context of remarks on the theater and circus as places where *amator* and *puella* can meet. He demonstrates how opportune a visit to the theater can be for such meetings by recounting the legend of the rape of the Sabine women (89–134). Then he gives a lesson on flirting at the circus by recapitulating a scene, vividly described in *Amores* 3.2, in which a *poeta/amator* woos a *puella* while they watch a chariot race (135–162).

The salient feature of the rape of the Sabine women—because Rome, the city he has just founded, is suffering from a shortage of females, King Romulus invites the Sabine women to the city and then to the theater so that his countrymen can drag them off during the performance—is the use of brute force; the Romans throw themselves on the *puellae* like wild animals pouncing on their prey. In contrast, the forms which, on the preceptor's instructions, his student should observe in carrying out his conquest of the *puella* at the circus are redolent of the school of high gallantry. Primitive hunting is thus contrasted with cultivated seduction. But does the one have nothing at all to do with the other? The *amator* at the circus is, after all, advised to cheer loudly for the same charioteer as the *puella* (145–146)—a deceptive maneuver that certainly bears comparison with a hunter's wiles.

What is only hinted at here and in one other passage in the first lesson (221–222) stands out the more sharply in the second and third. Most of the advice the preceptor dispenses on establishing and then sustaining a relationship is about keeping up false pretenses—indeed, about lying and fraud. But, if so, is what replaces the "coarseness" of the Romans' primitive ancestors simply "civilization"? In any event, what the preceptor holds out to his student as the art of love befitting cultivated Romans of the Augustan age is in no small measure a rather decadent *ars fallendi* (art of deception). Moreover, the preceptor not only teaches that art, but also practices it in his course, as can be seen at the very beginning of lesson two (263ff.). Here the professor claims that every woman will give in because sexual desire is much stronger in the other sex than in men. How does he prove it? Simply by producing a catalog of mythical women who stop at nothing in their frenzied passion: neither incest, nor sodomy, nor murder (283–344). But these are extreme cases, from which the student can hardly deduce a general rule. If he does, then he is letting the wealth of examples—doubtless, this is precisely what the preceptor wants—divert him from critically examining the argument.

The preceptor relates, and at great length, one of the myths he offers as an exemplum: the legend of Pasiphaë (289–326), a Cretan woman in love with a bull. The example of Pasiphaë's massive libido is supposed to show that all women are oversexed, those living in Rome around 1 B.C. not excepted. Thus it is actually quite appropriate that the preceptor should characterize his Pasiphaë as, in many respects, an elegiac *amatrix;* for instance, he has her call the bull her *dominus* (314). But this simultaneously generates the tension between the world of elegiac wish fulfillment and mythical reality already familiar to us from the *Epistulae Heroidum.* To that tension there corresponds, as I shall now go on to show, a discrepancy between appearance and reality that may also be discerned in the set of *praecepta amoris* discussed in the second lesson for the male student, which begins a few lines after the story of Pasiphaë (351ff.).

I should first point out that the teachings of the *Ars* and the *Remedia* are also attuned to the elegiac system, like the Ovidian version of the erotic myth we just glanced at. Thus the *praeceptor amoris* advises his student to shed tears while entreating the *puella* to hear him out (659–660). Tears are, in fact, a hallmark of the elegiac lover, since lament is basic to elegy. They therefore flow abundantly in Propertius and Tibullus. But nowhere in those two authors does an *amator* adopt the course of action that the preceptor recommends to his student in the passage cited above: if the tears do not flow on cue, he tells the young man, then he should wipe his eyes with a damp hand (661–662). Anyone reading that will surely wonder (if he does not simply laugh) whether this recommendation can contribute to the rational solution of romantic problems promised by the preceptor. If he doubts it, then he has created the field of tension between the text and the world of his experience that we evoked a moment ago. But he can find a similar tension *in* the world of the text as well. There the two poles are constituted by traditional elegiac motifs on the one hand, and, on the other, deceptive maneuvers that hardly square with the values associated with such motifs.

Let us now recall that, at the very beginning of the erotic novel, the *poeta/amator* of the *Amores* resorted to playacting to deceive the *puella* (p. 47). If the *praeceptor amoris* trains his student to act similarly, then he has not undergone any "metamorphosis" in this respect since the days when he was acquiring his practical experience. What *is* new, however, is that he sets a systematic, carefully organized strategy of deception over against the *poeta/amator*'s only occasional feints. Moreover, the preceptor calls his student's attention to a point that the *poeta/amator* does not consider when, as we have seen (pp. 51f.), he tries to sweep his *puella* off her feet with a flood of imposing talk:

quam populus iudexque gravis lectusque senatus,
    tam dabit eloquio victa puella manus.
sed lateant vires, nec sis in fronte disertus;
    effugiant voces verba molesta tuae.
quis, nisi mentis inops, tenerae declamat amicae?

Like the people and the stern judge and the select circle of the Senate
so woman [*puella*] too, vanquished by eloquence, will surrender.
But may your strength be hidden; do not make an open show of your rhetoric.
May your tongue beware of affected expressions.
Who, save a lunatic, would make speeches to his tender beloved?

(461–465)

That the preceptor admonishes the student to dissimulate his rhetorical gifts while warning him not to be long-winded squares with everything else he says about the need to playact. To be sure, in this case the preceptor's recommendation happens to comply with a requirement of the ancient theory of rhetoric, which calls for *dissimulatio artis,* that is, a style of discourse whose artificial nature goes unnoticed by the listener. Wilfried Stroh (1979b) has shown that the *Ars* and the *Remedia* allude constantly to the rules laid down by the Greek and Roman teachers of eloquence. As many of these rules also apply to the writing of verse, we have here another instance in which an elegiac speaker makes an indirect statement about poetics. For the rule laid down in 1. 463 of our text echoes a stylistic maxim that plainly mattered a great deal to the poet Ovid, as can be seen throughout his work. For example, the narrator of the *Metamorphoses* refers to this rule when, recounting how Pygmalion came to regard his statue as a real human being, he remarks (10.252) that "ars . . . latet arte sua" (art remains hidden thanks to its art).

Thus the lines just cited, among others, show that the preceptor can also mean poetics when he talks about erotics. Much the same thing holds for the metaphors of the ship and the chariot. The preceptor makes frequent use of both (*Ars* 1.3–4, 39–40, 41, 51, etc.), for the forward movement of these two means of transportation can be used to illustrate the student's progress in learning the art of love as well as the progression of the didactic poem. The second of the lessons for the *amator* briefs him on the path that will take him from his first contacts with the *puella,* established with the help of her handmaid (351–374), to his first attempts to have intercourse with her (669–722; ll. 723–754 offer him lessons on how to behave after his initial success; ll. 755–770 proffer some general advice by way of conclusion; ll. 771–772 provide a transition to Book 2). On the last point, the student learns that he may use force to stimulate the *puella*'s readiness to engage in love-play. We may again wonder what an art of love that includes the use of force has to do with reason or cultivated gallantry. To be sure, the preceptor contends that women actually want to be raped; but, here too, the only evidence he offers comes from myth.

The story of Achilles' rape of Deidamia, offered as part of the argument, has already been discussed in another context (see p. 9). This *puella* is, everything else aside, the victim of a trick, since the seducer wears women's clothing. Though the preceptor affirms that she too appreciated her *amator*'s way of going about things, one should keep in mind that, in the many different accounts of rape in the *Metamorphoses* and the *Fasti,* the instances in which the victim suffers emotionally outnumber the others. Thus there is at least room for the suspicion that the *praeceptor amoris,* who gives his student systematic training in deceiving the *puella,* wants, here as elsewhere, to deceive his student too so as to feed him on false hopes.

It is highly likely that the *praeceptor amoris* himself betrays doubts as to whether what he teaches actually works—this in a passage near the beginning of Book 2, almost exactly in the middle of the course for men, where he recounts the myth of Daedalus and Icarus (21–98). Just prior to the passage in question, in the proem to Book 2 (1–20), he even says that his student, in his joy at conquering the *puella* (thanks to lesson 2), declares the *Ars* to be more important than the works of Hesiod or Homer. Thus the teacher now girds up for a task that represents a special challenge to his art—teaching the student, in the third lesson, how to bind the *puella* to him. But that, says the preceptor, is no different from trying to keep the god of love, Cupid, from flying off, as he is wont to do at a moment's notice. He goes on to demonstrate how difficult *that* task is by recounting his myth. King Minos, he tells us, wants to prevent Daedalus from leaving Crete (which suggests that the king is the preceptor's counterpart). Daedalus tries to escape by making wings for himself and his son Icarus and then flying away. But when the boy disobeys his father's orders and flies too close to the sun, the wax holding his wings together melts and he goes plunging into the sea.

A number of Ovid scholars have convincingly argued that the conspicuous equivalence between the preceptor and Minos is in fact secondary, and that the real point of the text is to suggest that Daedalus stands for the preceptor. We cannot here linger over the many thematic and linguistic parallels between what we are told about this mythic creator of a "new work of art" (48) and what a work of poetics might well have to say about the preceptor and his *ars.* Let us content ourselves with pointing out that the metaphor of soaring flight was often used in antiquity to signify poetic activity; that the description of the wings as *leve opus* (light work, l. 46) might also serve as a description of the *Ars;* and that, by giving Icarus lessons in the *ars* of flying, Daedalus assumes the role of a "didactic poet." As he goes on to describe the disaster that ensued when this art was put into practice, the preceptor is, one suspects, indirectly indicating just how (un)likely it is that anyone who applies the *ars* the preceptor himself teaches will succeed. Of course, there is no way of deciding whether Icarus is supposed to represent the student, Cupid, the *Ars,* or all three. Thus there are no unambiguous answers to the following pair of questions: Is Icarus, considered as a student, the sole failure here, so that the only suggestion is that the *amator*'s attempt to apply the art of love will fail? Or is the preceptor characterizing the artist Daedalus as unreliable and thus suggesting that he himself is too? Whichever the case, the fact that he narrates the myth tends to imply that he is skeptical about what his art can actually accomplish.

The third lesson on acquiring that art is divided into two main parts. The first (2.99–336) is about firming up the liaison between the student and his new female conquest. The different sections of this part of the poem offer the *amator* suggestions on how to retain the favors of his *puella;* they unmistakably recall the forms the *poeta/amator* in Propertius and Tibullus observes in his dealings with his beloved in order to keep her firmly bound to him. But marked differences emerge as well—between, for example, "classical" *servitium amoris* and the services the *praeceptor amoris* enjoins his student to render the *puella*. Compare the prescriptions of the elegiac system with the following *praecepta:*

> iussus adesse foro, iussa maturius hora
> fac semper venias, nec nisi serus abi.
> occurras aliquo, tibi dixerit, omnia differ,
> curre, nec inceptum turba moretur iter.
> nocte domum repetens epulis perfuncta redibit:
> tum quoque pro servo, si vocat illa, veni.
> Rure erit, et dicet "venias": Amor odit inertes:
> si rota defuerit, ⬚ pede carpe viam.
> nec grave te tempus sitiensque Canicula tardet,
> nec via per iactas candida facta nives.

> If you are bidden to be at the Forum, then always arrive
> before the appointed hour and leave late.
> If she tells you that you should run to meet her somewhere, put
>   everything else off.
> Run! No crowd should hold you up on the way.
> At night, she wants to go home after a banquet;
> Go like a slave then too, if she calls you.
> She might be in the countryside and say that you should come.—
>   Cupid hates the lazy;
> If you have no chariot, make your way there quickly on foot.
> Let neither oppressive heat nor the Dog Star, who makes us thirsty,
>   hold you back,
> nor a street white with freshly fallen piles of snow.

(223–232)

When one recalls that, for example, the *poeta/amator* in Tibullus is even prepared to plow the fields if his *puella* tells him to—indeed, that he would not balk at being chained and whipped (2.3.79–80)—then the "slave-work" the preceptor's student is supposed to perform at his *puella*'s behest appears rather innocuous. One might even speak of a humanization of *servitium amoris*. But, in that case, it should also be borne in mind that that elegiac concept is basically meant only as a metaphor for the attitude of anti-establishment protest typical of a young intellectual with a countercultural lifestyle. It follows that the *servitium*'s inefficacy is in fact always one of its inherent features, a way of signaling that the antibourgeois pose is intended as a provocation. In Ovid, in contrast, what was at first primarily an image is again wittily taken at face value. It is as if the *praeceptor amoris*, who serves up an interminable catalog of *servitia* (the quotation above is a brief extract from a passage seventy-four lines long [177–250]), had begun by asking, "Dammit, is there no *servitium* that actually works?" At any event, the way he has his student positively overwhelm his *puella* with favors is very funny. It is just as funny to note that the *amator* manages to avoid a surcharge of effort and humiliation. Where quantity is on offer, "quality"—which has in any case proven ineffective—may be allowed to go by the boards.

Anyone who feels that the moderate variety of *servitium amoris* recommended by the *praeceptor amoris* is a contribution to the rational deflation of elegiac excess, and therefore cultivated and humane, should keep something else in mind: the above-quoted lines occur in a context in which there is again much talk of strategies of deception. This discussion reaches its climax at the end of the part of lesson 3 which prepares the *amator* for the eventuality that the *puella* might fall ill (315–336). He is unambiguously urged to take good care of her simply so that he can reap the fruits his efforts may be expected to bear, that is, in the hope that his patient will treat him well—not, say, feel well afterward! That is why the preceptor allows the student to offer only "psychotherapy"— kissing, for example—and to send for an old woman versed in ritual hocus-pocus. The *amator* must not give the *puella* medicine to drink, because the bitter liquid might make her hate him. He should therefore leave it to his rival to mix the medicine.

In the second part of lesson 3, the *amator* learns how to sustain a relationship with a woman once it has become a matter of habit (337–732). Two-thirds of this part of the lesson are given over to the problem of infidelities. After an introductory passage (337–372) comes a section that deals, first, with the *amator*'s infidelity (373–492) and then with his *puella*'s (493–600). The preceptor works the second of these two themes up into a demand that erotic activities be veiled over and hushed up (601–640). He next shows the student how he can delude himself into taking his beloved's flaws for virtues (641–662); then, after discoursing on the advantages of having a mature sexual partner (663–702), he teaches his student how to act in bed (703–732). The instructions he provides in this area—the last of his precepts bears on simultaneous orgasm as the ultimate objective of his course—are followed by a short epilogue. It tapers off into an advertisement for the course for *puellae* (733–746).

Like Book 2 of *Amores,* then, Book 2 of the *Ars* explicitly treats of the infidelity of both an elegiac *amator* and his *puella.* As we have already seen, the *poeta/amator* in the earlier work by Ovid does not have much luck in the role of Don Juan; indeed, he basically succeeds only in inducing the *puella* to "get her own back." So that the same fate will not, if at all possible, befall his student, the preceptor quickly runs through the myth of Agamemnon and Clytemnestra as an admonitory example (399–408), offering suggestions on how to dissimulate little infidelities (389–396). Should something reach the *puella*'s ears after all, the teacher recommends that the *amator* give the lie to the claim that he has slept with someone else by sleeping with *her* (413–414). The *amator* is being turned into a proper male chauvinist, and no mistake. Witness the next injunction: the student should, he is told, deliberately excite the *puella*'s jealously by airing his little secrets, so that, when she flies into a rage, he can restore domestic peace in bed by "pacifying" her there (425–466).

To demonstrate that this *praeceptum* has been "scientifically proven," the preceptor follows up with a cosmological and historico-cultural excursus (467–492). He begins by briefly describing how the world emerged from chaos and how the animals were created. Then he affirms that the first human beings, brutish creatures living in the wilderness, were civilized by mating. Yet they no more needed someone to teach them how to mate than the animals, among whom the females—as a long list of examples testifies—willingly offer themselves up to their males, or even, as in the case of mares, display frenzied sexual desire. Ovid's critics have spilled a great deal of ink over this section of the *Ars,* especially, of course, because it glances at didactic epic, which traditionally includes explanations of the origins of civilization. There can be no doubt that what we have here is a parody of similar passages in Lucretius' *On the Nature of Things* and Virgil's *Georgics.*

Those two didactic poems offer a very different assessment of the way love affects the behavior of men and beasts. In Virgil's exposition of the animals' love life (3.209ff.) as well as in the passages in which Lucretius philosophizes about human sexuality (4.1058ff.), erotic passion appears as a kind of madness. Indeed, the first men, on the Epicurean's view, were enfeebled by "Venus" (1011ff.). Comparing the passage in *On the Nature of Things* in which Lucretius says this with the excursus in the *Ars amatoria,* some critics have concluded that, in making love a shaping factor in the origins of civilization, Ovid is deliberately taking issue with

Lucretius' conception of eros. There is something to this, for the excursus is intended to show, with the help of examples drawn from the history of civilization, that sexual intercourse can have a calming effect and bring about peace. But what the preceptor really wants to say to his student in making this argument (see Bretzigheimer 1981, 21, for a similar view) is: "Look here, my dear fellow! The state of affairs you are supposed to bring about corresponds very precisely to the one that transformed our primitive ancestors from savages into genuinely human beings. Thus, every time you whip the *puella* into a frenzy and then sleep with her, you are staging a historical commemoration." Now there is a remarkably acute sense of history!

In his excursus, then, the "high-flying" preceptor has come forward as a veritable Daedalus of the elegy, at the level of both genre and content. That is why Apollo, the god of the poets, now puts in an appearance, calling the preceptor "to nearer matters" (511: *ad propiora*), as he does in the *recusatio* scenes in Virgil's sixth Eclogue (3–5), Horace's Ode 4.15 (1–4), and Propertius' Elegy 3.3 (13–16). These nearer matters turn out to be the lesson that the joys of love—the behavior the preceptor last recommended to the student is one of them—are rarer than the sufferings it brings (493–534). With that, we come to a key term in the poem, one crucial to the ensuing (535–600) discussion of the biggest problem facing the *amator:* the possibility of betrayal by the beloved, which as a rule implies suffering for the man.

What the *praeceptor amoris* recommends that the student do in this eventuality recalls something that, in *Amores* 3.14, the *poeta/amator* declares that he is prepared to do: namely, let the beloved cover up her infidelities (555–558). However, his justification for this is new. Whereas the *poeta/amator* shuts his eyes to the *puella*'s transgressions out of a desire to spare himself emotional pain, the preceptor's student is supposed to avoid catching his beloved in the act because, if he did, she and his rival would only make love with a vengeance thereafter (559–560). That was what happened to the God Vulcan, for example, when he exposed the adulterous relationship between his wife Venus and Mars by means of a trick. The *praeceptor amoris* here seizes the occasion to retell the story of the affair (561–592), first recounted in Homer's *Odyssey* (8.266–366).

Vulcan exposes the two adulterers in the myth very cunningly: he casts invisible snares over the bed in which Venus and Mars have taken to cuckolding him. Once they have been caught, Vulcan can call the other gods over to look upon them in their nakedness. But, since the two lovers carry on their affair quite openly from then on, the preceptor expressly forbids his student to set traps for the *puella* and his rival. He can leave that to legally wedded husbands (593–600). The allusion to the *lex Iulia de adulteriis* (see p. 43) is patent. The question as to what we might make of the preceptor's reference to the Augustan "context" (there are many such passages in the *Ars*) will be discussed in due time. Before we come to it, however, let us—now that we have surveyed the main features of the first two books of the poem—cast a glance at Book 3 and the *Remedia amoris*.

Ars Amatoria, Book 3: "Womanipulation"

At the beginning of the *Ars*, the *praeceptor amoris* announces only the course of instruction for the man (1.35–40). But, after finishing the course, he very surprisingly says: "Ecce, rogant tenerae, sibi dem praecepta puellae:/vos eritis chartae proxima cura meae!"; "Look, the tender young ladies are asking me to give them lessons./I shall attend to you in the next book" (2.745–746). Nearly all Ovid scholars see a contradiction here and conclude from it that the poet originally intended to write an *Ars amatoria* for men only. Then, they argue, a few years after this *Ars* saw the light, he wrote a "sequel" for women, and, without striking the indications of his original plan at the beginning of Book 1, created a loose link to this "sequel" by inserting 2.745–746. But it is much more likely that what we have here is a joke, not an unintentional clue for scholars studying the genesis of literary works. For the *Ars* is aimed at a student body made up of readers (1.2), one which already includes women in Books 1 and 2, as 2.745–746 shows. In Ovid's day, however, to "read" actually meant to "listen" (see pp. 27ff.); thus we may imagine the preceptor orally delivering a course to students who are really present. Being a man, he is naturally responsible for the men; but, bowing to "popular demand," he turns to the *puellae* as well after finishing his lecture course. There is a touch of condescension in this abrupt modification of the original plan: "Ah yes, the ladies are on hand too." Indeed they are; there would be no way of putting the *praecepta* of Books 1 and 2 into practice if they were not. The preceptor must therefore say a word about how they can contribute to the *amator*'s erotic success. But that is all: as will soon appear, the women are educated less in their own interest than in men's.

Women undoubtedly find it useful to be given expert advice on how they can make themselves look as attractive as possible. After a proem, therefore (1–100), the preceptor commences his new course with instructions on beauty care (101–250). But a real flesh-and-blood woman will hardly feel directly concerned by the counsel he proffers here. For a soulless image is mechanically constructed as we watch, one whose only purpose is to cater to male fantasies about what feminine beauty is. As if that were not bad enough, the preceptor caps his exposition on the most advantageous hairstyles (133–168), clothes (169–192), and cosmetics (193–250) by rehearsing with his female students, as if he were a stage director, how they should act in public. He makes demands like these, for example:

> sint modici rictus, parvaeque utrimque lacunae,
>   et summos dentes ima labella tegant,
> nec suo perpetuo contendant ilia risu,
>   sed leve nescio quid femineumque sonnet.

> Let the opening of one's mouth be moderate, and let no dimples
>   appear to either side,
> and let the bottom of the lips cover the top of the teeth.
> And they should not forever split their sides laughing,
> but it should somehow sound soft and feminine.

(283–286)

What the elegiac speaker engages in here, as he constructs the perfect *puella,* is no longer merely "womanufacture," it is "womanipulation." By the end of the course, things have gone so far that the preceptor can conclude that a woman's physique should dictate the position she adopts during intercourse:

> quae facie praesignis erit, resupina iaceto:
>   spectentur tergo, quis sua terga placent.
> Milanion umeris Atalantes crura ferebat:
>   si bona sunt, hoc sunt aspicienda modo.
> parva vehatur equo: quod erat longissima, numquam
>   Thebais Hectoreo nupta resedit equo.
> strata premat genibus, paulum cervice reflexa,
>   femina per longum conspicienda latus.
> cui femur est iuvenale, carent quoque pectora menda,
>   stet vir, in obliquo fusa sit ipsa toro.
> nec tibi turpe puta crinem, ut Phylleia mater,
>   solvere, et effusis colla reflecte comis.
> tu quoque, cui rugis uterum Lucina notavit,
>   ut celer aversis utere Parthus equis.
> mille ioci Veneris; simplex minimique laboris,
>   cum iacet in dextrum semisupina latus.

> A woman who has an especially pretty face should lie on her back;
> those whose backs please them should be seen from behind.
> Milanion was in the habit of resting Atalanta's thighs on his shoulders;

If they are shapely, they should be seen in this posture.
A short woman should ride: because she was very tall
his Theban wife [Andromache] never sat astride Hector.
A woman should press her knees to the bed, her throat arched slightly
     backwards,
If her long flank is agreeable to the eye.
If her thighs are youthful and her breasts without flaw,
The man should stand and she herself should lie diagonally across the bed.
Do not think it is unbecoming to loosen your hair like the mother
from Phyllus; arch your neck back while your hair cascades down.
You too, whose belly Lucina [the goddess of birth] has marked with wrinkles,
should ride, but like the swift Parthian, sitting backwards.
Venus knows a thousand games. It is simple and least tiring
for her to lie on her right side, half reclining on her back.

(773–788)

As one can see, the *puellae* are not provided the sort of lessons in vary-
ing their pleasures that might be of use to *them;* instead, they are installed
in their respective functions. The passage reads like a catalog of the famous *gabinetto pornografico* of Pompeiian wall-paintings in Naples. But it is
not only when it comes to adopting positions in loveplay that the preceptor's female charges have to behave as products of "womanipulation"
should; they must also do so during the act of intercourse itself. For
example, they are to fake orgasms, if necessary (797–804). One cannot
help thinking of one of those dolls that say "mama" when some sort of
built-in mechanism is activated.

The preceptor begins the long section of the poem on how a *puella*
should present herself in public with general remarks on beauty care,
which he calls *cultus* (101–132). The fact that a woman of his day cultivates her appearance seems to him to represent considerable progress
over the days of old, when *puellae,* or so he claims, adapted to the rough
soldierly demeanor of their men. He compares this form of progress
with that the architecture of his city has made since its beginnings and
counts himself lucky to be a child, not of that old Rome, but of the
Rome of his day and age. This passage in particular, which we have
already cited in another context (see p. 42), is very frequently interpreted as the speaker's profession of faith in a cultivated, "modern" way
of life and thus in cultivated eroticism. Well and good; but is this profession of faith meant to be taken altogether seriously? In looking at Books
1 and 2, we saw that the art of love taught there is in large measure an
ars fallendi. In the present instance, the *cultus* which the preceptor recommends to women in Book 3 is basically only affectation and facade.
If we bear this in mind, we will be more inclined to see the speaker's

celebration of the cultural progress made in the realm of beauty care as a confession of the frivolous pleasure he takes in fakery and fraud. As this passage also contains a profession of faith in the culture Augustus has created by mobilizing "the power of images," we have reason to suspect that, here too, appearances must be distinguished from reality.

The *puella* is trained in the art of creating illusions not only in the long section of the poem about the forms her culture should take, but, repeatedly, in the rest of the lecture as well. The structure of this part of Book 3 is manifestly patterned after that of the course for men. Here too, the preceptor first tells the *puella* where to find a sexual partner (381–432); then, how to win him (433–524); and finally, how to keep him interested in returning her love (525–746). In a sort of recapitulative appendix, which includes tips on how a *puella* should act at a banquet (747–768) and when making love (769–808), we are given a condensed version of an erotic novel with a happy ending, as in the sequence of elegies *Amores* 1.4–5. The preceptor then takes his leave of the ladies in a short epilogue (809–812).

The *praecepta* that follow the section of the poem about *cultus* enjoin the *puellae* to utilize various methods to deceive their partners; one might therefore be tempted to conclude that the professor has now, as it were, switched camps after all and selflessly made the interests of his female students his own. He himself, at any rate, deliberately cultivates this impression by twice branding himself a traitor to the cause of his own sex, one who voluntarily exposes himself to the "weapons" of the "foe" (577ff. and 667ff.). But these are "weapons" that the kind of *amator* the preceptor has designed and created is only too glad to be wounded by. When, for example, he advises women to repel their lovers often and leave them lying at their doors (577–588), this answers the heart's wish of an *amator.* The professor makes no bones about the fact. "We," he says, leaving no doubt about which side he is on, "cannot bear sweetness. Give us a bitter and rejuvenating potion." The *poeta/amator* in *Amores* 2.19 defends the same principle (see pp. 59f.).

Among the sexually stimulating feints the preceptor recommends to the *puella* is affected jealousy (677–678). To be sure, a *puella*'s real fear that her partner might betray her is likewise one of the subjects treated in the course; it is taken up immediately afterward. But if the professor is a past master in the art of disguise, he has, by the same token, precious little to say about sincere feelings. In the present instance, he can offer nothing more than the advice that the *puella* should neither lose her head nor believe everything she hears (683–685a). At all events, he has an impressive example at the ready to illustrate the negative effects of unfounded jealousy: the myth of Procris. When Procris is told that her husband, Cephalus, is forever asking "Aura" [*aura* means breeze] to come cool him off as he rests in a grove after a hunt, she takes it for granted that this personification of the breeze is a rival. Hiding behind a bush, Procris spies on her husband during his next "tryst with her"; when she realizes the truth, she starts up, rustling the leaves. Cephalus, assuming that an animal has made the noise, runs her through with his spear (685b–746). It is perhaps no accident that this myth, which shows the lethal consequences of mistaking appearances for reality, comes just before the preceptor hints that he will soon reach the end of his work (747–748)—no accident, in other words, that it occupies the prominent position it does. For this work sows all sorts of illusions.

The *Remedia Amoris:* The Systematic Dismantling of a System

The *Amores,* Ovid's first work, opens with a report by the speaker on how Cupid once horned in on his affairs. When he was setting out to write an epic, he tells us, the god changed him into a writer of erotic elegies by stealing a foot of his verse (1.1). In the first part of the proem to the *Remedia amoris,* the last of Ovid's erotic elegies with a male speaker, we are again told about an intervention of Cupid's (1–40). This time, however, the god of love does nothing; he merely objects to the title "*Remedia amoris.*" It suggests, he says, that there is a declaration of war against him in the air. By explaining why he has chosen this new theme, the speaker succeeds in persuading Cupid to let him write the work—indeed, in bringing the god to invite him to write it. But even if he manages to convince Cupid that he is still working in his service, he unintentionally reveals in his apologia that Cupid was right to step in. For, *pace* the speaker, the *Remedia* does not only offer therapy for unhappy lovers and thus, after the *Ars,* a supplementary course in sexual education. As Gian Biagio Conte (1989) was the first to see, it also systematically dismantles the elegiac system.

True, the speaker is still the *praeceptor* we know from the *Ars* (although we would do better not to call him *praeceptor amoris* from now on), as appears at the outset of the *Remedia* (9–10). His way of pleading his cause with Cupid also fits in nicely with the preceptor's idea of pedagogy. Love, he says, ceases to be a game when it causes so much heartbreak that it threatens to drive a lover to suicide. But love *has* been a game hitherto, as the preceptor last noted at the end of his course for *puellae* (*Ars* 3.809). Hence an end ought to be put to unhappy love affairs; a reading of the *Remedia* will help accomplish just that. In erotic elegy in its original form, however, love *must* be unhappy, for that is crucial to the functioning of the elegiac system. Consequently, in showing his students how to bid farewell to unhappy love, the preceptor is also show-ing them and his readers how to bid farewell to erotic elegy.

Of course, readers versed in the laws of the genre will be as amused by the dismantling of the elegiac system as they were by the playful transfor-mation of it that we observed in the *Ars*. For a game is played here too. The preceptor's opening gambit is already quite funny: after explaining the theme of his new work to his male and female students in the second half of the proem (41–78) and then invoking the aid of Apollo, god of poetry and healing, he proceeds to dispense some general medical advice (79–134). The humor stems from the fact that, by adopting the accents of a doctor, our elegiac speaker identifies himself as a figure who simply has no place in this genre. Propertius, for instance, once explicitly says, "The art of medicine can heal all human ills; but love does not love the one who heals the disease it causes" (2.1.57–58).

Thus one of the greatest pleasures the *Remedia* has to offer is that it lets us watch as the preceptor, progressing from one section of the poem to the next, steadily replaces the elegiac system with a new one, that of his course. Before looking at two examples of the way he plays his new literary game, let us briefly see how his course unfolds. The section of the poem just mentioned, in which the student body receives general medical counsel, is matched by another section on the same theme (795–810); all that comes after it is an epilogue (811–814). Taken to-gether, the two matching sections enframe the *praecepta,* which, in their turn, fall into two groups. The first contains advice on love therapy that is supposed to help unhappy lovers break with their partners (135–608); the second offers lessons on the period immediately follow-ing a separation (609–794). It is true that, in part two of the foreword (41–78), the preceptor announces not only to the men (whom he turns to first) but also to the *puellae* that he will be teaching them remedies for love; however, he then addresses himself almost exclusively to male stu-dents. As he does throughout the *Ars amatoria,* so here too the professor basically defends only the interests of his own sex. Furthermore, here as in the earlier poem, the *ars fallendi* holds a central place in the program of instruction. The sole difference is that here the art of self-deception, not very often taught in the *Ars*, thrusts the art of deceiving one's part-ner into the shadows.

But let us now look at the first instance of the dismantling of the elegiac system. In obedience to its rules, the *poeta/amator* in Propertius and Tibullus forgoes a political and military career, as was shown above (pp. 11–12); that is, he devotes himself not to *negotium,* but, heart and soul, to *otium*. It is therefore logical that the preceptor should, at the very start of his course, warn his students to avoid *otium,* the occasion and breeding ground for love, and turn instead to *negotium* in the forum or a military camp (135–168). To appreciate the wit of this *praeceptum,* we need to recall that the way of life the elegist chooses is meant to express protest against an urban upper-class society he considers morally degenerate. On the other hand, the preceptor takes *otium* to mean, in a very literal sense, "doing nothing," thus ignoring, comically, the deeper significance of an elegiac *amator*'s way of life. He can therefore prescribe "not doing nothing" as a cure. It is but a short step from this kind of trivialization of elegiac values to another: later in the poem, the preceptor uses examples from the experience of Tom, Dick, and Harry to show how certain problems that can come up in the world of *negotium* take people's minds off unhappy love affairs. He makes his demonstration by passing on the following lessons, which he claims to have been given by Cupid himself:

> qui Puteal Ianumque timet celeresque Kalendas,
>   torqueat hunc aeris mutua summa sui;
> cui durus pater est, ut voto cetera cedant,
>   huic pater ante oculos durus habendus erit;
> hic male dotata pauper cum coniuge vivit:
>   uxorem fato credat obesse suo.
> est tibi rure bono generosae fertilis uvae
>   vinea? ne nascens usta sit uva, time.
> ille habet in reditu navem: mare semper iniquum
>   cogitet et damno littora foeda suo.
> filius hunc miles, te filia nubilis angat;
>   et quis non causas mille doloris habet?

> He who fears the Puteal and Janus and the swift Kalends,
> let him be tormented by the sum of all his debts.
> He who has a strict father, even if everything else conforms to his wishes,
> let him keep his strict father before his eyes.
> This fellow lives in poverty with a woman who received a small dowry:
> let him believe that his wife adds to his misfortune.
> You have, on rich land, a vineyard that bears grapes
> in abundance: fear lest the grapes dry up as they ripen.
> That fellow has a ship that is homeward bound; let him think constantly
> of the adverse sea and the shore disfigured by his loss.
> That fellow should be worried about his soldier son; you, about
>   your marriageable daughter.
> And who does not have a thousand occasions for anguish?

(561–572)

These are the kinds of worldly problems that the elegiac *amator* defiantly flees for the alternative of making love, not war. They are indeed enemies of love! On your marks, then, you who are lovesick: make war, not love.

Before considering the second example, we should recall that the *puella* is the focal point of the world of elegiac experience and that, for the *amator,* she is as beautiful as a goddess. Thus, reporting on a rendezvous with her in 1.5, the speaker of the *Amores* exuberantly describes how lovely his goddess is in his eyes. He tells how, before sleeping with him, she stood naked before his gaze with her faultless body, in the half-light of a room whose window was partly closed. The preceptor in the *Remedia* is obviously alluding to this scene when he urges his student to leave the window wide open during love-making so that the *puella*'s "repulsive bodily parts" (*turpia membra*) will be in plain sight. And, whereas the speaker of *Amores* 1.5 brings his narrative to a close with a brief allusion to the mutual exhaustion brought on by his love-making with Corinna, the *praeceptor/medicus* makes no secret of what his patient ought to do once *he* is in the same state in the sun-filled room: he should mark all of his partner's blemishes, indeed, keep his eyes constantly trained on them (411–418). This patient certainly is given a room with a view!

Shortly after the preceptor starts in on the section of his lecture in which we read these instructions (357–440), he interrupts it to make a digression (361–396). Here he defends himself for choosing to write his elegiac poetry on erotic subjects. He addresses himself to the critics (without mentioning them by name) who, he says, have called his "books"—presumably Books 1–3 of the *Ars*—too "naughty" (362: *proterva*). He replies that tradition has established certain subjects as appropriate for each poetic genre, and that erotic subjects, precisely, are appropriate for elegy. In the didactic corpus on love comprised by the *Ars* and the *Remedia,* this is the one and only time that the preceptor makes an explicit statement about poetics. The fact that this digression is unique and also that it is so conspicuously inserted in the middle of a group of *praecepta* lends the statement special status in the four books. One has the impression, as one does not with comparable texts in the *Amores,* that the real author has temporarily doffed the elegiac speaker's mask and is here speaking in his own name. We do not know whether Ovid published the *Ars* and the *Remedia* separately or together. But we can easily imagine that, at some point in the publication process, his erotic didactic poems so offended part of his readership in Rome that he deemed it necessary to violate the literary fiction in the last book. We can only guess who might have criticized him and why. The most important aspects of this problem will be discussed in the last section of the present chapter.

What Besides *Crimen* Is Concealed in *Carmen*?

After asking Venus, in the proem to the *Ars,* to help him compose his work, the *praeceptor amoris* says:

> este procul, vittae tenues, insigne pudoris,
>   quaeque tegis medios instita longos pedes.
> nos Venerem tutam concessaque furta canemus,
>   inque meo nullum carmine crimen erit.

> Stay far off, you fine hair-bands, emblems of virtue,
> and you, you long border [on the stola] that half covers the feet.
> I shall sing of sure erotic pleasures [*tuta Venus*] and licit secrets,
> and in my poem [*carmen*] will be no crime [*crimen*].

(1.31–34)

Hair-bands and border represent the freeborn married women that they identified as such; the hair-bands also stand for unmarried women. Thus it is not for such women that the preceptor dispenses his lessons, which, as he hints in l. 33, will also cover the theme of adultery. The *lex Iulia de adulteriis,* indeed, made it a crime for such women to be unfaithful. The law did not, however, apply to libertines (emancipated female slaves). As we have seen, one can, if one likes, choose to hear a note of derision for Augustus' marriage laws in certain of Ovid's elegies (see p. 69). Does the *Art of Love* rule out that kind of intertextual play? By no means. Although the preceptor repeats the gist of the above-quoted lines in three other passages in the *Ars* (3.599–600; 3.57–58; 3.613–616) and once in the *Remedia* (386), he makes light, at several points in the *Ars* (Stroh 1979a), of the restrictions on sexual freedom that the *lex Iulia* imposed on married women. We have already touched on one of them (see pp. 102–103).

Is Ovid here criticizing the Roman ruler? If we can credit the exile's declarations in *Tristia* 2 to the effect that writing the *Ars amatoria* was one of the two reasons for Ovid's banishment (see p. 27), then it would seem that Augustus read the passages of the *Ars* just mentioned as a subversive call to violate the *lex Iulia.* But the emperor could level the accusation of being *obsceni doctor adulterii* (*Tristia* 2.212: "teacher of obscene adultery") only at the Ovid who assumed the fictive role of *praeceptor amoris,* not at the poet himself. In the elegiac letter to Augustus, in which the exile devotes a great deal of space to rebutting the count in the indictment constituted by the *Art of Love* (*Tristia* 2.211–572), he declares, and no mistake:

> crede mihi, distant mores a carmine nostri—
>   vita verecunda est, Musa iocosa mihi;
> magnaque pars operum mendax et ficta meorum
>   plus sibi permisit compositore suo.

> Believe me, my nature is different from my poem [*carmen*];
>   my way of life is decent, only my muse is lascivious.
> And a large part of my works is unreal and invented
> and has taken many more liberties than its author.

(353–356)

Augustus, then—if he actually identified Ovid's authorship of the *Ars* as one of the reasons for his banishment—failed to distinguish the elegiac speaker from the real author. The same would hold for the critics evoked in the digression on poetics in the *Remedia,* all of whom presumably defended Augustus' marriage laws. But even readers prepared to take the poetic masques in Ovid's works for what they are—Augustus and his partisans would certainly have had the education required to do so—must have asked, as we too do: Who is really speaking in the elegiac lines *Tristia* 2.353–356 about the need to distinguish between *carmen* and the author?

Quite simply, the (male) speakers of Ovid's works put on a poker face, as our speculations about Ovid's authorial intentions have made increasingly clear. Let us assume for the sake of argument that the voice we hear in *Ars* 1.31–34 is that of the real author, not the preceptor who, later in the text, pokes fun at the marriage laws. Does this mean that we should take seriously the profound respect for these laws expressed in 1.31–34? Hardly; for these lines too are ambiguous, as Stephen Hinds and Alessandro Barchiesi were the first to point out (in Sharrock 1994a, 111–112; see also Williams 1994, 207). Thus if one construes ll. 31–32 to mean that the speaker is quite literally asking that the hair-band and border, not the women who wear them, remain "far off," it seems clear that he is urging married women to take off their clothes. And, in fact, the woman whose infidelity is later described in detail *is* a naked married woman: Venus, in bed with Mars (3.583–584). Venus is, moreover, explicitly evoked just prior to 1.31–32 in her capacity as goddess of love, but not as patron goddess of the emperor's family, the role in which she was pictured wearing the Roman matron's robe (Bretzigheimer 1981, 32). The speaker goes on to promise *tuta Venus* in 1.33. However, if we read the expression he uses not figuratively ["sure erotic pleasure"] but literally ["safe Venus"], then this is a promise that goes unfulfilled: in 2.561ff., Vulcan catches his wife in a trap. As for 1.34, "inque meo nullum carmine crimen erit" (and in my poem there will be no crime), it is false to the extent that all the letters in *crimen* occur in *carmine.* What and whom can one actually believe here?

Fakery and fraud—but that is precisely what comprises the *ars* that the preceptor knows and teaches. Those who wish to wax indignant over the fact may, and no one can stop them from seeing the real author Ovid in the past master of the *ars fallendi.* But others may prefer to devote their energies to discovering the reality behind the appearances primarily at the level of the poetic enunciation; they will recognize, in the role-playing and intertextuality, the *poeta doctus*' "fakery and fraud," and will, first and foremost, be entertained and amused. This will not, however, prevent them from pondering the deeper meaning of such literary treatment of the classic theme of the discrepancy between illusion and reality. For the two erotic didactic poems invite us to think about that as well.

Of course, much of the literary charm of the *Ars* and the *Remedia* escapes readers who know little or nothing about the ancient world. But they will certainly notice at least one thing if they keep their eye trained, precisely, on the professor of love's *ars fallendi:* namely, that this art is by no means an insignificant element in the erotic commerce between men and women, even if it unmasks the professor's pose as advocate of a cultivated form of loving. Let us consider for a moment, from the vantage point of our modern, open society, the simple example of the man who holds a door open for a woman. He too is playing a role. For his act has basically lost all meaning in the age of equality between the sexes and must, as a result, seem like mere playacting. Yet, in the discursive exchange between the sexes, gestures of this kind have a certain function: for instance, man can "court" woman with them, even if the courting rituals of closed societies have long since disappeared from ours. Much of what transpires between an *amator* and an *amatrix* was and is similar— a studied form of behavior for which conventions thousands of years old furnish the text. Those who close an eye to the fact that the theatrics the *praeceptor amoris* recommends to his students often border on sheer hornswoggling—but someone who wants to make us laugh needs to exaggerate!—will detect, with Molly Myerowitz (1985), a version of that text in the *Ars* and the *Remedia.* And they will thus also be prepared to class both the preceptor's art of love and his love therapy under the rubric of what we today call civilization.

Poetic Explanation of Causes
as Mythological World History:
The *Metamorphoses*

Ovid's *Metamorphoses,* a poem in hexameter divided into fifteen books, is the poet's longest work. But it begins with the shortest of proems:

> In nova fert animus mutatas dicere formas
> corpora: di, coeptis (nam vos mutastis et illas)
> adspirate meis primaque ab origine mundi
> ad mea perpetuum deducite tempora carmen!

> The spirit moves me to tell of forms metamorphosed into new
> bodies. O Gods, look on my project—for you have metamorphosed
>   that [*illa*] too—
> with favor, and lead [*deducite*], from the very beginning of the world
> down to my own times, my continuous song [*perpetuum carmen*]!

A mere four lines; but four lines rich in important statements about the work—direct and indirect statements, which is what we have learned to expect from Ovid. To begin with, the subject of the work is identified here: this will be a work about metamorphoses—more precisely, mythical metamorphoses, as the apostrophe to the gods reveals in passing by taking it for granted that the gods caused them. Legends about changes take their place within a major subdivision of mythology known as mythical etiology (explanations of causes). Etiology provides answers to questions that men and women once asked when they pondered striking features of their culture or natural habitat. "Why do frogs croak?" was, for example, one of the things they wanted to know. The Greeks stated the reason (*aition*) in a legend that Ovid too recounts (6.313–381).

114

Lycian peasants refused to let the goddess Latona drink from their pond, though she was tormented by thirst; worse, they cursed her. Latona punished them by changing them into frogs. Thus they were condemned to curse "for all time" (369)—that is, to croak. A line of verse expresses this onomatopoetically:

QUAmvis sint sub aQUA, sub aQUA maledicere temptant.

Although they live under water, they try to curse underwater.

(376)

As we have seen (see p. 6), mythical etiology provided the subject matter of Callimachus' *Aitia* (Explanatory legends). It is true that the things Callimachus explains—rites and names—play a relatively minor part in Ovid's *Metamorphoses*. But, not long after Callimachus, Nicander of Colophon (who lived around the middle of the second century B.C.) probably devoted about as much space to nature as to culture in his (lost) *Heteroiumena* [Transformations], which is based directly on the *Aitia;* he provided mythical explanations for striking biological and geological phenomena, as Ovid would do after him. Ovid's great poem in hexameter, then, like his erotic elegies, belongs to the Hellenistic poetic tradition. The etiological works in this tradition were considered minor poetry. In the proem to the *Aitia*, a work composed in elegiac couplets, Callimachus pointedly contrasts his opus with a "unified, continuous song many thousands of lines long" dealing with "kings or heroes of yore." He thus distinguishes it, obviously, from narrative epics such as Homer's *Iliad*.

But it is precisely such a "continuous song" that is announced in the proem to the *Metamorphoses* (4: *perpetuum carmen*). Is this because Ovid now wants to abandon the paths blazed by Callimachus? Clearly, what is "continuous" in Ovid's etiological work is the plot, and plot is a defining feature of narrative epic. Of course, the action in the *Metamorphoses* is not dominated, as it would be in an epic, by a single king, hero, or—this too is conceivable—god. But, as is announced in the proem, the work recounts the history of the world from the beginnings of the universe down to Ovid's day, and the structure of a plot of this type is based on the deeds of gods, heroes, and sovereigns (Rieks 1980). The gods hold center stage in Books 1–5, that is, in the first pentad; the second (6–10) is mainly about heroes; because the third (11–15) opens with the founding of Troy, the men who figure most prominently here are (on an ancient view of the matter, at any rate) historical rulers.

Before deciding, however, which literary tradition to assign the *Metamorphoses* to, we must also give due consideration to the fact that the proem appeals to the gods to "lead" the *perpetuum carmen* from the origins of the world (down) to the present day. The Latin word used here, *deducere*, designates the spinning of wool threads, among other things; the word was employed in a metaphorical sense in theoretical statements on the composition of minor poetry. Well before Ovid, in Virgil's *Bucolics*, a pastoral poem is once (6.5) called a *deductum carmen* (finespun poem). Now, implicitly, the *Metamorphoses* is presented as a poem of the same kind, which it in fact is: as we shall see, long sections of the work even display "elegiac" features. Thus its author situates himself in the traditions of Callimachean minor poetry *and* narrative epic.

It follows that he has undergone yet another transformation, one he identifies in l.2 as the first metamorphosis in this book about metamorphoses. The *poeta* who is the speaker of the *Amores* is prevented from composing an epic, as he had initially planned to, by the god of love, who changes him into an elegist (1.1). Here it is the gods taken together who modify a "project" (2) of the poet's. Although he does not say what it consisted in, we might well imagine that it involved writing a new elegiac work. In any event, he has now been changed from an elegiac into a "proper" narrator. In discussing the *Metamorphoses*, I shall use the word "narrator" to designate the speaker so as to bring out the fact that Ovid is once again speaking to us masked.

Characteristically, the narrator of the *Metamorphoses* has a double function. On the one hand, he quite explicitly comes forward in a great many passages—very often parenthetically—as someone whose observation of the action he presents is colored by a strong moral and religious commitment. Thus when he uses the term "scoffer at the gods" to describe a character of his who, in contrast to himself, denies that the gods have the power to bring about metamorphoses (8.611–615), he is making a moral value judgment and, at the same time, once again giving us to understand that he believes the stories he tells. He only intimates doubts about the authenticity of a tale of metamorphosis—and rarely at that—when he calls a change "miraculous" (11.346, for example). On the other hand, the speaker of the *Metamorphoses* casts himself as a savant when, like the *praeceptor amoris* of the *Ars amatoria* and the *Remedia amoris,* he ranges himself in the company of Greco-Roman didactic poets. For this speaker too constantly resorts to the formulaic language of didactic epic; indeed, he employs didactic epic style throughout one whole section of his poem, the one on the origins of the world at the beginning of the first book (5–88). Thus two sharply antithetical narrative stances dovetail in the narrator's person: that of the etiologist who believes in myth and that of the scientifically enlightened didactic poet.

This contrast breeds the sort of tension that informs passages like the one in which the narrator tells how Hercules hurled Lichas into the Euboean sea:

> ille per aërias pendens induruit auras:
> utque ferunt imbres gelidis concrescere ventis,
> inde nives fieri, nivibus quoque molle rotatis
> adstringi et spissa glomerari grandine corpus,
> sic illum validis iactum per inane lacertis
> exsanguemque metu nec quicquam umoris habentem
> in rigidos versum silices prior edidit aetas.
> Nunc quoque in Euboico scopulus brevis eminet alto
> gurgite et humanae servat vestigia formae,
> quem, quasi sensurum, nautae calcare verentur,
> appellantque Lichan.

> He became hard as he hung in the air,
> and, as raindrops are said to be congealed by icy winds,
> so that they become snowflakes and this soft mass freezes
> in the whirling snow and is packed into solid hail,
> so he, as he was hurled through the void by the strong arms,
> is supposed, bloodless with fear and with no liquid left in him,
> to have changed into rigid stone, according to what was said in
>   olden times.
> To this day, in the Euboean sea, a small rock juts up
> out of the waves, preserving the outlines of a human form.
> Sailors are afraid to tread on it, as if it could feel that,
> and they call it Lichas.

(9.219–229)

Plainly, a mythical and a scientific causal explanation meet head-on here: on the one hand, we have a myth about the origins of a rock, and, on the other, scientific doctrine concerning the origins of snow and hail. The reader alert to the tension between the two will draw inferences that will shape her interpretation: unlike the narrator himself, she will be led to observe the events he depicts from an outsider's point of view. By the same token, however, the poem invites her to adopt a reflective attitude, so that, rather than becoming personally involved in the story, she can broaden her field of vision to include what seems to be "true to nature" in the *Metamorphoses:* the human, all-too-human dimension of the goings-on narrated there. Grasping this dimension of the poem may be even more gratifying than penetrating the secrets of the author's playful treatment of literary traditions. For, more than the erotic elegies, the *Metamorphoses* affords the reader fascinating insights into the psychology of human thought and action. It has therefore, and rightly, been called a poem of universal scope, or *Weltgedicht*.

Books 1–5: Chaos, Cosmos, Eros, and Chaos Again

A preliminary overview of the first pentad of the *Metamorphoses* yields the following picture. Book 1 opens with an account of the dawn of world history: beginning with the origin of the universe and the creation of humankind, it proceeds to describe the first catastrophe to break over the world—the Great Flood visited upon it by the gods—and the subsequent new departure in the life of the people and animals on earth (5–437). One of the creatures to emerge after the flood, the giant Python, was so great a "terror to the newly created peoples" that Apollo slew it. The brief report on this deed (438–451) gives way to a myth about the god's unsuccessful bid for the nymph Daphne's favors (452–567). That story is the first of several thematically related myths scattered throughout the rest of Book 1 and the remainder of this pentad (they are interspersed with others); they tell of further erotic liaisons between the gods and mortal women. The remaining myths (some of which are also erotic) evolve, in their turn, out of the legends about the gods, and, like them, continue the mythological history of humanity.

The next major event in this history is the second cosmic catastrophe, the universal conflagration that the narrator describes in the first half of Book 2 (1–400). He begins Book 3 by telling us, for the first time in the *Metamorphoses,* about the founding of a city—Cadmus' founding of Thebes—starting with its prehistory and following up with a series of legends that brings us three-quarters of the way through Book 4. Taken together, these legends might be called the myth of the early history of Thebes and of the dynasty of its founder (3.1–4.603). Then, in the first half of Book 5, we are given the first lengthy account of a fight between heroes: at his wedding with Andromeda, Perseus has to repel an attempt by his new bride's first fiancé to take her back by force (1–249). The narrator lets one of the nine Muses speak throughout almost all of the second half of Book 5 (250–678); she recites a number of myths, including the story of the rape of Proserpina. As I shall show later, this section of the poem, which crowns the first pentad of the *Metamorphoses,* constitutes a kind of metapoetical epilogue to the first third of the work. But here too we are told of an event that, like the first foundation of a city and the first big battle between heroes, can be called a landmark in the mythological history of the world: the introduction of agriculture by the goddess Ceres (341–343) and its extension over the face of the earth thanks to Triptolemus (642–649).

Most of the myths narrated in Books 1–5 and the following two pentads end in a metamorphosis. We saw at the start of this chapter that legends of transformation make up part of mythical etiology and that the *Metamorphoses* primarily provides etiological explanations of natural processes, unlike Callimachus' *Aitia,* which explains cultural phenomena. The changes Ovid depicts, almost all of which involve human beings, generally bring animals, plants, rocks, and streams into existence. In the last section of this chapter, we will speculate about what Ovid's preference for this type of etiology implies for an interpretation of the *Metamorphoses*. But, for now, let us attend to the fact, which can already be gleaned from our survey of the contents of Books 1–5, that the phenomenon of culture as such is very much a theme of the *Metamorphoses* too, even if Ovid's handling of it differs from Callimachus'.

Cosmos and Chaos

At the heart of the *Aitia* are mythological explanations of various institutions of merely local significance, such as festive celebrations. In contrast, the narrator of the *Metamorphoses,* to the extent that he takes an interest in cultural history, concentrates mainly on "primal events" in the history of the human race. We have already seen what comes under this heading in the first pentad: the first description of the foundation of a city, the first description of a battle between heroes, and the introduction and spread of agriculture. Again we see Ovid developing and modulating a theme announced in one of his early works, the *Ars amatoria,* where we were told the story of the first "pacification" of humanity through the act of love (2.467–488; see p. 102).

As in that passage of the *Ars,* so in the *Metamorphoses* as well, the creation of the universe prefigures that of civilization. In both cases, a chaotic state of affairs slowly gives way to an orderly one. Thus, just as we are told, in connection with the introduction of agriculture (5.343), that Ceres was "the first to give laws," so the emergence of the universe is presented as the result of the organizing activity of a creator who, starting out with a raw, amorphous mass—chaos—fashions it into a system that is carefully structured throughout (1.5–88). Separating out the four basic elements that are intermingled in chaos—earth, sea, dense air, and clear sky (ether)—the creator proceeds to give form to each one. Thus, immediately before we are given an account of the creation of human beings, who, as in the Old Testament, are the jewel of creation, we watch as life is infused into the cosmos:

neu regio foret ulla suis animalibus orba,
astra tenent caeleste solum formaeque deorum,
cesserunt nitidis habitandae piscibus undae,
terra feras cepit, volucres agitablilis aër.

And so that no realm would be without its own living creatures,
stars and divine forms occupied the firmament,
the waves fell to the shining fish as their dwelling-place,
the earth received the wild animals, and the mobile air, the birds.

(72–75)

What comes into being here is a veritable work of art, and it is precisely as such that the narrator presents the universe to his readers. For he portrays the creator as if he were a visual artist, underscoring the parallel with multiple allusions to Homer's description of the shield that Hephaistos makes Achilles in the *Iliad:* creation is depicted on it as well (18.483ff.). The upshot, if we continue to attend to the "polyphony" of the text, is that the cosmogony presented in the *Metamorphoses* begins to sound like a theoretical treatise on art. Thus, in Ovid's mythological history of the world, the creation of the universe itself appears as a founding event in the history of culture, with the creator playing the part of the first artist. In the rest of the poem, the narrator will often observe mythical artists like this creator as they go about their work, poets and storytellers in particular. In the section on the history of culture that rounds off the first pentad of the *Metamorphoses,* we learn about the first storytellers to make their appearance among men, the three daughters of Minyas, who live in Thebes. Significantly, as they tell their tales, they engage in another activity basic to human civilization, one that often serves Ovid as a metaphor for the composition of minor poetry: weaving (1–415).

If we now turn to those passages in the first pentad which depict orderly systems and thus artistic or cultural achievements, we see time and again that the narrator is concerned less to describe perfection as such than to show that it is ineluctably destroyed. For, in Ovid, the establishment of a harmonious order is always followed by its dissolution. Thus the description of the creation of the universe (1.5–88) is immediately followed by an account of the ongoing moral decline of the human race as one age succeeds another (89–150), until destruction threatens even the heavenly order (151–162, the battle of the Giants). The narrator likewise describes the chaos unleashed first by the Great Flood (163–415) and then the universal conflagration (2.1–400). And we learn that Cadmus, the founder of a city, along with several members of his family and the three Theban women who nimbly weave as they

nimbly tell their tales, were stripped of their human form and/or bru-
tally killed (3.1–4.603).

It is not only in the first pentad of the *Metamorphoses* that the narrator
shows us ordered structures falling apart; he often does so in the second
and third as well. As a rule, he spends less time on "cosmos" than on
"chaos." For instance, over against the above-quoted four lines, which
describe with epigrammatic brevity the way the four regions of the world
were infused with life (1.72–75), he puts another twenty that paint a detailed picture of the collapse of this system during the Great Flood
(1.291–310). There is no lack of comedy in the narrator's description of
this process. Witness the following passage:

> mirantur sub aqua lucos urbesque domosque
> Nereides, silvasque tenent delphines et altis
> incursant ramis agitataque robora pulsant.
> Nat lupus inter oves, fulvos vehit unda leones,
> unda vehit tigres; nec vires fulminis apro,
> crura nec ablato prosunt velocia cervo,
> quaesitisque diu terris, ubi sistere possit,
> in mare lassatis volucris vaga decidit alis.

> The Nereids [water nymphs] admire, under water, groves and cities
>   and dwellings,
> and dolphins inhabit forests, bumping into high
> branches and colliding with the trunks that are thus set shaking.
> The wolf swims among the sheep, the waves carry tawny lions,
> the waves carry tigers, and the boar's strength, which is like
>   the lightning's, avails him not at all,
> nor do his swift thighs help the stag as he is swept away,
> and after long seeking land where she might alight,
> the fleeing bird sinks into the sea with exhausted wings.

> (301–308)

It should be clear by now that the changes related in the *Metamorphoses* include, besides the transformation of human beings into other
kinds of creatures, the alternating emergence and disappearance of ordered systems in nature and culture. Often, when such a system is
destroyed—by the Great Flood, for example—it is human iniquity which
has provoked the wrathful gods to retribution. Yet one is not left with
the impression that Ovid is inviting his readers to ponder the underlying theological and ethical reasons for the metamorphosis of a "cosmos"
into a "chaos." His main object is plainly to depict the phenomenon itself as vividly as he can. What the lines just quoted show also holds for all
the other passages in the *Metamorphoses* in which an order disintegrates:

the comic aspect and literary playfulness of such descriptions are so pronounced that, if only for this reason, we feel no call to ponder the
"moral of the story." We saw something similar in the erotic elegies.
There too we have a god who brings "chaos" into people's lives—
namely, Cupid. As he is also forever wreaking havoc in the world of the
Metamorphoses, this is a convenient place to turn to a consideration of
the erotic myths in Books 1–5.

Eros and Chaos

In Greek cosmogonies, Eros usually takes a hand in the creation of
the world. In Ovid, however, Eros' Roman counterpart Cupid gets down
to work only after life on earth has been first destroyed and then regen-
erated and the first new threat to the security of the human race, the
Python, has been neutralized. At this point Apollo, who has triumphed
over the monster and is bursting with pride over his exploit, tells the
god of love that he alone is entitled to wield a bow and arrow because he
has slain the dragon; a little lad like Cupid, he says, has no business with
such weapons. But Apollo straightaway learns how well Cupid can
handle them, for the god wounds him with an arrow that awakens love
in his heart. His desire soon alights on the nymph Daphne. Cupid, however, strikes her with an arrow that makes her indifferent to love, so that
Apollo woos her in vain (1.452–567).

Unmistakably, this Cupid too creates a situation typical of elegiac love.
The lines that paint the scene between Apollo and Cupid are a direct allusion to *Amores* 1.1. Just as, in that poem, the god of love first changes
the author of a heroic epic into an elegist and then shoots him with an
arrow to make him fall in love (see pp. 46f.), so he here wounds the
doer of a heroic deed with an arrow, whereupon his new victim begins
conducting himself exactly like an elegiac *amator*. Although Daphne
turns out to be a *dura puella* (hard-hearted beloved) and even runs away
from Apollo, the god, in pursuit, makes her a speech of a kind we are
eminently well acquainted with, thanks to the *poeta/amator* of the *Amores*.
It is rich in motifs familiar from Ovid's early elegiac poems, among
them the idea, which we know from the *Ars amatoria*, that the relationship between *amator* and *puella* should be regulated in rational fashion.
For, on a splendid inspiration, Apollo says, "aspera, qua properas, loca
sunt: moderatius, oro,/curre fugamque inhibe, moderatius insequar
ipse"; "Rough is the region you are rushing through. Run more slowly,/I
beg you, and hold back your flight! And I will pursue you more slowly"
(510–511). Daphne does not take at all kindly to the suggestion; she
simply keeps on running. Apollo, quickening his pace, now undertakes
to do something that the *Ars* also recommends (1.669ff.), namely,

raping the *puella*. But he does not quite manage to, because, in extremis, Daphne's father, the river god Peneus, heeds her plea and changes her into a laurel tree.

In this text too, then, a tension is created between elegiac love and mythic reality in a way familiar to us from the *Epistulae Heroidum*. This happens here under two conditions peculiar to the world of the *Metamorphoses*. In the myth of Daphne and Apollo, first, the "real" event that puts paid to the *amator*'s attempted conquest of the *puella* is a metamorphosis of the kind that the myths in this poem usually culminate in. We are told about this metamorphosis, in turn, because it provides the answer to a question posed by Greco-Roman religion: "why is Apollo, to whom the laurel is sacred, especially fond of these leaves?" Thus it is the etiological strand in the myth of Daphne and Apollo which creates the reality confronting elegiac love in this story.

Second, the myth of Daphne and Apollo is woven into the discourse on the history of civilization in this mythological history of the world. For we are told that Apollo had, before dispatching Python, tested out his bow and arrow "only on fleeing stags and deer" (1.441–442); thus he is given the role of the first hunter to appear in the *Metamorphoses*. Changing him into a lover, Cupid brings "disorder" to an activity that ranks among one of humanity's earliest cultural achievements; indeed, he puts an end to it, at least for the nonce. In the rest of this mythological history of the world, it is always mortal hunters of both sexes whose orderly lives are destroyed by the power of Eros. That is what befalls Callisto (2.401–530) and Narcissus (3.339–510) in the first pentad. Actaeon too should be mentioned here, even if the erotic activity that terminates his existence consists simply in seeing the goddess Diana naked, whereupon he is changed into a stag and torn to pieces by his own dogs (3.131–252).

The set of erotic myths scattered throughout Books 1–5 of the *Metamorphoses* is also similar to Ovid's earlier erotic poems in that its structure too recalls the tripartite structure of a Greek erotic novel. Leading off this series of myths is a narrative, the myth of Daphne and Apollo, which portrays the behavior of a young man who has just become a slave to love. Correspondingly, at the end of the series, a young man celebrates his wedding. The bridegroom is Perseus, the hero of the legend placed just before the "epilogue" to Books 1–5, the Muse's tale (4.604–5.249). Of course, the celebration of the hero's marriage to Andromeda is not exactly comparable to the happy ending of a novel whose story line conducts hero and heroine to conjugal bliss. For, at his wedding banquet, Perseus has to square off with Andromeda's former fiancé Phineus and his followers; and when, after doing diverse heroic deeds, he nevertheless finds himself about to succumb to the aggressor's superior strength, he has to use the head of the Medusa fixed to his shield to turn his surviving foes to stone. Thus the first heroic battle described at length in the *Metamorphoses* does not conclude as one might expect. True, images of the wedding banquet are, "as is only proper," preserved for posterity, as, in our day, they are preserved by the wedding photo. But the images that make this possible in Perseus and Andromeda's case are made of marble—and are identical with the bodies of the people whose features they wear.

The erotic myths placed between the account of Apollo's first experience of love and the story of Perseus' wedding day have a common feature: in all of them, mortals have negative experiences of Eros. One of them is the suffering caused by separation from one's beloved; this is a theme that typically occurs in the middle section of Greek erotic novels, where whole oceans can lie between lovers. The story of Narcissus (3.339–510) works a most unusual variation on it. Beholding his own image in the limpid waters of a fountain, the handsome young man falls in love with it. He complains that his love can never be fulfilled—his delusion notwithstanding, he is quite keenly aware of that—and finds it especially agonizing that his beloved, though right before his eyes, is forever beyond his reach:

> quoque magis doleam, nec nos mare separat ingens
> nec via nec montes nec clausis moenia portis;
> exigua prohibemur aqua! Cupit ipse teneri!
> nam quotiens liquidis porreximus oscula lymphis,
> hic totiens ad me resupino nititur ore;
> posse putes tangi: minimum est, quod amantibus obstat.

> And this makes my pain still greater: no vast sea separates us,
> no street or mountains or walls with bolted gates;
> only a little water keeps us apart! He himself longs to be embraced!
> For, as often as I try to kiss the clear water,
> he strains toward me with upturned countenance.
> You would think I could touch him. It is almost nothing, that which stands in
>   the lovers' way.

(448–453)

This paradoxical situation resembles an elegiac lover's to the extent that Narcissus' plaint recalls a *paraklausithyron* (see p. 11). That lends Ovid's tale something of a comic air, which in turn leaves one wondering whether the psychoanalytic interpretations that are, of course, on offer by the carload, can contribute to a better understanding of the text.

Some of the erotic myths in Books 1–5 of the *Metamorphoses* do not, on first sight, seem to have anything to do with the world of elegy, since they narrate the rape of a mortal woman by a god. But if we bear in mind that the *Art of Love* recommends violence as one means of conquering a *puella* (1.669ff.), we will have no trouble making connections. For the *Ars* offers only theoretical instructions on how to bring about forced intercourse, whereas the *Metamorphoses* repeatedly affords us glimpses of the actual practice. In so doing, it makes what the lessons on love have to say on this head seem highly questionable indeed. What is more, the *Metamorphoses* usually details the consequences the practice can have for the victim. The passage that does both these things most compellingly is the myth of Callisto (2.401–530). Callisto, a hunter, is one of the followers of the goddess Diana, who admits only virgins to her suite. In a grove, Jupiter approaches her disguised in Diana's form. Thus, before resorting to force, he tries a ruse, quite in the spirit of the *Ars*. The narrator unambiguously adopts Callisto's standpoint in describing the rape, stressing the god's vastly superior physical strength:

> Qua venata foret silve, narrare parantem
> inpedit amplexu nec se sine crimine prodit.
> Illa quidem contra, quantum modo femina posset,
> (adspiceres utinam, Saturnia, mitior esses!),
> illa quidem pugnat, sed quem superare puella,
> quisve Iovem poterat? Superum petit aethera victor
> Iuppiter: huic odio nemus est et conscia silva;
> unde pedem referens paene est oblita pharetram
> tollere cum telis et, quem suspenderat, arcum.

> Just when she tries to tell in which wood she has gone hunting,
> he stops her with an embrace and, not without crime, reveals himself.
> To be sure, she resists, as best a woman can—
> if you had witnessed that, Juno, you would have been kinder!—
> to be sure, she struggles, but whom could a young woman overcome,
> and who could overcome a Jupiter? Jupiter soars up to the highest
>   ether victorious.
> Bur for her, the grove and woods are hateful, for they are accessories
>   to the crime.
> Turning her steps from that place, she nearly forgot to take
> the quiver with the arrows and the bow she had hung up.

(432–440)

The narrator describes the aftermath too primarily from Callisto's standpoint. In 64 lines (441–504), he makes the reader feel the mental anguish that the raped girl, who becomes pregnant, must endure both

before and after Diana ostracizes her, as is inevitable, and then again
after she is punished by Jupiter's wife Juno, who changes her "rival" into
a bear. Her suffering ceases only when Jupiter transforms her and her
son into constellations. We need not review that in detail here. One more thing, however,
should be noted. From the ancients' point of view, it was by no means
obvious that the narrator should empathize with a rape victim. For, in
Ovid's day, forced intercourse with a free Roman woman was regarded
as something negative in only one respect: it was prejudicial to the interests of a father or husband (Doblhofer 1994). Thus people had less sympathy for the woman than for the man she was legally subject to. This
being so, it is especially noteworthy that Ovid, the only ancient author to
have thematized the problem of rape in the manner we have briefly described, showed the "chaos" that Eros could cause in this way as well.

The Muse's Tale

Exactly three hundred lines before the first pentad of the *Metamorphoses* comes to an end, the god of love lets fly with yet another arrow
(5.379ff.). It strikes the god of the underworld, Pluto. He proceeds to
carry Proserpina off to his kingdom, whereupon her mother Ceres
makes a long journey over land and sea in quest of her daughter. Failing
to find Proserpina, she blights Sicily's agriculture and makes the island
infertile. When she is at last informed of Proserpina's whereabouts by
the fountain-nymph Arethusa, she manages to secure the right to have
her daughter with her for six months every year. Now she has the leisure
to listen to Arethusa tell how she was saved from being raped by the
river god Alpheus: she was changed into water (572–641). Ceres then
orders the Athenian Triptolemus to revive agriculture and introduce it
to those regions where it does not yet exist (642–661).

The narrator does not, however, give us a direct account of all this; he
has the Muse Calliope relate these stories in a song. What is more, he
arranges for the song to be cited by another, unnamed muse in the
course of a report to the goddess Minerva about a song competition between the nine Muses and the nine daughters of Pierus, who lose
(294–678). Minerva encounters the Muses on Mount Helicon, where
the goddess learns first how the winged horse Pegasus brought forth the
spring of the Muses and then how King Pyreneus once threatened them
in vain (250–293).

As Rudolf Rieks (1980) was the first to see, the Muse's tale, as well as
Orpheus' song in Book 10 (143–739) and the frame put around Book
15 by Pythagoras' speech and the narrator's epilogue (75–478;
871–879), all round off five-book pentads of the *Metamorphoses;* this sig-

nificantly shapes the structure of the work. Moreover, the passages featuring the Muses, Orpheus, and Pythagoras serve (like Sappho's letter in the *Epistulae Heroidum*) as substitutes for metapoetical epilogues to the individual pentads. Indeed, if only because of the meter it is written in, hexameter, the *Metamorphoses* is generically related to the epic, which means that the narrator is supposed to efface himself as much as possible (although, as we have seen, he does not really do so). He therefore seizes the occasion afforded by the "epilogues" to reflect at least indirectly on his own activity.

How does he go about this in Book 5? He makes the whole of the Muse's narrative, down to the end of the song by Calliope cited in it (661), mirror the section of the poem which runs from 1.5 to 4.249. Thus the most important themes in the earlier section are repeated here in roughly the same order. I cannot show this in detail here. Let us simply note that that the passage which contains the myth of Pyreneus and quotes the Pierides' song (about the gods' battle with the Giants [250–340]) corresponds to the story of the early history of the world told in 1.5–451. Similarly, Calliope's song (341–661) corresponds to the section of the *Metamorphoses* that opens with the legend of Daphne and Apollo and ends with that of Perseus (1.452–4.249). In both parts of the poem, the second narrative segment begins with Cupid shooting an arrow and ends with the flight of a hero. Triptolemus is not the only one to sail off into the air; Perseus does too. And, like the "epilogues" to the other pentads, this one as well is not a single, unified narrative but rather contains several narratives intercalated into the main text.

Thus the Muse's report is also a *perpetuum carmen* (continuous poem). That, however, as the proem to the work already indicates, is a novelty in the world of poetry, as new as the spring on Mount Helicon to which Minerva pays a visit (compare 1.1, *nova*, with 5.256, *novi*). That one of the Muses who dwell beside the spring now recites a miniature *perpetuum carmen* is her way of intimating that she much appreciates this new type of poetry. With that, the Muses' "consecration" of the author of the *Metamorphoses* takes place, as it were, post festum, at the end of the first pentad. For his part, the author perhaps means to hint at something by having the Pierides, whose song rings a change on one of the themes of the early history of the world, lose the singing competition with the Muses: namely, that his understanding of his own poetry inclines him to identify more closely with the part of his *perpetuum carmen* mirrored in Calliope's song. For the matter and manner of the *Metamorphoses* changes with the series of primarily erotic myths inaugurated by the myth of Daphne, so that the work now resembles Callimachus' *Aitia* and Ovid's earlier works more closely than does the history of the beginning of the world. In the latter, in contrast, mythic and didactic epic are combined as they were in Hesiod's *Theogony*.

It is, however, the Muse's narrative as a whole, from 5.269 to 5.661, which corresponds to the new kind of poetic work found in the rest of Books 1–5 of the *Metamorphoses*. Since Minerva listens to the Muse beside the new spring, it seems appropriate to identify this spring too with the new work. At all events, the goddess conspicuously admires the spring and, while looking at the magnificent, blooming natural world surrounding her, calls the Muses "happy" "because of their artistic pursuits and the place they live" (5.264–267). What does the patroness and protector of all artists mean to say by that? What if not "Keep up the good work, Ovid"?

Books 6–10: Framing Heroes and Frothing Heroines

In the second pentad of the *Metamorphoses*, we again find the tripartite division we noticed in the first: here too we have a "prologue" (in this case, the history of the beginnings of the universe), a long main section containing a series of legends, and an "epilogue" on poetics. The early history of the universe revolves around the punishment of the whole human race by the company of the gods, who have been angered by men's iniquity. The "prologue" to the second pentad recounts, in four myths, how a few individual mortals or a group of them incur the ire of certain deities through their impious disrespectfulness, and how they are made to pay for it. Arachne has the audacity to engage in a weaving competition with Minerva, who turns her into a spider (6.1–145). All too proud of the fact that she has brought fourteen children into the world, Niobe mocks Latona for having borne only Apollo and Diana, who punish her by taking all her children from her and then changing her into a woman of marble (146–312). The Lycian peasants are turned into frogs (313–381) for reasons we have already seen (see pp. 114–115). Marsyas is flayed alive by Apollo for daring to engage him in a musical contest (383–400).

The theme of this set of myths is the retribution of the gods, and yet, here again, we are not really inclined to lose ourselves in theological or ethical ruminations. On the other hand, it seems to me impossible to overlook a metapoetical statement lurking between the lines. It harks back to the "epilogue" to Books 1–5 and bears, first and foremost, on the distinction between "major" poetry in the epic tradition and "minor" poetry in the tradition of Callimachus. In the first myth—this one example will have to suffice—Minerva weaves into her tapestry images of the gods "in exalted dignity" (6.73) and the human beings they have punished. Arachne weaves into hers images of the lords of the sky raping mortal women. Thus two sets of themes in the *Metamorphoses* are again brought face-to-face. However, as neither of the competitors can clearly be said to emerge victorious from this weaving contest, it is impossible to tell whether the narrator means to hint at a preference for one or the other of the two themes.

The main section of the second pentad (6.412–10.142), to which a condensed version of the legend of Pelops serves as a transition (6.401–411), is again framed by myths that exhibit thematic affinities with the beginnings and endings of Greek erotic novels. This time, in fact, we have two pairs of legends which tell of budding love or else describe a wedding feast. At the beginning of the pentad, it is Tereus and Medea (between their two myths we find, as a comic "intermezzo," the legend of the abduction of Orithyia by the wind god Boreas [6.675–721]), who are each depicted as newly entangled in an erotic passion (6.455ff.; 7.9ff.). At the end of this series of legends, in the myth of Iphis and Ianthe (9.666–797), we are given a happy ending in the guise of a marriage feast. On the eve of his marriage with Ianthe, Iphis, a man disguised in woman's clothing, is changed into a proper groom by the goddess Isis (who played an important role in the ancient novel). The myth of Orpheus and Eurydice (10.1–105), on the other hand, gives us a wedding with a tragic outcome: the bride is bitten by a snake and dies. The narrator proceeds to spin the "epilogue" to the second pentad out of this myth. Orpheus appears before the rulers of the underworld, Pluto and Proserpina, and, invoking their own "romance" (10.28–29)—the reference to the "epilogue" to the first pentad is plain enough—negotiates Eurydice's return to the world of the living. But he loses his wife again while climbing back up to it, because he turns around to see if she is following him. To his lament over this misfortune, he adjoins a lengthy song (10.143–739). It is another *perpetuum carmen*.

In the main section of the second pentad, which is framed by the myths of Tereus and Orpheus, the mythological history of the world is continued in a way familiar to us from the first pentad. For one thing, myths which are erotic and others which are not are strung together here. For another, this section exhibits parallels to one of the major "historical" sections in the first pentad, the one about the early history of Cadmus' dynasty. For, here too, genealogy and family chronicles provide the "historical" backdrop for a sequence of myths. As we now find ourselves in the age of the heroes who preceded the generation that fought at Troy, the narrator's themes are taken from the best known of the legends about these early heroes: the expedition of the Argonauts, the Calydonian Hunt, and the adventures of Theseus and Hercules. But we are not told about the deeds of the two last-named heroes for their own sake. The myth of Theseus serves primarily as a frame narrative for a number of myths in the Callimachean tradition, so that little space is left for an account of the hero's life. As to Hercules' exploits, they are mentioned only in the form of a brief catalog (9.182–199) that is woven into a report on the hero's death and apotheosis (9.134–272).

Thus the heroes are barely recognizable as such, because the myths that recount their heroism are intertwined with others. We do, however, learn a great deal about the spectacular deeds of the heroines. In the very first two myths of the second pentad, we encounter, in the persons of Arachne and Niobe, women who behave in unusual ways. The kinds of things the heroines of the main part of the pentad do exceed all the limits that custom and decency put on human action, in particular those that were imposed on feminine activity by Roman social norms. For some of these women lose their self-control to the point of displaying uninhibited sexual passion; one—Byblis—goes so far as to tell her brother of her passion for him. Others do not balk, in their furor, at murdering members of their own family. Thus, as far as the women go, sex and crime play a central role in Books 6–10 of the *Metamorphoses*, as they do in the third pentad of the *Epistulae Heroidum*. Let us now look first at the way this theme is framed by the legends of the heroes and then at the series of frothing women.

The Heroes

War is first mentioned in the mythological history of the world at the beginning of the main section of the second pentad. Athens is waging war against barbarians (we are not told which ones) who are finally put to flight by the king of Thrace, Tereus (6.421–425). But, just as Apollo changes from hero to lover at the beginning of the main section of the first pentad, so in Tereus' case too the war, as soon as it is over, gives way to love. (The process is described in detail in a myth that we shall examine more closely later [6.426–674]). We do not hear about any other significant event in the history of civilization until we reach the end of the following myth, that of Orithyia (6.675–721)—which is to say, a full three hundred lines later, at the very end of Book 6. The event in question is the journey of the *Argo,* the "first ship," as is mentioned in, for the time being, just two (720–721) lines on the new theme. The reader who hopes to find a more detailed account of the heroic exploits of the Argonauts when the next book opens is in for a disappointment: after providing a scant eight-line report on their expedition, the narrator proceeds to give a detailed account of the first stirrings of Medea's love for Jason, the rejuvenation of Jason's father Aeson by the sorceress, and the murder of Jason's foe Pelias by Pelias' daughters, an affair stage-managed by Medea (7.1–393).

After Medea has murdered her children, an act the narrator mentions only in passing, she marries the Athenian king Aegeus (394–403). Her foiled attempt to poison his son Theseus (404–424) provides the transition to the long section of the mythical world history centered on Theseus, which runs down to line 97 of Book 9. Yet this part of the poem is no "Theseid," as we have already said. For, of the 1,443 lines it contains, only 75 (7.404–452; 8.169–176, 8.260–269, 8.403–410) chronicle the hero's deeds. The rest of this section of the poem consists of myths intercalated into the story of Theseus, and the passages leading up to them. There are ten stories here, one of which is even about a subject drawn from the world of heroic epic: the legend of Meleager and the heroes' hunt for the Calydonian Boar (8.260–546). But here, as we have already seen (p. 3), the heroes pursuing the beast are portrayed quite unheroically—are, indeed, made to look ridiculous. Not only does Theseus cut an embarrassingly poor figure as a hunter; he also prefaces his appearance on the scene with a rather suspicious statement about the kind of heroism to be expected from a hero:

> ibat in adversum proles Ixionis hostem
> Pirithous, valida quatiens venabula dextra;
> cui "procul" Aegides "o me mihi carior" inquit
> "pars animae consiste meae! Licet eminus esse
> fortibus: Ancaeo nocuit temeraria virtus."
> dixit et aerata torsit grave cuspide cornum;
> quo bene librato votique potente futuro
> obstitit aesculea frondosus ab arbore ramus.

> Ixion's son Pirithoüs wanted to charge straight at the foe,
> brandishing the hunting spear in his strong right hand.
> Aegeus' son spoke to him: "Oh, you who are dearer to me than
>   my own self,
> and a part of my soul, stop where you are! One can be brave
> at a distance. Ancaeus' rash manliness has proven his bane."
> He spoke and hurled the spear made of cornelwood, heavy with its
>   bronze tip.
> In its way, though it was well cast and should have reached it mark,
> stood the leafy branch of an oak.

(403–410)

None of the other interspersed myths in the section about Theseus has anything even remotely to do with heroic epic. The first is in the tradition of the Roman didactic poem (7.518–660: the plague at Aegina). The next two legends are elegiac/erotic (7.690–862: Cephalus and Procris; 8.6–151: Scylla). Then comes the legend of Daedalus, which carries metapoetical connotations, like the version of the story found in the *Ars amatoria* (8.183–259; see p. 98). After the report on the Calydonian Hunt, we find a pair of short myths that provide etiological accounts of the origins of some islands (8.577–589; 8.590–610) and a pair of somewhat longer ones whose subjects are largely borrowed from tales by Callimachus (8.618–724: Philemon and Baucis; 8.738–878: Erysichthon). Capping the sequence is a narrative that leads into the section of the poem about Hercules; it describes the hero's single-handed combat with the river god Achelous, relating how he breaks off one of the god's horns (9.1–88).

What is doubtless the best known of these stories tells how the gods Jupiter and Mercury, after assuming human form, knock on a thousand doors in vain before finally being offered food and drink by an old married couple, the poor but pious Philemon and Baucis. After sinking the couple's neighbors in a swamp, the gods appoint the two old people priests of a golden temple, and, at their request, change both into trees at exactly the same moment at the end of their lives. When the person who tells this uplifting myth, a companion of Theseus' by the name of Lelex, brings his tale to a close, his listeners, "especially Theseus" (8.725–726), are visibly moved. The reason for Theseus' emotion, brought to light by Stephen Hinds (1987a, 19), is that, in Callimachus' *Hecale* (see p. 6), Theseus is given a similarly frugal but hospitable reception. The allusion underscores the fact that the "Theseid" is merely a frame narrative in the *Metamorphoses*.

The same holds, with certain qualifications, for the "Herculeid." Here the only story we are told about Hercules while he was still among the living concerns his marriage with Deianira: he first wins her in combat with Achelous (9.1–88), then prevents the centaur Nessus from taking her from him (98–133). Ultimately, however, his flesh is slowly eaten away by a tunic, soaked in Nessus' poisonous blood, that Deianira sends him; in his agony, he builds a pyre and tries to burn himself alive (134–238). None of this casts Hercules in a very heroic light, and, indeed, nothing more is said about him for his own sake in the rest of the Hercules section of the *Metamorphoses*. For the main order of business in the next part of the poem, an account of Hercules' apotheosis (239–272), is to pave the way for the series of apotheoses described in the Roman section of the history of the world (see pp. 143f.). The remainder of the "Herculeid" deals only with members of the hero's family; it is the women who figure most prominently here (273–401). The narrators dwells in particular on the *la-*

bores (labor pains) that Hercules' mother Alcmena suffers in bringing him into the world (285–305). Indeed, he devotes more lines to them than he does to the hero's *labores,* cataloged in the first part of the section on Hercules, who, pursued by his stepmother Juno's inveterate hatred, has to perform these labors at Eurystheus' bidding (182–199). Rarely in the *Metamorphoses* is it as obvious as it is here how much the narrator's interest in what men and women feel outweighs his interest in the feats supposedly performed by the heroes of yore.

The Heroines

The first in the series of heroines driven to their acts by uncontrolled emotion is a woman who does a gruesome deed: Procne, an Athenian. With the help of her sister Philomela, she slaughters her son Itys and serves him up to his father Tereus, king of Thrace, for dinner (6.636ff.). She is not the only one of Ovid's heroines to kill members of her own family; the theme also appears in the stories of Medea (7.1–403), Scylla (8.6–151), Althaea (8.445–532), and Deianira (9.134–238).

Procne does her bloody deed to revenge herself on Tereus for raping Philomela in a forest in Thrace. Tereus is the only mortal in the *Metamorphoses* to have forced intercourse with a mortal woman. When, after the rape, Philomela threatens to reveal what has befallen her, something else happens:

> quo fuit accinctus, vagina liberat ensem
> adreptamque coma flexis post terga lacertis
> vincla pati cogit; iugulum Philomela parabat
> spemque suae mortis viso conceperat ense:
> ille indignantem et nomen patris usque vocantem
> luctantemque loqui conprensam forcipe linguam
> abstulit ense fero; radix micat ultima linguae,
> ipsa iacet terraeque tremens inmurmurat atrae,
> utque salire solet mutilatae cauda colubrae,
> palpitat et moriens dominae vestigia quaerit.
> Hoc quoque post facinus (vix ausim credere) fertur
> saepe sua lacerum repetisse libidine corpus.

> He draws the sword girded on his side from the sheath,
> drags her along by the hair, twists her arms behind her back,
> and ties her up. Philomela offered him her throat—
> at the sight of the sword, she had hoped for death—
> but, with pincers, he seized the tongue that resisted and kept
> calling on the name of her father and struggling to speak,
> and chopped it off with the savage steel. The rest of the root of her
>   tongue is still twitching,

the tongue lies on the black earth and, palpitating, murmurs
   something into it.
And, as the tail of a mangled snake is wont to jerk about,
it too writhes and, perishing, seeks its mistress' feet.
Even after this shameful deed—I hardly dare believe it—he is supposed
to have often, in his craving for pleasure, indecently assaulted her
   mangled body.

(6.551–562)

Tereus' behavior here is like Apollo's in the story about Daphne, where
the god, before resorting to force, comports himself like an elegiac lover.
Philomela catches the king's attention when, after five years of marriage
with Procne in Thrace, he goes to Athens at his wife's request in order to
invite his sister-in-law to pay a visit to his court. Enflamed with passion
from the moment he lays eyes on Philomela, he immediately begins plotting to win her for himself by bribing her nurse and attendants and giving
her presents (6.451–463), thus demonstrating that he is eminently well
acquainted with the strategy of conquest taught in the *Ars amatoria*. The
same applies to the rhetoric and tears that he mobilizes to persuade
Philomela to make the journey to Thrace (469–471). Yet the narrator
sees nothing but pernicious false pretense in the fact that Tereus assumes
the role of an elegiac lover, as his comment on the king's behavior shows:
"pro superi, quantum mortalia pectora caecae/noctis habent!"; "Oh ye
immortals! How much dark night rules in the hearts of mortal men!"
(472–473). Once again, Ovid confronts elegiac themes with mythical reality to generate tension. Throughout the main part of the second pentad
of the *Metamorphoses,* he continues to do so in the myths portraying female
passion. It is not only Medea (7.9–158), Procris (7.796–862), Scylla
(8.6–151), and Deianira (9.134–157) who exhibit some of the character
traits of an elegiac *puella;* this is true even of Byblis, who is in love with her
brother Caunus (9.454–665).

   The narrator has the heroine present herself in direct discourse in
122 of the 212 lines making up the story of Byblis, including three fairly
long, uninterrupted speeches, two of them oral and one written, interspersed with narrative passages. A monologue she delivers on waking
from an erotic dream (474–516) is followed by a letter to her brother in
which she declares her love for him (530–563), and then by another
monologue touched off by Caunus' angry rejection of her suit
(585–629). What we have here are three erotic elegies composed in
hexameter. The first monologue is reminiscent of the poem *Amores* 1.2,
in which the *poeta/amator* realizes, after a sleepless night, that he is in
love. The situation that gives rise to the second corresponds to *Amores*

1.12, in which the lover laments that his letter to Corinna seeking a rendezvous was in vain. Byblis' letter, finally, is quite obviously conceived on the model of the *Epistulae Heroidum;* the style of argument it uses closely resembles that found in Phaedra's letter (4).

The narrator observes Byblis as she writes:

> dextra tenet ferrum, vacuam tenet altera ceram.
> incipit et dubitat; scribit damnatque tabellas,
> et notat et delet, mutat culpatque probatque
> inque vicem sumptas ponit positasque resumit.
> quid velit, ignorat; quicquid factura videtur,
> displicet; in vultu est audacia mixta pudori.

> The right hand holds the stylus, the other holds the empty wax tablet.
> She begins and hesitates, she writes and rejects what is written,
> and she inscribes and effaces, changes and criticizes and approves,
> alternatively laying down the tablets she has picked up and, hardly
>   has she laid them down, picking them up again.
> She does not know what she wants; everything it seems right to her to do
> then displeases her. In her features is boldness mixed with shame.

(9.522–527)

Besides offering further compelling testimony of Ovid's gift for psychologically insightful description of human behavior, the passage indicates how we are to imagine the heroines of the *Epistulae* writing their letters.

Byblis' persistent advances ultimately drive her brother to flee. Like a frenzied Bacchante, she tracks him so long that, after traversing a number of different countries, she collapses, weeping violently, and dissolves into the fountain that bears her name "to this day" (664). Thus the fires of her passion are quenched in the most literal sense. Plainly, a metamorphosis can be read not only as etiological explanation, but also as metaphor. We shall come back to this point in the final section of the present chapter.

Orpheus' Song

Orpheus' song, which stands at the end of the second pentad of the *Metamorphoses* (10.143–739), is a miniature *perpetuum carmen* [continuous song], like the Muse's tale at the end of the first pentad. Orpheus begins his song with a proem announcing his theme: earlier he sang of Jupiter and the Giants, but now his song will be about "boys loved by the gods, and young women [*puellae*] who, driven out of their senses by the flames of forbidden passion, merited punishment for their lust" (148–154). Thus, like the text of the second pentad, which precedes Orpheus' song, this *perpetuum carmen* too lacks a section on the earliest history of the universe. The singer refers back only to the themes of the series of erotic stories in the section of the *Metamorphoses* that runs from 6.1 to 10.142.

Among the love stories Orpheus recites, some are, thematically, of a kind almost without precedent in the *Metamorphoses*, for they turn on the erotic relationship between a divinity and a mortal youth. Immediately before Orpheus' song, we find the legend of Apollo and Cyparissus (106–142); included in the song are the legends of Jupiter and Ganymede (155–161), Apollo and Hyacinthus (162–219), and Venus and Adonis (503–739). Of the women featured in the remaining erotic myths—the Propoetides (220–242), Myrrha (298–502), and Atalanta (560–707)—one bears an unmistakable resemblance to a woman who appears in Books 6–10, before Orpheus' song: Myrrha. Myrrha's story, like the myth of Byblis, deals with the theme of incest. Myrrha is in love with her father; the way the narrator has Orpheus tell us her tale differs somewhat from the way he himself tells us Byblis'. In Myrrha's story, direct discourse is eclipsed by narrative passages containing such graphic, gripping descriptions that one is reminded of a tale by Boccaccio.

A comparison of the two incest stories reveals that Ovid has assigned Orpheus' song too the function of prompting the reader to metapoetical reflections on the *perpetuum carmen* as a new form of verse narrative. But the myth of the greatest interest in this connection is precisely the one that Orpheus fails to mention in announcing his theme: the story of Pygmalion, who falls in love with an ivory statue he himself has carved (243–297). What this text obliquely tells us about Ovid's writing refers, however, not to the *Metamorphoses*, but, as Alison Sharrock first observed (1991b), to the *Amores*, or rather, more generally, to the type of elegy that that work exemplifies.

Pygmalion is not satisfied to kiss the statue, speak to it, and cradle it in his arms; he also flatters it and brings it all sorts of gifts, "of the kind that please young women [*puellae*]" (259), including clothes and jewelry. After mentioning presents of this sort, Orpheus goes on to say:

> cuncta decent; nec nuda minus formosa videtur.
> conlocat hanc stratis concha Sidonide tinctis
> appellatque tori sociam adclinataque colla
> mollibus in plumis tamquam sensura reponit.

> All that becomes her, but she is no less beautiful naked.
> He lays her on blankets dyed with Sidonian purple,
> and he calls her his bedfellow, and lays her reclining neck
> back on the feathers, as if it could feel that.

(266–269)

When we read how Pygmalion treats his statue, we have constantly to bear in mind that, on the literal meaning of *durus* (hard, hard-hearted), the statue is truly a *dura puella*. If we do, we will recognize in the man who makes the statue and then falls in love with it an elegiac poet, or, rather, his fictive embodiment as *poeta/amator*. As we have seen, the *poeta/amator* too fashions his beloved by dint of "womanufacture" (see pp. 48–49); as *dura puella*, she then has him woo her as Pygmalion woos his statue. In Propertius' and Tibullus' "classical" elegiac erotic novels, however, the *poeta/amator* eventually stops dancing attendance on the *puella* and puts an end to his relationship with her. Things take a different turn in the story of Pygmalion: the beloved—who, after all, cannot make the slightest response to her creator's and lover's suit—"softens up," for Venus changes her from a statue into a flesh-and-blood woman. Myth, with its own "reality," makes it happen.

Books 11–15: From Troy to Rome and From There to Eternity

In Books 1–10 of the *Metamorphoses*, we find only a handful of *aitia* about religious rites, interspersed with legends explaining natural phenomena. The same holds for most of Books 11–15. However, the final section of the third pentad of Ovid's poem, which is framed by the two apotheoses that Venus persuades Jupiter to bring about—Aeneas' (14.581–608) and Caesar's (15.745–851)—offers explanations for natural phenomena only in Pythagoras' speech (15.75–478). Moreover, Pythagoras is a Greek philosopher who teaches in southern Italy, and his lecture is an interpolation in the ongoing narrative, like the "epilogues" to the first and second pentads. The narrative proper is about the Roman period in the mythological history of the world; the myths it contains offer etiological explanations for rites and ritual objects and nothing else.

The history of Rome related at the end of the *Metamorphoses* is thus sharply set off from the rest of the work. It constitutes, within the third pentad, the continuation of a section of the poem (13.623–14.580) that corresponds to Virgil's *Aeneid;* this long passage is preceded by another that traces the history of Troy from its founding to its destruction (11.194–13.622). The Trojan section of the poem comes on the heels of a "prologue" to the third pentad which, unlike the analogous passages in Books 1 and 6, contains only two myths. One relates the murder of the singer Orpheus, who, after Eurydice's death, eschews the love of women; he is slain, we learn, by Maenads from Thrace who are then punished by Bacchus (11.1–84). The other is about King Midas, who, for a brief period, turns everything he touches into gold; because he declares, after a musical competition between Apollo and Pan, that Apollo has been unjustly awarded the palm, Apollo fits him out with ass's ears (11.85–193). Both myths are akin to the "prologue" to the second pentad in that they are more easily read as metapoetical pronouncements than as statements on theology and ethics. But the attempt to read them that way would take us too far afield here.

After only twenty-seven lines, the narrative that follows the legend of Midas, an account of the history of Troy, is broken off to make room for a 575 line-long passage containing mainly erotic myths (11.221–795). This passage begins with a myth about Peleus' rape of the goddess Thetis (221–265) that is, in its turn, one of the twin cornerstones of the set of erotic myths stretching from one end of the pentad to the other. This time, the last myth–the legend of the seduction of the nymph Pomona by the god Vertumnus (14.622–771)—bears a striking similarity to the first. In both, one half of the couple involved is a god who likes to change into various forms—Thetis in the first case, Vertumnus in the second. Unlike all the love stories that come between them, both these myths end happily.

However, if we are alert to what precipitates the happy ending in each case, we will notice an important difference which again indicates that Ovid sets the Roman section of the mythological history of the world—including the legend of Pomona—off against the rest of the poem. Peleus founds his marriage with Thetis on a rape, that is, a form of "conquest" of a woman depicted a number of times before Ovid begins to tell the story of Rome and often represented as a source of great suffering for the woman. Vertumnus, in contrast, first tries his luck with trickery. He takes on various forms in an attempt to seduce Pomona, finally appearing in the guise of an old woman who tells a love story with elegiac features, the myth of Iphis. Iphis hangs himself at the door of a *dura puella* named Anaxarete; she, fittingly, turns to stone (698–761). After all Vertumnus' efforts have proven vain, he appears before Pomona in his own form, that of a youthful god, whereupon the following transpires: "vimque parat: sed vi non est opus, inque figura/capta dei nympha est et mutua vulnera sensit"/"And he made ready to do violence to her, but there was no need for violence, and the nymph/was smitten by the god's form and felt the same love pangs" (770–771). What a surprising turn of events at the close of the last love story in the *Metamorphoses!* Because an *amator* puts aside all dissembling and is entirely himself, he can renounce the use of force and immediately win the affections of a *puella*. In the first erotic myth in the poem, Apollo plays the elegiac lover's part; but neither that nor his attempt to use force get him anywhere. In the following myths, other *amatores* try to achieve their ends by trickery and/or coercion, but we are never told that a *puella* returns their love. Because the *Ars amatoria* counsels both dissimulation and violence, the myth of Pomona reads like a counterexample to the doctrine preached by the *praeceptor amoris*. While Vertumnus is still in the process of changing from one form to another, he makes arguments like the *praeceptor*'s, taking a myth with elegiac motifs as his example— and all for naught. Then, in the rustic atmosphere that prevailed before the Rome was founded, he puts his talent for disguise aside, thus appearing as the very opposite of the crafty, ever-changing *amator* of "cultivated" Rome. The "reality" that here contrasts with the world of false appearances conjured up by the *praeceptor amoris* is that of a Roman, not a Greek myth. And this occurs in the Roman section of the *Metamorphoses*, which consequently proves different from the rest of the work in its treatment of erotic themes as well.

From Achilles to Aeneas

The series of erotic myths in the third pentad opens with the myth of Peleus. This myth is bound up with the history of Troy, the founding of which is narrated in the preceding legend. For the union of Peleus and Thetis produces Achilles, the greatest of the Greek heroes to fight at Troy. At the very beginning of the myth of Peleus, there is a reference to the fact that Peleus' son will be greater than his father (11.222–223); at the end of Book 15, the narrator says the same about Augustus, Caesar's (adoptive) son, forging a link that spans four books (850ff.). Hence one expects that the story of Peleus' rape of Thetis will open out into an account of the events leading up to the Trojan War. Instead, from 11.226 on, the myth of Peleus gradually modulates into the myth of Ceyx and Alcyone, which runs almost to the end of the book, as if Troy had been quite forgotten. For what we now hear about is the elegiac love of a married couple: when the wife finds the body of her husband on the shore near their home after he drowns in a shipwreck, man and wife are both changed into kingfishers (410–748).

However, the violent storm that sinks Ceyx's ship is depicted in such detail that the reader is now, at all events, in the right frame of mind to step into the world of epic, of which the battle for Troy is an integral part. For, since Homer, storm scenes had been a traditional feature of epic, and the narrator of the *Metamorphoses* offers us a particularly fine specimen (474–572). Moreover, he mentions the "warring winds" (491) and compares the waves that come breaking over the ship with the act of storming a besieged city (508–509; 525–536). At the same time as the narrator thus sets the stage for the lengthy epic section that begins with the first line of Book 12, he closes off, with a portrait of Alcyone, a line of action initiated at the beginning of Book 7: Ceyx's wife is the last in the series of elegiacally amorous heroines in the *Metamorphoses*. We are given, immediately after the account of her tragedy, a brief love story in which Aesacus, the son of the Trojan king Priam, is assigned the *amator*'s role (11.749–795); the love story provides a transition to the narrative of the battle for Troy.

This section of the poem, which encompasses not only the whole of Book 12 but 622 lines of Book 13 as well, is, like Homer's *Iliad*, basically an "Achilleid." For, as in the *Iliad*, Achilles is at the heart of the action here too. Of all the events that revolve around the hero, however, Ovid relates only those that occur before or after the phase of the Trojan War which is chronicled in the *Iliad*. The narrator begins by very quickly relating the Greeks' departure from Aulis and the single combat between Achilles and Cygnus (12.1–145) and then brings his narrative down to a several days' lull in the fighting, during which Nestor tells stories to the Greeks Achilles has invited to a banquet (146–579). Next, he reports Achilles' death (580–619) and then has Ajax and Odysseus make their long speeches in the dispute over which of the Greeks is to inherit Achilles' weapons (12.620–13.398). The section of the poem on Troy is rounded off by two narratives. The first is a detailed account of the fate of Priam's wife Hecuba, who, after the Greeks have taken the city, must witness, among other things, the sacrifice of her daughter Polyxena to appease Achilles' ghost (399–575). The second is a myth that tells how the ashes of the hero Memnon, slain by Achilles, are changed into birds (576–622).

Thus the events of the *Iliad* are simply skipped over here. Yet the place-filler that Ovid puts where they would normally have gone calls for special attention: it is Nestor's account of the bloody fight that breaks out between the Lapithae and the Centaurs at Pirithoüs and Hippodamia's wedding (12.210–535). Here, as in Homer, we are presented with detailed descriptions of single-handed combat between valiant heroes. But the level of the heroism of the brawling wedding guests is located well below that of Homer's braves; what they engage in is ultimately only a kind of wild free-for-all. Thus the weapons they use are the sort of objects one finds to hand at a banquet, indoors or out: wine pitchers, candelabras, or stumps, for instance. No doubt, these weapons too meet the desired end. Thus a tree trunk brought crashing down on a Lapith's skull procures the following effect:

> fracta volubilitas capitis latissima, perque os
> perque cavas nares oculosque auresque cerebrum

molle fluit, veluti concretum vimine querno
lac solet utve liquor rari sub pondere cribri
manat et exprimitur per densa foramina spissus.

The writhing head was split wide open, and, through the mouth
and nostrils and eyes and ears, the brains
came gushing out, soft like the curdled milk
that wells out of a weave of oaken withes, or the juice that, when
    pressure is put on the sieve,
drips down and is squeezed out of narrow openings.

(434–438)

Yes, such a blow is most impressive. In the *Iliad* too, the scenes in which the heroes are wounded or killed are described quite as graphically. But what the narrator offers us along these lines, in various passages in the story of the fight between the Lapithae and the Centaurs, is a caricature of Homeric battle scenes so grotesque that Homer's battles end up seeming absurd. The manifest point of the caricature, as Joachim Latacz (1979) was the first to point out, is to dismantle a literary system. Here, by making it abundantly clear what the use of force can lead to, the narrator undercuts the sublimity of stirring heroics. What is called into question is, of course, not Homer's poetry, but the sort of hero worship that finds his portraits of battle scenes uplifting.

The "Homeric" section in the mythological history of the world gives place to a "Virgilian" section that tells the story of Aeneas' adventures (13.623–14.580). But little of the *Aeneid* survives in the *Metamorphoses*. Of the 926 lines in this section of the poem, only some 200 are given over to retelling Virgil's epic. The others present a number of myths that Ovid works into his version of the legend of Aeneas. Thus, like the "Theseid" in Books 7–9, the "Aeneid" in Books 13–14 provides nothing more than a frame narrative. Moreover, it leaves out almost everything Virgil's *Aeneid* has to say about the significance of the myth of Aeneas for the history of Rome and the Augustan state. Only readers familiar with Virgil's epic—it may of course be presumed that readers of Ovid's day were—will understand the rare allusions to Aeneas' *pietas* (sense of duty; cf. 13.624 and 626, for example) and fulfilment of a divine mission that Ovid sprinkles through the text of the *Metamorphoses*.

The *Aeneid* serves primarily as the basis for intertextual games here, as it does in many other passages of the *Metamorphoses*. Consider, for instance, the passage in Ovid in which we are told that Aeneas, returning with the Sibyl to the world of the living after his descent into Hades, made the arduousness (*labor*) of the difficult ascent a little easier to bear by engaging the seer in conversation (120–121; see Smith's dissertation 1990, 28–30). Virgil's Sibyl had announced before leading him down into the underworld that, unlike the descent, the return to the world of the living would be a *labor* (6.125–129). Given the religious intensity of her declaration, it is very funny that, in Ovid, the *labor* is so trifling that a pleasant little chat can put it out of mind: once again, the *Metamorphoses* reduces heroics to human proportions. The contrast between the kind of conversation Ovid's Sibyl makes with Aeneas and the religious solemnity of what she says in Virgil puts an even greater distance between Ovid and his predecessor: in the *Metamorphoses* (130–153), the Sibyl recounts how Apollo once vied for her favors. (She did at least turn him down.)

The flow of the story is broken by various other erotic myths that, like the one the Sibyl recounts, are intercalated into Ovid's "Aeneid." Here again, tension is generated by the gap between elegiac love and mythical reality. This is done to especially witty effect in the description of the Cyclops Polyphemus, enamoured of the nymph Galatea (13.750–897). For, in this case, our *amator* is an oafish one-eyed giant. To be sure, he too pretends to be cultivated, but, to do up his hair and beard as recommended in the *Ars amatoria* (1.518), he uses a rake and sickle (765–766). As to what comes out when he tries to use the metaphoric language of the elegiac lover, we have an example in the passage that describes his encounter with a prophet:

> terribilem Polyphemon adit, "lumen" que, "quod unum
> fronte geris media, rapiet tibi" dixit "Ulixes."
> risit et "o vatum stolidissime, falleris" inquit,
> "altera iam rapuit."

> He stepped toward the terrible Polyphemus. "That one eye that
> you wear in the middle of your forehead—Odysseus will," he said,
>   "take it from you."
> But Polyphemus laughed and said, "O you most stupid of all seers,
>   you are mistaken.
> Another, a woman, has already taken it."

> (772–775)

Polyphemus makes his *puella* a particularly prolix declaration of love (789–869); but, like the speaker of the *Amores* before him, he woos her in vain. Like Apollo in the myth of Daphne and Apollo, he then resorts to brute force; it is, however, not Galatea, but Acis, the handsome young man she is in love with, who bears the brunt of it. Yet Acis does not die when Polyphemus buries him under a mass of rock; he is changed into a river god.

In addition to the Cyclops, other figures familiar from Homer's *Odyssey* appear in the myths inserted into Ovid's "Aeneid." The sorceress Circe is one of them; thus the intertextual game takes in the third great epic as well. Since Roman tradition has it that Circe lived in Latium, Ovid can choose a region that was later conquered by Aeneas as the setting for a myth in which she falls in love with a man. Here, in her rage over the fact that King Picus does not return her love, Circe changes him into a woodpecker (14.320–434). But this is the only time in the *Metamorphoses* that a story set in Latium describes how a woman's passionate love is transmuted into frenzy. The myths about Latins and Romans narrated in the Roman section of the work are of a very different order.

From Aeneas to Augustus

The word *deducere* (lead down), which the narrator uses in the proem to the *Metamorphoses* in entreating the gods to "lead" his work from the origins of the world down to his own day, can serve as a metaphor not only in weaving, but also in navigation, where it may designate, for example, the piloting of a ship from the high seas into a port. Seen in this light, Augustan Rome appears as a port that offers the narrator and reader a haven after their journey through the mythological history of the world. It is therefore fitting that two rather long passages in the last three books should chronicle a sea voyage. One of these passages is about Aeneas' journey from Troy to Latium (13.623–14.157). The other, placed just before the section of the poem on Caesar and Augustus, depicts a journey taken by Aesculapius, the god of healing, who appears to men in the form of a serpent; he sails from his old temple in Epidaurus to his new sanctuary in Rome (14.697–728).

As Alessandro Barchiesi (1994, 227) has pointed out, a passage in the latter narrative which describes how the serpent slithers along manifestly alludes to the act of unrolling (*explicare*) a roll containing writing (*volumen*):

> . . . deus explicat orbes
> perque sinus crebros et magna volumina labens
> templa parentis init.

> . . . the god unrolls [*explicat*] his coils,
> and, gliding forward in countless curves and broad loops [*volumina*],
> he enters his father's temple.

(720–722)

Someone reading this passage in ancient times would have been very close to the end of the last of the *volumina* the *Metamorphoses* was written on. After reading a few more lines, she would have unrolled Book 15 far enough to have reached the goal of the "journey" represented by the work: the narrator's own times.

The myth of Aesculapius is followed by an account of Caesar's apotheosis (745–851), the last in a series of four descriptions of apotheoses linked by their conspicuously similar wording. Three of these descriptions occur in the Roman section of the *Metamorphoses,* which opens with Aeneas' apotheosis (14.581–608). There follow a catalog of the kings who ruled Latium after Aeneas (609–621), the story of Pomona (622–771), and a section on Romulus, the founder of Rome, which concludes with an account of the apotheosis of the king and his wife Hersilia (722–851). Then, after mentioning Romulus' successor Numa, who studies the "nature of things" (15.6), the narrator makes a transition to Pythagoras' speech (15.1–478). Following the speech, a series of myths that explain Roman rites and ritual objects (479–744) culminates in a description of Caesar's apotheosis, the narrator's prayer that the gods postpone Augustus' apotheosis for as long as possible, and the epilogue to the work as a whole (745–879).

If we take Hercules' apotheosis, already described in Book 9 (239–272), in conjunction with the three accounts of apotheoses in the Roman section of the *Metamorphoses,* then we have a set of four myths. In each of them, an important role is assigned one of the four elements of which the world is, at the beginning of the work, said to have been made (Davis 1980). Hercules becomes a god after his body has been consumed by fire. The water of the river Numicius washes Aeneas free of every last trace of mortality. Romulus' body evaporates into the air (melting into what are obviously the lower levels of the atmosphere), while Caesar's soul is changed into a star, that is, attains immortality in the ether. Thus the reader is led from the four elements of the cosmogony through the four apotheoses they make possible to the apotheosis of Augustus, which the narrator evokes only indirectly—"from the very beginning of the world down to my own times" (1.3–4). Does it follow that the history of the world has reached its culminating point with Augustus' reign? Before essaying an answer, I need to consider the epilogue to the *Metamorphoses.* But that presupposes a discussion of Pythagoras' speech, which itself represents a kind of epilogue.

Pythagoras' Speech

Pythagoras' speech is divided into three parts. The first and the third taken together (15.75–175, 453–478) are about half as long as the second (176–452). They treat the same theme: both warn against eating meat, basing what they say on the doctrine of metempsychosis. In the long middle section, Pythagoras explains that everything in the world is constantly changing. He shows this by considering, first of all, the alternation of day and night and the changing seasons (186–213); the fact that people grow old (214–236); and the constant separation and recombination of the four elements (237–251). Then he mentions changes that affect the surface of the earth (252–360); mutations in the plant and animal world (361–417); and changes in the political map over the course of history (418–452). He caps the last section of his speech with the words of the Trojan seer Helenus, who is supposed to have prophesied to Aeneas that Rome would achieve the status of a world power and that Augustus would become a god (439–449).

To the present day, many critics take Pythagoras' speech as the key to interpreting the *Metamorphoses,* arguing that Ovid here reveals the philosophy underpinning his work. At the same time, they say, he engages in a scientific discussion of the phenomenon of change, which he has so far treated in fictional narratives. However, what Pythagoras here offers us by way of philosophy is limited to the doctrine of the transmigration of souls, which the historical Pythagoras is also thought to have professed. And it is Pythagoras himself, not Ovid, who presents this doctrine here. As for Pythagoras' "scientific" explanations of processes of transformation, they can at best be termed pseudoscientific, even from the standpoint of antiquity, as Sara Myers has rightly insisted (1994, 133ff.). For Ovid has obviously borrowed many of Pythagoras' examples of geological and biological transformations from Greco-Roman paradoxography, a literature that entertained its readers with cataloges of natural miracles. But such miracles belong to the realm of fiction no less than the mythical *Metamorphoses* themselves. Accordingly, the same phenomenon often appears in Ovid both in Pythagoras' speech and elsewhere. Thus in Book 4, for example, the myth of Salmacis and Hermaphroditus (271–388) is offered as an explanation for the fact that the pool of Salmacis unmans the men who bathe in it; Pythagoras mentions precisely the same body of water as an illustratation of nature's capacity to work transformations (15.317–319).

The juxtaposition of mythology and pseudo-learned natural science in the *Metamorphoses* is not limited to the juxtaposition of Books 1–14 with Pythagoras' speech. Myth and pseudoscience also rub elbows early in the poem—in the cosmogony, for instance, which leaves open the question as to whether human beings were created from divine sperm or a combination of the four elements (1.78–83). In the further course of the narrative as well, we often find a mythical transformation alongside one presented as a natural phenomenon—the description of Lichas' metamorphosis, cited at the beginning of this chapter, is a case in point (see p. 117). Pythagoras, for his part, by no means excludes mythology from his doctrine. Thus it is quite impossible to interpret his explanations as scientific rectification of the mythological worldview purveyed by the rest of the *Metamorphoses* and, on those grounds, to identify the philosopher's voice with Ovid's.

To do so would be to overlook the fact that the character who narrates the mythological history of the world and the one who tells us about natural miracles stand side by side in the poem. Both narrators recite a *perpetuum carmen* [continuous song]. For Pythagoras' speech too is a condensed *perpetuum carmen*. Like the Muse's tale in Book 5 or like Orpheus' song, it is structurally and thematically similar to the larger work in which it occurs. Indeed, the *Metamorphoses* as a whole is mirrored in Pythagoras' speech, which exhibits thematic parallels with the story of the origins of the universe in Book 1, both in the first part and at the beginning of the long middle section. Thus Pythagoras' admonition against eating meat, which he depicts as a barbarous, bloody deed, finds its pendant in the narrator's sermonizing on the decline of the human race from the innocence that marked the generation of the Golden Age—which Pythagoras too portrays as morally pure (15.96–103)—to the bloodlust of the mortals of the Iron Age (1.89–150). After Pythagoras has, in the course of his lecture, mentioned any number of different transformational processes that the mythological narrator also treats—I have already mentioned the example of the power to "emasculate" attributed to the pool of Salmacis—he brings the middle section of his discourse to a close, like the narrator of Book 14, with an allusive reference to Augustus' apotheosis.

Hence Pythagoras' speech, like the Muse's tale or Orpheus' song, can be read between the lines as a metapoetical "epilogue," one which prompts the attentive reader to take a closer look at the narrator of the *Metamorphoses*. For, like the narrator, Pythagoras too strikes us as a rather garrulous, Polonian sort; indeed, he stresses, on three different occasions, that he has much more lecture material to hand than he actually manages to cover (15.307–308, 418–420, 453–454). Pythagoras' demeanor thus drives home the point that we should not take his near look-alike, the narrator, any too seriously. Moreover, a careful reading of his speech reveals that this philosopher's effort to provide an intellectual explanation of the phenomenon of metamorphosis does not yield particularly compelling results. That too holds for the narrator. To be sure, both engage in lively, lengthy discussions of the principle of change; yet neither the narrator's mythology nor Pythagoras' natural philosophy explains its root causes well enough to enable the reader to discern "what, at its very core, holds the world together."

But even if what the *Metamorphoses* has to say about the history of the world as a process of permanent change does not hold water philosophically, the work does convey something like a conception of history. And it does so in the Rome of Augustus, although one of the notions underpinning the ideology of Augustus' principate had it that, with the emperor's reign, the history of the city-state had reached a stage not susceptible of further change, that of Rome's eternal world rule. Let us, then, return to the question of whether the *Metamorphoses* too presents Augustus' principate as the highest and ultimate stage in world history.

Augustus and the Power of Metamorphosis

After entreating the gods to postpone Augustus' apotheosis, all the narrator has left to say is this:

Iamque opus exegi, quod nec Iovis ira nec ignes
nec poterit ferrum nec edax abolere vetustas.
cum volet, illa dies, quae nil nisi corporis huius
ius habet, incerti spatium mihi finiat aevi:
parte tamen meliore mei super alta perennis
astra ferar, nomenque erit indelebile nostrum,
quaque patet domitis Romana potentia terris,
ore legar populi, perque omnia saecula fama,
siquid habent veri vatum praesagia, vivam.

Now I have finished a work that neither Jupiter's wrath, nor fire,
nor iron, nor gnawing age will be able to destroy.
If it wants to, let the day that has power
over nothing but my body put an end to the uncertain span of my life.
With my better part, I will yet, enduring forever,
leap high above the stars, and my name will be imperishable,
and as far as the power of Rome stretches over the conquered lands,
I shall be read out from the mouth of the people, and shall, through
      all the centuries—
if there is any truth to the poet's premonitions—live on in fame.

(871–879)

The passage is clear. Alluding to the four apotheoses already mentioned, those of Hercules, Aeneas, Romulus, and Caesar, and taking as its immediate point of departure the preceding allusion to Augustus' expected deification, it prophesies the apotheosis of the author of the

Metamorphoses: he announces, speaking in the narrator's voice, that what is noblest in him will live on, high above the stars. It follows that he will rise even higher than Caesar, Augustus' (adoptive) father, who was changed into a star (15.850). That has the ring of an affront to the emperor. Is it?

The attempt has repeatedly been made to construe the *Metamorphoses,* particularly the last two sections of the poem—the one about Caesar/Augustus (15.745–870) and the afterword—as the literary manifesto of an anti-Augustan. Inasmuch as Augustus is compared with Jupiter toward the end of the section on Caesar/Augustus (858–860), line 871, predicting as it does that Jupiter's wrath will prove powerless to destroy the work, has been interpreted as a "warning" from Ovid to the emperor. In the *Tristia* and *Epistulae ex Ponto,* the emperor's anger toward the banished poet is often called the wrath of Jupiter; this has emboldened some critics to speculate that the epilogue was composed while Ovid was in exile. Many of Ovid's critics have taken this assumption as a starting point for their reading of the passages in the section of the *Metamorphoses* on Caesar/Augustus glorifying the emperor's deeds: these lines are construed as veiled criticisms of the system, or, at least, ironic statements about it. They do indeed lend themselves to such an interpretation. For, on the one hand, this praise of the Roman ruler is grossly exaggerated, and, on the other, it leaves us with the impression that the narrator is merely attending to a chore.

Siegmar Döpp has, however, offered a convincing reading of Ovid's panegyric as the reflection of a cautious attitude toward Augustus (1992, 129–130). As the *Metamorphoses* was being written, the Roman Empire was entering a period of crisis (see p. 43), so that one was well advised, in making public statements, to lavish as much praise as possible on an emperor uneasy about the future of his monarchy. That is what our text does. But, even if we take due account of the inclination to flatter, the fact remains that the narrator portrays Augustus as a great ruler and depicts his reign as the high point of the history of the world down to the time the *Metamorphoses* was composed. Pythagoras' speech had quoted Helenus' prophecy to the effect that Augustus would make Rome mistress of the world (15.447–448); the narrator has Jupiter confirm it (830–831). Why should we not read this as an expression of his positive attitude toward Augustus? As we have seen, he sets the Roman section of the mythological world history apart from the rest of the text, marking it off as a collection of edifying myths by offering us only apotheoses and *aitia* about rites. The aim is manifestly to pave the way for a presentation of Augustus' principate as a historical climax.

Certainly, the fact that Ovid's verse is marked by constant wordplay and intertextual references must by itself have encouraged contemporary readers to comb the *Metamorphoses* for politically ambiguous statements. Certainly, one can—for example, by drawing comparisons between the punishments meted out by the gods and by Augustus— manage to construe long sections of the text as anti-Augustan allegory. Perhaps contemporaries, and, with them, Augustus did indeed do so. But is such an interpretation justified? In any event, those of Ovid's modern readers who detect criticism of the principate at every turn in the *Metamorphoses* have yet to offer conclusive evidence that Ovid really intended to voice such criticism.

Let us return to the poem's epilogue. Stephen Wheeler was the first to point out that the narrator's remarks about the powers incapable of destroying his work can be brought into relation with specific sections of that work (1992, 193ff.). In the *Metamorphoses*, fire, iron, and Jupiter's wrath are three of the many forces that destroy the universe and human civilization. This theme is taken up on several occasions in the first pentad; it undergoes variation in the rest of the poem, where it appears as the theme of the destruction of an existing order. Again, fire and Jupiter's wrath are to blame for two cosmic catastrophes, the Great Flood and the universal conflagration. In the myth of the ages of the world (1.89–150), the narrator calls iron, or rather weapons forged of iron, threats to human civilization; he also repeatedly portrays the devastating effects of the use of armed force. Among the cultural achievements that are destroyed, we find art and, with it, poetry. But if some artists fall victim to divine wrath or violence as the mythological history of the world unfolds—Arachne and Orpheus are cases in point—the narrator, as he himself predicts, will survive along with his work. Thus he exempts that work from the law which dictates that culture comes into existence only to decline and disappear.

Augustus too will live on after his apotheosis. But what of his work, which made Rome mistress of the world? If the princeps' contemporaries believed his propaganda, then they also believed that the state he had remodeled would last forever. With the Secular Games of 17 B.C. and in other ways as well, Augustus had stated his claim to having led the Roman people back to a Golden Age, ensuring that its empire would long endure. In the *Aeneid,* Jupiter makes a remark very much in the spirit of this teleological conception of Rome when he declares before Venus, ancestral mother of the emperor's dynasty, that he has imposed neither spatial nor temporal limits on the Romans and has given them an empire without end (1.278–279). It is true that the narrator of the *Metamorphoses* has Pythagoras say that, after the downfall of Troy, Sparta, Mycenae, Athens, and Thebes, Roman domination of the world is imminent, and that, according to Helenus' prophesy, Augustus will establish it (15.420–448). But he does not have Pythagoras say that Rome will rule the world forever. The reader has no reason to expect him to, after everything she has heard in the narrator's myths and Pythagoras' speech on the principle of the mutability of all things.

As the *Metamorphoses* moves toward its conclusion, the narrator also declines to have *Jupiter* say anything to the effect that Roman domination of the world will last forever. Thus we may draw the inference that, in the *Metamorphoses*, Augustus' reign is treated as the first but not the final climax in world history. For nowhere is it said of the world domination which Augustus secures for Rome that it is exempt from the law that all things come into being and pass away, and thus not subject to the dominion of mutability. Yet Ovid's major work, the *Metamorphoses, is* accorded that privilege. I asked a moment ago if the wording of the epilogue to the poem constituted an affront to the emperor; I will now hazard the response that one could indeed speak of an affront here. But nobody knows if Augustus also saw the matter in that light.

In the *Metamorphoses,* it is not only the mutations that cosmos and culture undergo in the course of the mythological history of the world which contribute to making the world of the poem one caught up in a process of constant change; the more than two hundred transformations of human beings do too. But there is something that the metamorphoses of people into animals, plants, and inanimate things have no part in, unlike the transformations of cosmos and culture: the cycle of further change. Byblis remains the fountain that she was changed into, and the croaking frogs who were once foul-mouthed peasants still croak today. Thus there *is* something which, once it assumes a certain form, stays the same. But what is it, precisely? And what role does it play in the world of the *Metamorphoses?* What significance do the transformations of people into other kinds of creatures or things have there?

There exists a voluminous literature on the theme of change in Ovid's great poem. So far, none of the attempts to trace the frequent recurrence of this theme back to a single underlying intention have proven persuasive. In the light of Ernst August Schmidt's (1991) particularly thorough study of the problem, however, one thing can be said with some confidence: many of Ovid's myths of transformation recast a metaphor in the form of an etiological narrative. Thus, as we have already seen, the water flowing from the fountain of Byblis is a metaphor for the flowing tears of a woman unhappy in love—namely, Byblis, who, as the mythical story has it, was changed into the fountain that bears her name once she could do nothing else but weep. This fountain is now, in the form of the metaphor "fountain of tears," an integral part of humankind's stock of metaphors. In that sense, it is something that, within the world of the *Metamorphoses,* is no longer subject to change. The same applies to all the people who appear in the work and can, in their altered form, be read as metaphors for human character traits, emotions, and good or evil deeds.

We can now see why natural phenomena are the main subject of the poetic explanations of causes found in the *Metamorphoses.* This kind of etiology makes it especially easy for the narrator to build a story around metaphors that help him keep the reader's eye trained on human psychology. In its turn, human psychology is, like the metaphors which reflect emotions that stir the human soul, a constant amid the permanent change that marks the mythological history of the world. For, from one end of the *Metamorphoses* to the other, Ovid's characters think, feel, and act in the same way, before and after the destruction of the cosmos and culture. The particular charm of the work lies precisely in its psychological insight, its unvaryingly faithful portraits of the human soul. This is a hallmark of Ovid's earlier works too, as we have seen. But what is new here is the fact that, first, the metaphors conveyed by the myths of transformation extend our powers for describing the impulses of the human soul; and, second, that the people and anthropomorphic gods who appear in the *Metamorphoses* are the agents of a mythological world history that considerably extends the relatively narrow limits imposed on the description of human behavior by the erotic themes of the earlier works.

Ernst August Schmidt is thus altogether right to begin the first chapter of his book with the words, "the theme of Ovid's *Metamorphoses* is man" (1991, 12). But this formulation fails to indicate that the man at the center of the poem is one whose actions are observed in the course of a mythological world history marked by constant change. I have tried to show that that is of no small importance for the interpretation of the *Metamorphoses* and the impact the Augustan context has on it. It follows that the theme of the work is, rather, man in a world caught up in a process of constant change—even if there is no saying so in a sentence as elegant as Schmidt's.

Poetic Explanation of Causes as Commentary on the Calendar: The *Fasti*

The last myth in the *Metamorphoses* before the section on Caesar and Augustus tells how the cult of Aesculapius was established in Rome (15.622–744). This is the first of two events that the *Fasti* (Festival calendar) commemorates on January 1 (1.289–292). In a sense, then, the *Fasti* begins where the *Metamorphoses* leaves off. Moreover, in the proem to the earlier work, the narrator had announced that his theme would be the history of the world from its origins "down to [his] own *tempora* [times]." Now *tempora* is identified, in the very first of the elegiac couplets that make up the *Fasti*, as one of the two themes of the new work: "Tempora cum causis Latium digesta per annum/lapsaque sub terras ortaque signa canam"; "The times with their causes, ordered throughout the year in Latium,/and the stars, as they glide under the earth and rise, shall I sing." Like "Fasti," "Tempora," the first word in the text, served in antiquity as a title for the whole poem; thus one can also take the *Metamorphoses*' announcement of its theme to mean that it will pursue the story it tells down to the beginning of the *Fasti* (Barchiesi 1991, 6). This elegiac work in hexameters does indeed establish thematic links with the *Metamorphoses*. The Roman section of the *Metamorphoses*, the finale, contains *aitia* that explain rites and ritual objects alone. The *Fasti* carries on in the same vein: it provides etiological explanations for ritual traditions associated with the holidays of the Roman calendar year, proceeding in the order prescribed by the calendar. The poem's other main theme is the mythical etiology of the constellations that appear in the heavens over the course of the year.

Thus the *Fasti* is, like the *Metamorphoses,* an etiological *perpetuum carmen* (continuous poem), but with even closer thematic affinities to Callimachus' *Aitia.* In the *Fasti* as in the *Metamorphoses,* mythical "history" is a theme, because the majority of the rites explained in the *Fasti* were instituted, according to legend, in the early days of Rome. Since the structure of the *Fasti* is based on the chronology of the Roman calendar, the "protohistorical" events the work recounts are naturally not presented in chronological order. Nevertheless, a continuous reading of the six books covering the months from January to June—the only books we have—gives one the impression that the development of Latium and Rome from their earliest beginnings down to the liberation of the city from the Gauls (387 B.C.) provides a rough chronological framework for the poem.

How does Ovid manage to create this impression? We should keep in mind that what he proffers in the *Fasti* is not the calendar as such, but merely a gloss on it; this allows him to make choices within the structure laid down by the course of the year, to focus on certain events and not others. Since, in Rome, certain myth cycles were associated with various festivals scattered throughout the year, Ovid could, to begin with, often pick the day and month with which to associate the telling of a given myth. Second, he was free to choose how fully he would describe each festival and the events it commemorated. He took advantage of both kinds of poetic license in order to accommodate "historical" chronology to some extent. Thus it is that Book 1 can feature the early history of Latium, Books 2–5 focus mainly on the period immediately preceding the founding of Rome and the reigns of the first two kings, and Book 6 highlight certain events of the later monarchy and early Republic.

Structural analysis of the individual books shows how much care Ovid took to superimpose other forms of organization on the chronology of the calendar while respecting the limits it imposed. In each of the first four books of the poem, an introductory section combines the etiology of the name of the month with strategies directing the reader's attention to one of the book's central themes. The poet also forges structural links between the introductions to pairs of successive books and thus between the books they introduce—creating, in this way, three pairs of books, 1/2, 3/4, and 5/6. The *Fasti* as it has come down to us thus has the structure of a triptych. But this way of organizing the poem's contents is not the only point of resemblance between the *Fasti* and the other works by Ovid that we have examined. The way the *Fasti* handles its themes is also similar: in the stories about the origins of Roman festivals, the "reality" of the mythical worlds of the gods and men is repeatedly brought into relation with the "value system" of the erotic world of the elegy, so that, once again, areas of tension arise.

From the very beginning of the *Fasti,* the dedication addressed to Augustus' (adoptive) grandson Germanicus, the poet unmistakably alludes to a central theme of his erotic elegies. After explaining that he will also speak of holidays associated with particular events in the history of the imperial family, he says: "Caesaris arma canant alii: nos Caesaris aras,/et quoscumque sacris addidit ille dies"; "Let others sing of Caesar's [here, Augustus'] arms; I sing of Caesar's altars/and all the days he has added to the holidays" (1.13–14). This rings a change on the identification of the idea "make love, not war" with a *recusatio* (refusal): the *Fasti* intends to be not an epic about Augustus' war exploits, but an elegiac poem in the tradition of Callimachus' *Aitia,* even when it offers us etiological accounts of holidays honoring the emperor. That sounds familiar and thus innocuous enough on a first reading, but it harbors a potential for conflict of a special kind. For if the literary game governed by the elegiac system is to be expanded to include the Augustan discourse as well, the elegiac world will be counterposed not to the world of myth, but to an actually existing reality. Can that work within the framework of a game?

As we shall see, Ovid does not exempt the passages of the *Fasti* that are about Augustus and his family from the game the poem plays. What we shall *not* be able to see are signs pointing unambiguously to the intention informing that choice. One thing, in any case, seems to me to be highly likely: that the poet very consciously abandoned his game at halftime. If so, we may hazard the guess that he considered a continuation of the game—and thus, probably, what he had already accomplished as well—to be somehow problematic. It would follow that the game had proven unmanageable in his eyes.

The text does contain what may be a hint to this effect, even if it is a poetically stylized one. Ovid, of course, once again addresses the reader in the guise of a fictive first-person speaker. In the *Fasti,* however, he has endowed his fictive double with a feature that his other incarnations do not have. Like the *praeceptor amoris* in the *Ars* and the *Remedia* and the narrator of the stories about metamorphosis, who also sometimes come forward as didactic poets, the commentator on the calendar whom Ovid plays in the *Fasti* is a fairly questionable authority in his field. But, as Carole Newlands first observed (1992), he strikes us as much less reliable than the other two teachers. For he alone makes no secret of the fact that he does not consider himself entirely competent. Thus he tells us on several occasions how he tries to obtain information by conversing with specialists. Indeed, he sometimes appears all but overwhelmed by his task in both of the last two books of his commentary on the calendar. But before discussing what that might imply about Ovid's way of approaching the *Fasti,* let us have a look at the poem.

Books 1 and 2: From Janus to Terminus and Beyond

The *Fasti* begins, after a proem to Germanicus (1.1–26) which finds its pendant in the proem to Augustus in Book 2 (1–18), with preliminary comments on the history of the Roman calendar and the related terminology (27–62). These are followed by a gloss on the 1ˢᵗ of January, Janus' day (63–294). A link that arches across the whole of Book 1 to the end of Book 2 connects this gloss to the section on the 23ʳᵈ of February, Terminus' Day (2.639–684). The gods in charge of these two days have something in common: both can look forward and backward at the same time. Janus, the god of all beginnings, always sees what lies behind him as well; Terminus is the personification of a border stone. The day sacred to Terminus was the last day of February and thus also, during the period when the Roman year commenced in March, the last day of the year. In Ovid's times as in ours, the 23ʳᵈ of February was followed by five or six more days; one of them, the 24ᵗʰ (the day of the "flight of the king") is elucidated at length in the *Fasti* (2.685–852). In this gloss, the commentator on the calendar gives us, in a powerful finale to the first pair of books, his version of the story of the rape of Lucretia and her suicide.

In accordance with the function of the god Janus, whose day is the subject of the longest section in Book 1, the theme of sources and beginnings dominates this book. To start with, we may range under this rubric a piece of information that Janus himself provides: he was once chaos, a formless lump, from which he changed into his present form (103–112). The same theme is illustrated by the god's backward glance at the early history of Latium (191ff.), supplemented in the commentary on the 11ᵗʰ of January with the account the commentator gives us of the arrival of the seer Carmentis and her son Evander, Aeneas' "herald," in the still thinly settled area where Rome would later spring up (461–542). The section of the poem on the 9ᵗʰ of January takes up a chapter from the earliest history of human civilization. The subject is origins of animal sacrifice (335–456). Here we also find the first erotic story in the *Fasti.* It explains why donkeys are sacrificed to Priapus: a donkey betrayed the phallic god by braying as he was about to rape the sleeping nymph Lotis (393–440).

Because February was originally the last month in the Roman calendar, it was, even in Augustus' day, a time of festivals that were commemorated with the kind of atonement rituals typically celebrated at the end of a

cycle of months. This provided Ovid a ready occasion to contrast February, the month when things ended and various procedures were officially
concluded, with the antithetical month of January, the month of beginnings. Atonement, on the ancients' conception of it, absolved an individual of responsibility for the injustices she had committed and thus often
purged a violent criminal of guilt; a number of mythical examples are ad-
duced at the beginning of Book 2 (39–44). It is presumably no accident,
then, that we often hear about violent crime in Book 2. Two cases of attempted murder aside (79ff.; 381ff.), the crime involved is always rape: we
are told of six cases, in some of which the rapist achieves his ends, while
he is prevented from doing so in others (153ff.; 303ff.; 457ff.; 585ff.;
599ff.; 721ff.). The story of Lucretia thus serves as the finale both to the
first pair of books in the *Fasti* and also to a series of thematically related
narratives in Book 2.

Violence in the form of acts of war is also frequently evoked in Book
2. Both here and in the first quarter of Book 3, one early Roman stands
out—after the many accounts in Book 1 focusing on the protohistory of
Rome, the period just before and after the foundation of the city is now
a recurrent theme—as a personage symbolizing militarism and brute
force: Romulus, the first Roman king. Aside from the fact that he is to
blame for the death of his brother Remus (2.143) and grants asylum in
his grove to criminals who have fled to Rome (2.140), he masterminds
the rape of the Sabine women, touching off a war between their husbands or male relatives and Rome (2.433; 3.179–228); divides the year
into ten months because he knows more about war than about the stars
(1.27–42; 3.99–134); names the first month after his father Mars, the
god of war (3.71–98); and orders the Romans, after Mars has changed
him into the god Quirinus, to cultivate the art of warfare because that
was the art their fathers practiced (2.508). The history of civilized Rome
begins only with his successor Numa, for Numa gives his subjects laws,
teaches them religion, and sees to it that "right is mightier than arms"
(3.277–284).

As the *Fasti* presents matters, however, it is only with Augustus that the
Romans can become genuinely cultivated, pious, and peace-loving. In
Books 1 and 2, in passages on the holidays honoring him and his family
(1.587ff.; 637ff.; 705ff.; 709ff.; 2.55ff.; 119ff.), and in other passages as
well (1.13–14.; 67–68.; 277ff.; 529ff.; 701–702), the emperor is extolled
for reviving religion and preserving the peace. The praise culminates in
the gloss on the 5th of February, the day the title *pater patriae* (father of
the fatherland) was conferred on Augustus. After averring that, as an
elegiac poet, he does not feel equal to the task now before him
(2.119–126), the commentator on the calendar goes on to say:

sancte pater patriae, tibi plebs, tibi curia nomen
  hoc dedit, hoc dedimus nos tibi nomen, eques.
res tamen ante dedit. sero quoque vera tulisti
  nomina, iam pridem tu pater orbis eras.
hoc tu per terras, quod in aethere Iuppiter in alto,
  nomen habes: hominum tu pater, ille deum.
Romule, concedes: facit hic tua magna tuendo
  moenia, tu dederas transilienda Remo.
te Tatius parvique Cures Caeninaque sensit:
  hoc duce Romanum est solis utrumque latus
tu breve nescio quid victae telluris habebas:
  quodcumque est alto sub Iove, Caesar habet.
tu rapis, hic castas duce se iubet esse maritas:
  tu recipis luco, reppulit ille nefas.
vis tibi grata fuit, florent sub Caesare leges.
  tu domini nomen, principis ille tenet.
te Remus incusat, veniam dedit hostibus ille.
  caelestem fecit te pater, ille patrem.

Venerable father of the fatherland, the people, the Senate have given you
this name; we equestrians have given you this name.
But first history gave it to you; only later did you receive the true
name, but you had already long been the father of the world.
Here on earth you have this name which, in the high heavens, Jupiter
bears: you are the father of men, he, the father of the gods.
Romulus, you must quit the field: with his protection, he gives strength to your
walls; you let Remus spring over them.
Your power was felt by Tatius and the little towns of Cures and Caenina;
under his leadership, everything from sunrise to sunset is Roman.
You owned only a little strip of conquered land;
everything that lies under Jupiter's heaven belongs to Caesar.
You abduct women; he orders them to live as virtuous wives under his rule.
You grant asylum in your grove; he has repelled injustice.
You welcomed violence; under Caesar, laws thrive.
You were called Lord; he is called Princeps.
Remus accuses you; he has forgiven his enemies.
Your father made you a god; he, his father.

(127–144)

It has been said that Augustus could not have taken pleasure in such
praise, because he is known to have identified with Romulus, the
founder of the city, whose deeds here serve as a foil. But what holds for
the panegyric to Augustus at the end of the *Metamorphoses* applies to this
passage as well: the crisis-ridden political situation in which Rome found
itself in the last decade of Augustus' reign doubtless accounts for the

way the emperor is here glorified. It is therefore conceivable that Ovid thought he was writing what was expected of him.

Yet there is a difference, and no small one, between this passage and the panegyric to Augustus in the *Metamorphoses*. Only the passage in the *Fasti* is brought into relation with generic traditions: the commentator on the calendar modestly states that, as an elegiac poet, he feels that the task of writing an encomium to Augustus is above him. But what effect does his confession have? It gives the reader all the more reason to believe that the elegist will now transcend the limits of his genre. Yet he fails to do so, proceeding instead to give us a catalog full of allusions and witticisms, of the kind we find again and again in Ovid's elegiac verse; one need only recall the comparison between the *amator* and a soldier in *Amores* 1.9 (see p. 14). In the light of this tradition, the comparison between Augustus' and Romulus' exploits has a rather comic ring to it. That, however, may not have sat very well with the emperor.

Furthermore, considered in context, this glorification of the *pater patriae* can seem rather ambivalent. At the end of the passage, we read that Romulus' father made him a god, whereas Augustus made his father (Julius Caesar) a god. But the following lines evoke two mythical personages who were elevated to the firmament: the "Idaean boy," that is, the Trojan Ganymede, whom Jupiter made love to and then changed into a constellation (145–146), and Callisto, whom Jupiter raped before placing her and her son among the stars (153–192). As the commentator on the calendar expressly compares the *pater patriae* Augustus with the father of the gods, one may, if one likes, conclude that Augustus too is thereby retrospectively likened to Jupiter, who is in the habit of first committing adultery and then immortalizing his amours. One is in an even better position to do so if one realizes that the two astronomical legends did not have to be placed at this point in the *Fasti:* some constellations rise and set and others do not, so that Ovid had considerable latitude when it came to picking the days with which to associate astral myths.

It follows that the poet also deliberately chose to place the astronomical legend preceding the panegyric to the *pater patriae* where he did. In question here is a myth that, once again, revolves around an artist who falls victim to violence, the singer Arion. On a ship whose crew threatens to kill him, he leaps overboard and is saved by a dolphin (the future constellation) (79–118). Before making the leap, he sings one last time, "flebilibus numeris veluti canentia dura/traiectus penna tempora cantat olor"; "just as, in plaintive [*flebilibus*] tones, when his white temples [*tempora*]/are pierced by a hard arrow, the swan sings" (109–110). This passage quite plainly characterizes Arion's song as a *flebilis elegia* (plaintive elegy). One should recall here that "tempora" means "times" as well as "temples," so that it can designate the *Fasti*, as we have seen; one should also bear in mind that, in the elegies of exile which may have been composed at the same time as this text, the banished poet confesses his fear of barbarian arrows. One can then imagine all sorts of things in view of the fact that the story about the "elegist" threatened with death stands side by side with the panegyric to the emperor.

Of course, these considerations by no means prove that Ovid meant to find fault with the emperor between the lines either of the passage about the anniversary of the day Augustus received the title *pater patriae* or of other glosses on holidays honoring him. All that can be shown is that the poet mingles elegiac and Augustan discourse and thus, intentionally or not, produces a certain effect: the reader not only pricks up his ears, but even feels that he is being issued an outright invitation to probe the text for a veiled critique of the principate.

The same holds for other passages in the *Fasti* that are placed far from those on Augustus. Ovid's version of the myth of Lucretia is a case in point (2.685–852). It forms a conclusion to this part of the commentary on the calendar, one which is somewhat detached from the rest of the first pair of books. If one notices that the narrative has a rather pronounced elegiac coloring, one may at first be inclined to assume that the narrator, whose commentary on the festival of Terminus (639–684) has led him to cross what was once the dividing line between the old year and the new, imagines that he has, as it were, temporarily stepped outside the regime of the calendar—and that he takes this as an opportunity to rip off a good story, mining a greater number of elegiac themes than he has so far. But the Augustan context can be discerned here too, though not within the *Fasti*. A reader of Ovid's day ran straight into it, if he compared—as he could hardly avoid doing—Ovid's text with its model, the story of Lucretia in Livy's *History of Rome* (1.57–59).

The historian presents the heroine in such a way that Augustus could hold her up as a shining example of the kind of Roman wife his marriage laws called for. During her husband's absence, Lucretia is raped by Sextus Tarquinius, a son of the Roman king, who breaks into her bedroom at night. In Livy, she sends for her husband, her father, and their friends Valerius and Brutus the very next morning and makes them an extremely emotional speech. She says that her chastity (*pudicitia*) has been lost, calls on the men to punish the prince, and declares, before punishing herself by putting an end to her days, that she wants to make it impossible that, "in future, any unchaste (*impudica*) woman [can] live by citing Lucretia as her example" (58.7–10). This Roman matron is the very personification of *pudicitia*.

After Lucretia's death, Ovid's narrator calls her a "matron with manly spirit" (847); however, he has gone so far as to call her a *puella* on one previous occasion (810) and, what is more, consistently portrays her as such. Like Laodamia, the author of Ovid's *Epistula* 13, she is very uneasy about her husband, who has gone off to war (745ff.). Outwardly, she resembles a *poeta/amator*'s beloved, as becomes especially clear when Sextus Tarquinius fervently brings her beauty before his mind's eye after seeing her for the first time:

> sic sedit, sic culta fuit, sic stamina nevit,
>   iniectae collo sic iacuere comae,
> hos habuit voltus, haec illi verba fuerunt,
>   hic color, haec facies, hic decor oris erat.

> So sat she there, so elegant [*culta*] was she, so she spun the threads,
> so her loose hair fell onto the nape of her neck,
> this was the expression on her face, these were her words,
> this was her coloring, this her figure, this her charm.

(771–774)

In the scene with the men, she behaves in especially "elegiac" fashion by weeping more than speaking:

> illa diu reticet pudibundaque celat amictu
>   ora: fluunt lacrimae more perennis aquae.
> hinc pater, hinc coniunx lacrimas solantur et orant
>   indicet, et caeco flentque paventque metu.
> ter conata loqui ter destitit, ausaque quarto
>   non oculos ideo sustulit illa suos.
> "hoc quoque Tarquinio debebimus? Eloquar" inquit,
>   "eloquar infelix dedecus ipsa meum?"
> quaeque potest, narrat; restabant ultima: flevit,
>   et matronales erubuere genae.
> dant veniam facto genitor coniunxque coactae:
>   "quam" dixit "veniam vos datis, ipsa nego."
> nec mora, celato fixit sua pectora ferro
>   et cadit in patrios sanguinulenta pedes.

> She is silent for a long time and, full of shame, buries her face
> in her dress. Her tears flow like a fountain that will not run dry.
> Here her father, there her husband seek to quell the stream of
>   tears, and they ask
> for a sign and, in uncertain fear, they weep and are overwhelmed.
> Three times she tried to speak, three times she faltered, and when,
>   the fourth time, she dared to,

she did not raise her eyes for that.
"Do I have this too to thank Tarquinius for? Must I utter," she said,
"Utter my own disgrace in my misfortune?"
And what she can tell, she tells, leaving out the end. She wept,
and the woman's cheeks turned red;
Her sire and her husband forgive her the deed she was forced to do.
"The forgiveness," she said, "that you grant, I refuse to grant myself."
And straightaway she pierced her breast with a dagger that she had
    hidden on her person,
and fell, covered with blood, at her father's feet.

(819–832)

This is neither a sermon nor a moral appeal addressed to all wom-ankind. It is easy to imagine that Augustans regarded this Lucretia, when they compared her with Livy's, as an eminently un-Augustan cry-baby. Modern readers are likely to notice that Ovid has acutely observed a psychological phenomenon often mentioned in discussions of vio-lence against women: the speechless consternation of a victim who, sum-moned to testify about what has befallen her, imagines that she is experiencing the rape all over again. Elegiac narration does not always strike us as just a game.

Books 3 and 4: Mars without and Venus with Arms

The second pair of books in the *Fasti* is, like the first, framed by two interrelated sections. In the introduction (1–166) to Book 3, which is about the month of March, named after the god of war Mars, we learn that Mars raped the Vestal Virgin Rhea Silvia, that she gave birth to twin sons, Romulus and Remus, and that the twins grew up—this part of the story is run through very quickly—to build Rome (9–70). The conclud-ing couplet leaves us eager to learn the sequel: "moenia conduntur, quae, quamvis parva fuerunt,/non tamen expediit transsiluisse Remo"; "Walls are built, which, low though they were,/Remus would have done better not to jump over" (69–70). We are not told what happened—that Remus paid with his life for jumping over the wall—until we reach, near the end of Book 4, the commentary on the 21st of April, the day com-memorating the founding of Rome (807–862). All we find in the re-mainder of the book is a few short etiological sections on the Vinalia and Robigalia festivals (863–900; 901–942), together with brief remarks on the 28th of April that introduce the subject of the sections on the Flo-ralia in Book 5 and the Vestalia in Book 6, the longest sections in those two books (943–954).

It is appropriate that these books are so structured as to highlight the founding of Rome, given that Books 3 and 4 are assigned to the two divinities who, says the legend, created the essential conditions for the founding of the city: respectively, Mars, the father of the twins, and Venus, the mother of their ancestor Aeneas. The commentator engages in direct conversation with both gods, dialoguing with Mars at the beginning of Book 3 (1–8; 167–252) and Venus at the beginning of Book 4 (1–18). In the very first couplet in Book 3, he asks the god of war to lay down his arms. This hints at the theme of what lies ahead: the book on Mars will unfold under the sign of a Mars without weapons, because war will scarcely be mentioned in it. On the other hand, the book will frequently deal with things erotic, some of which will even involve the god of war. As for the goddess of love, it is true that the commentator on the calendar assures her that he is still devoted to her service (4.7–8). But he never speaks of her power in the book about her month—he derives "April" from "Aphrodite," the Greek name for Venus (61–62)—except in a hymn to her included in the introduction (91–132). And, of all the books in the *Fasti*, this is the only one in which not a single story turns on erotic love.

Mars makes two personal appearances as *amator* in the erotic tales in Book 3: in the account of his rape of Rhea Silvia (9–22) and in the myth about his love for Minerva (675–694). In the first legend, he proves quicker at making-love-not-war than Caesar at making war on Pharnaces in the famous sequence *veni, vidi, vici* (I came, I saw, I conquered). Here is how he proceeds with Rhea Silvia: "Mars videt hanc visamque cupit potiturque cupita"; "Mars sees her and desires her whom he sees and possesses her whom he desires" (21). It all takes place so quickly that the woman, who happens to be sleeping, never realizes what is happening (22). Later, with Minerva, matters take a very different turn. Here Mars plays the elegiac lover forced to bide his time and engage a go-between, an old woman he often has to get after to carry out her task. When everything is finally set and he can proceed to unveil his beloved in the bridal chamber, he discovers—oh, horrors—not Minerva, but the old woman!

Our commentator relates this farce in the context of a rather lengthy gloss on the festival of Anna Perenna, celebrated on the Ides (the 15th) of March. Later it is his turn to be horrified, when it is suddenly brought to his attention that he is on the point of forgetting Caesar's assassination:

> Praeteriturus eram gladios in principe fixos,
>   cum sic a castis Vesta locuta focis:
> "ne dubita meminisse: meus fuit ille sacerdos;
>   sacrilegae telis me petiere manus."

I was about to leave out the dagger that was thrust into the prince,
when, from her pure hearth, Vesta spoke up:
"Do not hesitate to recall it. He was *my* priest,
the impious hands attacked *me* with their weapons."

(697–700)

Vesta relates how she transported her Caesar heavenward while the daggers plunged into a phantom shadow (701–704). Was Augustus, if he ever read the *Fasti*, pleased to see this rather casual transition from a story in which Mars appears as a fool in love—the god held an important place in Augustan religion—to a passage on the emperor's (adoptive) father? It hardly seems likely. At any event, when the *Fasti* was being composed, Augustus himself was the priest of Vesta and had been since 6 March 12 B.C. There is a short passage in the poem about the day he assumed his new office (415–528). It is the only passage in Book 3 to elucidate a day honoring the emperor, although, to be sure, the thematic orientation of the book may help explain this.

Legend has it that Numa introduced the worship of Vesta to Rome. As we saw in the preceding section of the present chapter, this king is introduced in the second quarter of Book 3—the first is still dominated by his warlike predecessor Romulus—as the founder of the Rome which was civilized by legal institutions and reverence for the gods (277–284). That, in turn, fits in very well with the unmartial book on Mars and is equally appropriate for the section of the poem on the Mamuralia festival (the 1st of March), in which the main role falls to Numa (259–392). Here we are given an etiological explanation for the traditional dance of the Salii in their battle dress. But, in his commentary on the calendar, the commentator says little about the ritual itself; in contrast, he lingers over the *aition* (explanatory legend) that tells how Numa pries a major concession from Jupiter, the father of the gods, with trickery and fast talk.

Finally, it also seems to me in keeping with this "demilitarized" book on the god of war's month that it should contain three fairly long stories centered on women. In the first of these myths, Roman wives actually manage to stop a war. These women are the ones who were earlier wrested from the Sabines. Because they do not want to see their husbands and fathers engage in mutual slaughter (179–228), they and their children stage a procession across the battlefield. Here is what it accomplishes:

tela viris animique cadunt, gladiisque remotis
   dant soceri generis accipiuntque manus,
laudatasque tenent natas, scutoque nepotem
   fert avus: hic scuti dulcior usus erat.

The men let their weapons and their mettle fall, and, having laid
    by their swords,
the fathers-in-law shake hands with their sons-in-law and receive
    their handshake,
and they praise and embrace their daughters, and the grandfather carries
his grandson on his shield. He preferred using the shield that way.

(225–228)

Just as this story is a sequel to the story of the rape of the Sabine women in
the *Ars amatoria* (1.101–134), so another myth in Book 3 of the *Fasti*
shows us how Ariadne fares after she marries Bacchus in a ceremony that
is also described in the *Ars* (1.527–564). Before her wedding, she had
Theseus' infidelity to complain about; now she must put up with the
god's. He consoles her, however, by inviting her to have intercourse with
him in the heavens and changing her crown into a constellation
(459–516).

The third story about women in Book 3 of the *Fasti* also provides a sequel to a well-known myth. The story recounts how, after Aeneas has already been crowned king of Latium, Dido's sister Anna flees Carthage,
occupied by the Numidians. During her flight, a storm washes her up on
the shores of the land ruled by the hero, who gives her a hospitable reception. But when his wife begins plotting against the refugee's life, Anna
flees again, and, after the river god Numicius carries her off to his watery
realm, is changed into a nymph (543–656). It is quite impossible not to
notice that we are here presented with a new "*Aeneid*," with, however, a
female Aeneas. Ovid has not only replaced familiar episodes of Virgil's
epic with their equivalents, but has also added a scene analogous to the
apotheosis of Aeneas depicted in the *Metamorphoses* (15.581–608). The
poet's delight in staging role reversals is often evident in his work. Here it
yields a story that will intrigue feminists—and others as well.

While Book 3 offers sequels to myths that Ovid relates in other works,
Book 4 offers us a reprise: a retelling of the story of Proserpina, which
takes up 231 hexameter lines in the *Metamorphoses* (5.341–571) and
runs for nearly the same length, 102 couplets, in the *Fasti* (4.417–620).
One of the many differences between the two versions (which we cannot discuss further here) resides in the fact that it is only in the *Metamorphoses* that Pluto, god of the underworld, falls in love with Proserpina
because Cupid has pierced him with an arrow at his mother's behest
(363–384). That, of all things, is what is left out of the book about Venus
in the *Fasti*. But, as we have already seen, Venus' power as goddess of
love is not a subject of Book 4, except in the hymn to her. Indeed, she is
even made to embody the antithetical principle here, and that right

from the commentator's gloss on the 1st of April, the day the temple of Venus Verticordia was inaugurated (133–162). We are told that the Romans erected this shrine on the Sibyl's instructions, at a time when the virtue of chastity was on the decline in the city. Venus, mistress of the temple, "changed the hearts" (whence *Verticordia*) of the Roman women, who were urged to worship her in this shrine because she watched over beauty, virtue, and one's good name.

The virtue of chastity is the theme of several tales in Book 4. A boy by the name of Attis, who breaks the vow of chastity he has made the goddess Cybele, punishes himself for what he has done by castrating himself (223–244). The Roman noblewoman Claudia Quinta is widely denounced for her immorality, but declared chaste after a trial by ordeal. When the ship that is to bring the idol representing Cybele to Rome gets bogged down in the muddy bed of the Tiber, the men are not strong enough to set it afloat again; yet Claudia does so unaided, after beseeching the goddess to grant her success in pulling it out of the mud only if she is chaste (291–328). King Numa, who wishes to ask the god Faunus for counsel because Rome's soil and livestock have long been infertile, refrains from sexual intercourse (657: *usus Veneris*) as part of the ritual preparations for consulting the god. When Ceres learns that Pluto has carried off her daughter and protests to Jupiter, she does not, it is true, explicitly indicate that the god of the underworld has violated the rules of common decency, but she does say that this is hardly the proper way for her to come by a son-in-law (591–592).

The commentator on the calendar does not make Venus responsible for Pluto's state of sexual excitement, but he certainly does see to it that she exercises her power in another context. His gloss on the 15th of April, in which he also evokes Numa's "renunciation" of Venus, ends with these words:

Hanc quondam Cytherea diem properantius ire
    iussit et admissos praecipitavit equos,
ut titulum imperii cum primum luce sequenti
    Augusto iuveni prospera bella darent.

Cytherea [Venus] once ordered this day to pass more quickly,
and drove the unbridled horses [of the sun] into the depths [of the evening],
so that on the following day the title of Imperator would, as soon as possible,
be bestowed on the young Augustus by a successfully terminated war.

(673–676)

In other words, Venus was responsible for hastening the day of the ceremony in which the victorious Octavian/Augustus was named Imperator (commander). This is the second of the two passages in which the *Fasti* begins to refer to the sovereign as a military leader; earlier he has been celebrated only for having revived the worship of the gods and guaranteeing that peace will be preserved. In the first of these passages, we find a brief remark about the triumph evoked, presumably, in l. 676: the Roman victory at the battle of Mutina in 43 (627–628, for the 14th of April). The commentator mentions Augustus' special relationship with Venus at the very beginning of the book. Immediately after his brief exchange with the goddess (1–18), he directly addresses the sovereign, declaring that, because of the emperor's origins, April is his month and should therefore be of special interest to him (19–22). As proof, he provides a genealogy in which Venus, patron goddess of the month of April, is identified as Julus' grandmother and, accordingly, an ancestor of the Julio-Claudian dynasty (23–60). Near the end of the introduction, he also turns to the citizens of Rome, reminding them that Venus once took up arms for "their Troy" and was wounded in the hand as a result (119–120). Thus she did something he asked the god of war Mars to refrain from doing at the beginning of Book 3; here, however, he manifestly approves such acts.

Should we conclude, now that we have looked at all the passages in the book on Venus from which we can piece together a "de-eroticized" image of the goddess, that Ovid organized this book as he did out of respect for Augustus? That, in so doing, he gave due account to both the myth that the imperial dynasty was descended of the goddess and also the princeps' attempt to regulate Roman sexual mores? Let us suppose—plainly, nothing will ever be certain here—that such was the case. The fact remains that two souls dwell in the breast of the commentator who addresses us in this text—one Augustan, but the other, unmistakably, elegiac. This casts doubt, whatever the author's intentions, on the sincerity of those of his declarations that can be interpreted as favorable to the principate. I shall try to show that this holds for Book 4 by way of an examination of two passages.

There is, first, the hymn to Venus. It occurs in the introduction not long after the list of Augustus' forebears, is about as long, and consists mainly of a representation of erotic love, personified by Venus, as the force responsible for civilizing humanity (91–132). The hymn, a kind of sequel to the "history of civilization" in Book 2 of the *Ars amatoria* (2.467–492; see p. 102), affirms that Venus, or rather Love, awakened in humankind a talent for poetry, elegant speech, and a thousand other things. Unambiguously, what is meant here is *elegiac* love, not, say, the form of conjugal love that Augustus was endeavoring to put on solid institutional foundations with his moral legislation.

Second, when the commentator on the calendar, again in Book 4, presents Venus as bearing arms for the victorious emperor and furthering his aims, he unwittingly reveals that he cannot really muster much enthusiasm for the subject of weapons and victories. This seems to me to be implied by a passage in which he comments on the 6th of April, the anniversary of Caesar's victory at Thapsus in 46 B.C.:

> Tertia lux (memini) ludis erat, ac mihi quidam
>   spectanti senior continuusque loco
> "haec "ait" illa dies, Libycis qua Caesar in oris
>   perfida magnanimi contudit arma Iubae.
> Dux mihi Caesar erat, sub quo meruisse tribunus
>   glorior: officio praefuit ille meo.
> hanc ego militia sedem, tu pace parasti,
>   inter bis quinos usus honore viros."
> plura locuturi subito seducimur imbre:
>   pendula caelestis Libra movebat aquas.

> It was—I remember very well—the third day of the games,
>   and one or another
> elderly man sitting next to me said to me, while I watched,
> "This is the famous day when, on the Libyan coast, Caesar
> smashed arrogant Juba's perfidious army.
> Caesar was my imperator; I am proud to have served him
> as colonel. When I was doing my duty, he was my commander.
> I acquired this seat through military service, you acquired yours in peace,
> because you held office in the College of the Ten."
> We were about to say more when we were parted by a sudden rain-shower;
> the constellation of the swinging Balance set heavenly torrents in motion.

(377–386)

Days come and go. On one, a king is defeated in battle; on another, two Romans are soaked to the skin in a rain-shower. Someone who comments on the calendar can also show that everything is constantly changing. But this particular commentator shows that in an age which the (adoptive) son of the victor at Thapsus claims to have made into an Age of Gold.

Books 5 and 6: "Summanus—Whoever That Is"

The third and last pair of books in the *Fasti* as we have it begins and ends with a set of questions that the commentator on the calendar puts to the Muses (5.1–110; 6.797–812). In Book 5, the sisters give divergent answers because they disagree among themselves (5.9:

dissensere); they concur in Book 6 (6.811: *adsensere*). The first time our commentator questions them, it is because he is in a tight spot:

> Quaeritis, unde putem Maio data nomine mensi?
>   non satis est liquido cognita causa mihi.
> ut stat et incertus qua sit sibi nescit eundum,
>   cum videt ex omni parte, viator, iter,
> sic, quia posse datur diversas reddere causas,
>   qua ferar, ignoro, copiaque ipsa nocet.

You ask whence May derives its name, in my opinion?
The reason has not become sufficiently clear to me.
As a traveler stands there and is unsure and does not know where to go
when he sees roads running in all directions,
so I do not know, because it is possible to recite different aitia,
where to turn, and the multitude of possibilities is standing in my way.

(5.1–6)

This is not the first time that our commentator feels unsure of his subject. In Book 4, he had already said that his sources offer such a welter of explanations for the origins of a given rite that they are confusing and hold up his project (783–784). In Book 6, he even confesses four times that he has insufficient knowledge of his subject (1; 503; 571–572; 731–732). In a short gloss on the 20th of June, for example, he remarks: "they say a temple was consecrated to Summanus—whoever that is" (731–732). What does the etiologist's increasing uncertainty signify? It is further reflected in the fact that, toward the end of the extant poem, the number of expert gods and men he consults, or who volunteer information unasked, is clearly on the rise. In Book 1, the narrator needs three informants (89ff.; 465ff.; 657ff.); in Book 2, he mentions an oral source only twice (269; 584); in Book 3, again, three specialists provide him with information (167ff.; 259ff.; 697ff.). In contrast, there are already five specialists in Book 4 (195ff.; 377ff.; 687ff.; 807ff.; 905ff.), five again in Book 5 (1ff.; 183ff.; 447ff.; 635ff.; 697ff.), and as many as eight in Book 6 (1ff.; 213ff.; 225ff.; 249ff.; 399ff.; 481ff.; 651ff.; 799ff.).

Here too, then, it becomes clear that the commentator is finding it harder and harder to carry out his task. There is reason to suppose—Carole Newlands (1992) was the first to speculate along these lines—that Ovid wanted his fictional alter ego to seem increasingly unsure of himself because he had no intention to write the second half of the *Fasti* and was setting the stage for the work's premature end. Thematic and structural comparison of Books 5 and 6 with the other books buttresses that assumption; it shows that the last two books of the *Fasti*, unlike

Books 1–4, do not have a general theme derived from the name of their month and contain no narratives of any length. Moreover, the way Books 5 and 6 link their separate sections to individual holidays reminds us of a catalog much more than do Books 1–4.

What creates this impression in Book 5 is the fact that Greek astronomical myths alternate with etiological explanations of Roman rites in strictly mechanical fashion. Like Books 1–4, Book 5 opens with an introduction about the origins of the name of the month. Here it is easy to see what blocks the development of an organizing theme: the Muses, presented as experts, offer the commentator on the calendar three alternative etymological explanations of the word *Maius*—it may be derived from *maiestas* (majesty), *maiores* (elders), or Maia (the mother of Mercury)—and he is unable to choose among them (1–110). Whereas, in Books 1–4, one or another aspect of the history of Rome from its origins in Latium down to warlike Romulus and cultivated Numa provide the central subject matter, we find only two rather short narratives in Book 5: the gloss on the 9th of May takes up the legend of the foundation of Rome where Book 4 left it (4.807–862/5.445–492), and, for the 14th of May, we are offered a sequel to the story of the visit Hercules pays Evander in Book 1 (1.543–586/5.621–662).

One section of Book 5 stands out for both its length and its especially "elegiac" content: the commentary on the Floralia, a festival in honor of Flora, the goddess of bloom (183–378). The festival was celebrated in Rome from the 28th of April to the 3rd of May. The goddess, whose rite is characterized by the fact that the celebrants are even livelier, lewder, and tipsier than on other holidays (331–354), claims that she once bore the Greek name Chloris (195), which might well be the name of a *poeta/amator*'s beloved. Indeed, although Flora, comically, puts on the airs of a dignified matron, she resembles a *puella* in many ways and thus also the personified elegy we know from *Amores* 3.1. The phrases the goddess uses to describe her flower garden contain expressions that Ovid also uses as metapoetical metaphors (209–228). Among Flora's flowers—this provides another link to the rest of Ovid's work—are people who have been changed into flowers. Narcissus is one of them. Full of pity for him, the goddess says: "infelix, quod non alter et alter eras"; "You unfortunate, who were not both the one and the other" (226). Then, after she has finished presenting herself and her festival, we are told:

> omnia finierat: tenues secessit in auras,
>   mansit odor: posses scire fuisse deam.
> floreat ut toto carmen Nasonis in aevo,
>   sparge, precor, donis pectora nostra tuis.

> She had quite finished her speech. She drew off into the light air,
> only fragrance remained; you could tell a goddess had been there.
> So that Naso's poem may bloom for all time,
> strew, I beg you, your gifts in my heart!
>
> (375–378)

Of course, someone named Naso (*nasus* means "nose" in Latin) will know how to appreciate divine fragrance (Barchiesi 1994, 123). It is, in contrast, the sound of clanking weapons which tells the commentator on the calendar, later in Book 5 (545–598), that the god of war, Mars in person, is approaching for the second time in the *Fasti*. He arrives on the 12th of May in order to visit the temple of Mars Ultor (Avenger) consecrated on the 12th of May in the year 2 B.C. Observing the way the temple is decorated gives the god and the reader a good sense of the "power of images" (Zanker 1987) in Augustan Rome. The princeps had vowed to build the temple if he was granted victory over Caesar's murderers. In the *Fasti*, he cries out before the battle, "Mars, ades et satia scelerato sanguine ferrum"; "Mars, stand by me [*ades*] and glut the iron with criminal blood" (575). This is at antipodes from what the commentator tells Mars at the outset of Book 3 (1–2). There he appeals to the god to lay down his arms for a while, using, as he does here, the words *Mars, ades*. Once again there appears a discrepancy between the Augustan and elegiac worlds.

In Book 4 and again in Book 5, the commentator on the calendar evokes a battle won by Octavian/Augustus; now, in Book 6, he repeatedly takes up the theme of war. A full five of the days he glosses commemorate battles—the 9th, 11th, 17th, 22nd, and 23rd of June—and another seven touch upon various military operations (185–186; 193–194; 201–202; 203–204; 241ff.; 349ff.; 731–732). To be sure, all seven cases involve wars fought before Octavian/Augustus' day; the imperial family appears rarely in Book 6 and then only when temples (455ff.; 637–638) or Livia's colonnade (639ff.) are mentioned. Nevertheless, it is odd that so much attention is devoted to warfare in this elegiac verse. It would seem that elucidation of the calendar is now, over long stretches of the poem, simply a chore the author must perform and that he doesn't much care what he writes about in performing it. Moreover, Book 6 is the book of the *Fasti* which contains the largest number of passages that are nothing but short notes. Thus it seems even more like a catalog than Book 5.

In the case of June as well, our commentator fails to settle on one of three possible explanations for the name of the month—the available etymologies turn on Juno, *iuniores* (younger ones), or *iungere* (unite)

(1–100)—and thus lets slip another opportunity to derive a general theme for the book. He does, however, continue to bring early Roman history alive here. In Book 6, we find passages about King Servius Tullius (569–636), the period during which Rome was occupied by the Gauls (349–394), and the departure of the flute players from the city (651–692). All three are based on texts in the first Decade of Livy's *History of Rome*. In addition, the commentator tells how (in 241 B.C.) Lucius Caecilius Metellus, Vesta's priest, extinguished a fire that broke out in her temple (437–454); he also recalls, as was noted above, a series of wars fought in the Republican period of Rome's history. Missing here, however, is a theme linking the narratives of historical events, in contrast to Books 1–4, in which one can make out the general outlines of an evolving cultural history.

Two of these narratives, the story of the Gauls' occupation of Rome and the account of the fire in the temple of Vesta, make up part of what is by far the longest section of Book 6, the commentary on the Vestalia festival (249–460). I have already pointed out that Augustus was the priest of Vesta when the *Fasti* was being written; in that capacity, he bore the title *pontifex maximus* (chief priest). One notes time and again that, in the passage on Vesta, our commentator makes no effort to exempt the patron goddess of the hearth from his playful treatment of the themes of erotic elegy, although she was held in particular reverence by the Romans, who honored her as a divine virgin. Thus, as Carole Newlands was the first to see (1995, 136ff.), the story about how the fire in her temple was put out contains a series of witty double entendres. They revolve around the fact that Metellus, being a man, had no right to set foot in the temple, which was confided to the charge of female priests who were under obligation to remain virgins. But the emergency caused by the fire required him to do so; this affords the commentator an opportunity to evoke a classic "elegiac" scene, the *amator*'s forced entry into the *puella*'s house. When we read in the text that "Vesta burned" (437–438: *Vesta arsit*), we can construe the phrase metaphorically to mean "Vesta was aflame with passion." Again, when the words *intrare* (burst in), *adire* (charge toward), and *irrumpere* (enter by force) are used in connection with Metellus' act, their obscene connotations resonate along with the others. Augustus too knew this; thus, if he read the text, he was perhaps none too pleased.

Another story in the section on Vesta relates how Priapus was foiled in the attempt to rape the sleeping goddess when a braying ass gave him away (319–348). Thus we see the commentator on the calendar returning to a theme already exploited in Book 1 (393–440). We can even discern a certain dependence on the thematic structure of the first book here. Before we are told the story of Priapus, Janus too reappears (119ff./1.89ff.) and, as in his speech in Book 1 (171ff./1.199ff.), we are given a description of the frugal mode of life of the early Romans. Later in Book 6, another Greek woman settles with her son in pre-Roman Latium—in Book 1 it was Carmentis and Evander, now it is Ino and Melicertes—where she functions as a seer (481ff./1.469ff.); once again, the construction of a temple to Concordia is recalled (6.637ff./1.637ff.). And if the setting of the sign of the Crab is mentioned at the beginning of Book 1, the end of Book 6 makes explicit mention of its rising (1.313–314/6.727–728), although our commentator by no means systematically charts the nocturnal movements of the heavenly bodies.

Thus Book 6, taken in conjunction with Book 1, puts a frame around the *Fasti* as we have it. Ovid may have employed this device too, which makes Books 1–6 look like a self-contained whole, because he wanted to gloss only the first half of the calendar year. The suspicion that such is indeed the case is strengthened when we note that Book 6 is the only one containing several anticipatory allusions to the end of the month, in the glosses on the 19th, 22nd, 24th, and 29th of June (725; 768; 774; 795). Our commentator introduces his gloss on the 24th of June with these words: "Tempora labuntur, tacitisque senescimus annis,/et fugiunt freno non remorante dies"; "The times [*tempora*] glide away and we grow older with the silent years/And the days flee, and no bridle curbs them" (771–772). Does he mean to suggest that the *Fasti* is gliding away from him, since the word *tempora* can be used to refer to the work as well? His gloss on the 30th of June begins as follows: "Tempus Iuleis cras est natale Kalendis:/Pierides, coeptis addite summa meis"; "Tomorrow is the birthday of the Kalends [the 1st] of July;/Pierides [Muses], set [*coeptis*] the crown of perfection on my beginning" (797–798). That sounds like the prelude to a section concluding an entire work, especially when one recalls that, in the proem to the *Metamorphoses* (and the *Fasti* is a kind of sequel to that work), *coepta* is used to refer to the text as a whole. Moreover, the final lines of Book 6, which follow an appeal to the Muses, contain thoughts and allusions which make it seem altogether plausible that Ovid meant these lines to be the very last in his commentary on the calendar. For one thing, they form a pendant to the proem addressed to Germanicus in the *Fasti*: the muse here sings the praises of a member of the imperial family, Marcia, a cousin of Augustus' who also happened to be married to Ovid's friend Fabius Maximus. For another, the temple of Hercules and the Muses, whose restoration by Marcia's father Lucius Marcius Philippus is the occasion for Clio's song, has, as it were, metapoetical significance. Originally erected by Marcus Fulvius Nobilior, a friend of the poet Ennius (239–169), the temple harbored a calendar, presumably painted on one of its walls and perhaps accompanied by a commentary. And Ennius, in the last lines of Book 15 of his (lost) *Annals,* whose first edition ended at this point, probably described Fulvius' consecration of the temple.

Ovid and the Power of the Calendar

Like Ennius' contemporaries, the Romans who lived in the Augustan state could examine copies of their calendar in places open to the public. After Caesar reformed the calendar in 46 B.C.—as is well known, the new system for dividing up the year served as the basis for the revised calendar commissioned by Pope Gregory XIII in 1582—a number of copies of the reformed calendar, with commentaries attached, were engraved in stone and exhibited in various localities in the Roman Empire. Shortly after 6 A.D., or, in other words, about the time Ovid is likely to have begun writing the *Fasti,* stone tables, fragments of which have come down to us, were set up in Praeneste; a calendar and commentary written by the grammarian Verrius Flaccus were exhibited on them. The commentary was doubtless also available in book form, and Ovid obviously made use of it for his *Fasti.*

An important function of the Roman calendar with its series of holidays was to remind Romans throughout the course of the year of their community's history and its self-image. Thus the collections of myths and the explanations of the various festivals available in commentaries on the calendar were not random accumulations of curiosities, but rather a compendium of individual interpretations of Rome and its people organized by the state. These interpretations could be supplemented by others and thus partially modified or revised whenever new holidays were added to the calendar. Since Augustus too increased the number of festivals by introducing days honoring the emperor, he exercised an influence, in his own fashion, on the way the annual religious rituals represented Rome and the Romans. That is, one of the ways he propagated his state ideology was to mobilize the "power of the calendar," as Roman authorities had done from time immemorial.

Without a clear appreciation of this, we cannot measure the importance of Ovid's decision to compose his own version of a commentary on the calendar. Certainly, as a writer of elegy, the verse form in which his *Fasti* too is composed, he belonged to a literary tradition that encouraged his readers to expect not serious contributions to the interpretation of Roman history, religion, and politics, but an amusing, entertaining game making use of the narrative material the calendar offered. Indeed, in his role as commentator on the calendar, Ovid repeatedly emphasizes that he continues to feel bound by the elegiac "value system" that by definition rules out interference in matters of state. But it was quite impossible consistently to exclude this domain; the fact was that, with the holidays commemorating the emperor, contemporary political discourse made its way into the calendar.

In the *Fasti*, as we have seen, our commentator does indeed incorporate the imperial holidays and the ideology they convey into his explanations. But we also saw that praise of the sovereign could be cast in an ambiguous light by the context in which it was embedded, that of elegiac narrative. If, in the *Metamorphoses*, Roman history and, with it, the panegyric to Augustus at the very end of the work are sharply set off from the rest, the praise of the emperor in the *Fasti* is in such close proximity to playful reinterpretations of old myths and rituals that tension inevitably springs up between these two realms. It springs up, at any rate, for those readers who suspect that the author of the *Fasti* is capable of attempting, in his turn, to exercise the "power of the calendar" over his public.

We do not know if that was Ovid's intention. It is entirely conceivable that, when he formed the plan to write the *Fasti* as a kind of sequel to the Roman section of the *Metamorphoses*, he had not quite realized the kind of problems that the composition of a commentary on the calendar in elegiac couplets would pose. However, as is suggested by structural and thematic analysis of the *Fasti*, especially Books 5–6, he did become aware of the problem at some point and consequently abandoned the work after finishing the first half of it. Of course, one can imagine other reasons for the fact that the work has come down to us in fragmentary form; for example, Ovid may have died after completing Books 1–6 as they stand. But it is difficult to believe that the fact that there are exactly six books—in other words, that we have a complete commentary on the first half of the year—is due to chance. To which it must be added, first, that these six books form a skillfully composed whole, and, second, that they create the fiction that the commentator was not in a position to pursue his explanations because—to a certain extent in Book 5 and then definitely in Book 6—he was at his wits' end.

Assuming that Ovid deliberately broke off the *Fasti* with his gloss on the 30th of June, the question arises as to why he did so on that particular day. The explanation may be that what he would have had to comment on next were Julius Caesar's and Augustus' months. Perhaps the poet feared that he would have to subordinate two whole months to an Augustan theme, with the concomitant risk of succumbing completely to the "power of the calendar." Or he may have wanted to continue to confront the elegiac and Augustan worlds, but then have realized that a sharp collision between the two systems could no longer be avoided. It is striking that, of the three passages in the *Fasti* which anticipate the discussion of events in the second half of the year (3.67; 3.199; 5.147), two have to do with Augustus, and that the third (3.199) heralds the treatment of a myth already recounted in the *Ars amatoria:* the Rape of the Sabine Women (1.101–134). Did Ovid really want to give us another rendition of that episode? In Book 3 (179–228), he had, after all, already presented a sequel to the story included in the older work.

The *Fasti* too is the creation of a poet who underwent a "metamorphosis." To the extent that he here rang changes on the poetry he had so far produced in the elegiac tradition, he often succeeded not only in thinking up new, witty variations on the old literary game, but also in extending the series of his extremely sensitive portrayals of human psychology. However, as a commentator on the Augustan calendar writing from the elegist's standpoint, he ran into difficulties that, so it seems, could not quite be resolved even by the past master of the art of poetic transformation that he was.

Exile as an Elegiac World Out of Joint: The *Tristia* and the *Epistulae ex Ponto*

In what was presumably the last role Ovid played as a first-person speaker in his works, we have a poetic reflection of the real situation in which the writer Ovid found himself: like the speaker of the *Tristia* (Elegiac laments) and the *Epistulae ex Ponto* (Letters from the Black Sea), he too had been banished to Tomis on the Black Sea coast, where he was living when he composed these two collections of poems in elegiac couplets. Yet, even in these works, we hear the voice of a poetic speaker, not the author's. In the chapter on Ovid's life, we saw that the account the banished speaker of the elegies of exile gives of his plight could only be a fictionalization of the poet's real experiences (see pp. 25f.). Thus the speaker's claim that, in Tomis, he is living in the midst of very primitive savages in a region beset by an interminable winter does not correspond to historical reality. And although Ovid's alter ego repeatedly tells us that the quality of his poetic production has declined as a result of his banishment, it is in fact at the same high level as in his earlier works.

The collections *Tristia* and *Epistulae ex Ponto* further resemble Ovid's other writings in that the poet plays a literary game here too. Like the *poeta/amator* in the *Amores*, the exile—that, quite simply, is how we shall refer to the speaker of these elegies—is the central figure in a world that operates by the rules of the elegiac system (see pp. 10ff.). But it is an elegiac world thrown out of joint, even more radically than is the elegiac world of the *Epistulae Heroidum*. The latter is out of kilter in the sense that *women* assume the *amator*'s role, while the fictionalized Roman atmosphere of the *Amores* has been replaced by the "reality" of myth. Yet, like the elegiac lover, the heroines too complain about how love has made them suffer. Their suffering is caused by their separation from the men they love. The exile's stems, it is true, from a similar situation; however, *he* complains about being separated not only from the woman he loves—his wife, in this case—but also everything else he has lost as a result of his banishment from Rome. As the elegiac *amator*, whenever the *puella* refuses to see him, prostrates himself at her threshold and complains about how hard it is and how hard she is too, so the exile feels that his lot is a hard one, and, like the *amator*, begs that someone alleviate his pain. However, the person to whom he appeals and who remains hard in the face of his pleas is not a woman, but Augustus. Thus, in the dislocated elegiac world of exile, the emperor is cast in the role of the *dura puella* (hardhearted beloved); and, as the exile piously submits to the capriciousness of the "god" in Rome (the *amator* too treats his *puella* as if she were a goddess!), he finds himself in a situation akin to *servitium amoris* (erotic servitude). His elegies are "poetry of courtship" (Stroh 1971) and, as such, as unsuccessful as those of a *poeta/amator* or the heroines.

In addition to the elegiac *themes* of the poems of exile, their richly metaphoric language, familiar from Propertius, Tibullus, and Ovid's *Amores,* also constantly recalls the world of erotic elegy. When the exile falls ill, or, as often happens, longs for death, his way of describing his feelings often reminds us of a lovesick *poeta/amator*. His wife too can sometimes appear in the *puella*'s role—when, for example, coaching her as to how to act during their separation, he employs the diction of the *Ars amatoria*'s *praeceptor amoris* (professor of love). Moreover, when he promises her, as a *poeta/amator* does his beloved, that his elegies will win her fame, he is engaging in a theoretical discussion of his poetic art. He does so in various contexts in the *Tristia* and the *Epistulae ex Ponto,* both directly and indirectly. Among his indirect statements on the subject are certain passages in which he describes the barbarians on the Black Sea coast. Here the Getae's bows and arrows replace Cupid's weapons. In *Amores* 1.1, the god of love changes the *poeta/amator* into an elegist when he sets out to sing of arms and wars—that is, to compose a sort of *Aeneid*. In contrast, the barbarians of the Black Sea region incarnate the world of the heroic epic, and the elegist, in his exile, is drawn into that world after all. Betty Rose Nagle (1980) was the first to study this kind of intertextual play in depth.

Ovid may have been prompted to engage in this game by a Greek literary genre, the historical novel in letter form. Although, in the *Tristia,* the transition from elegies addressed to an individual to elegiac letters is effected only gradually, one can most assuredly call both this collection and the *Epistulae ex Ponto* a collection of letters from exile. In the *Tristia,* as we shall see, the speaker's experiences are retraced in chronological order over a period of several years; precisely the same thing happens in Hellenistic and Imperial collections of fictional Greek prose letters, which may be considered forerunners of the modern epistolary novel (Holzberg 1994). Their authors, whose names we do not know, pose as prominent Greeks of the sixth to the fourth centuries writing letters in which they provide chronological reports on a certain period in their lives, accompanied by their reflections. Some of these men also write their letters from exile.

Besides the constant alternation between report and reflection, which characterizes the discursive mode adopted by the exile in the *Tristia* as well, the Greek epistolary novels have a good deal else in common with Ovid's poetic work. Both the elegies in the *Tristia* and the letters in the Greek corpuses are tied together by different strands of frequently recurring themes. The result, in the Greek texts, is that certain events the letter-writers refer to come into sharper focus as their letters accumulate; much the same thing occurs in Book 1 of the *Tristia*. At the end of a Greek epistolary novel, or of a series of letters contained in it, the various thematic strands converge in a lengthy letter—the corresponding section of the *Tristia* is Book 2, the letter to Augustus—which explains matters the reader has so far not quite grasped. Thus, in his seventh letter, Plato retrospectively provides a great deal of information omitted from the reports on his experiences with the tyrants of Syracuse Dionysius II and Dion contained in letters 1–6. In Plato's letters (which many scholars consider to be partly authentic) as in all other Greek epistolary novels, the relationship between an intellectual and someone in a position of power is a major theme. That too holds for the *Tristia*. Let us, then, began by having a look at this "epistolary novel."

Tristia, Books 1 to 4: Odysseus in the Land of the Getae

Book 1 of the *Tristia* opens with a poem in which the speaker tells the book, which is traveling to Rome without him, how it should approach its audiences and how it should address them. He combines this with a report to the reader on his personal situation. He has been banished (3) and is, even as he writes, aboard a ship being buffeted by a winter storm (42). Plainly, he is on his way to his place of exile, but he does not say precisely where that is. At the end of the poem, he reveals only that he will be living at the "end of the world" (127–128). Again, he divulges almost nothing about the reasons for his banishment, aside from a brief remark about *crimina* (offenses): they have earned him the reputation of a "public enemy" in Rome, but his book is not to defend him against these charges (23–26). He also hints that the three books of the *Ars amatoria* had something to do with his punishment (67–68; 111–116). But here too he contents himself with comparing these books to mythical parricides.

At the beginning of Book 1 of the *Tristia*, then, the reader is faced with a number of riddles. But if she is hoping to discover the solutions to them by reading the eleven elegies which make up the work, she is in for a disappointment. At the end of the series of elegies, she knows little more about the poet's place of banishment than its name; about the reason for his banishment, she knows virtually nothing at all. In the process of reading, she has accompanied the exile on his way to his place of banishment, for he has, in the poems written during his journey, told the reader both of the adventures he has had on the way and also of the thoughts and memories recorded in elegies addressed to friends (5, 7, and 9), his wife (6), and an enemy (8). His travelogue opens with the description of a storm he experiences at sea. Extending over two poems (2 and 4), it is interrupted by a particularly vivid account of his memories of his departure from Rome (3). After incorporating the reflective elegies into his travel report, the exile gives us detailed information on his itinerary (10). In the last poem in the book (11), which we are obviously supposed to imagine him writing shortly before he reaches his destination, the exile, again beleaguered, at that very moment, by the wind and waves, tells us that he is apprehensive about his place of banishment. He imagines, he says, that the coast to his left is inhabited by barbarian robbers and killers.

Meanwhile, the reader has learned from very summary indications in Elegies 2, 3, 5, 8, and 10 that the exile will be taking up residence in the city of Tomis on the "Getic shore" (10.14). Not until she reaches Book 2 of the *Tristia*, the letter to Augustus, does she find a section of any length with a preliminary account of the population and the climate of the region (187–206). Information about the reasons for the exile's banishment is supplied in much the same fashion. All that the exile says of the "offenses" evoked in the first poem in Book 1 is that he deserves to be punished for them, but that he committed them as the result of an error and out of naïveté; he adds that he did nothing of a criminal nature (2.63–64, 2.95–100; 3.37–38; 5.42). In the letter to Augustus, on the other hand, he says the following:

> cur aliquid vidi? cur noxia lumina feci?
>   cur imprudenti cognita culpa mihi?
> inscius Actaeon vidit sine veste Dianam:
>   praeda fuit canibus non minus illes suis.

scilicet in superis etiam fortuna luenda est,
    nec veniam laeso numine casus habet.

Why did I see something? Why did I let my eyes become guilty?
Why did I, unsuspecting, learn of guilt?
Actaeon saw Diana without her clothes unwittingly;
He did not become the prey of his own dogs any less for that.
Certainly, among the immortals, one has to pay for misfortune as well,
and accident, when a deity is offended, is no excuse.

(103–108)

Thus the speaker inadvertently glimpsed something he ought not to have, offending the "god" Augustus as a result. But the speaker has done something else to disgruntle the sovereign: he has composed the *Ars amatoria*. To the question of what this work has to do with the banishment decree, the reader is given an answer only when she comes to the letter to Augustus. After throwing out mere hints in Book 1 of the *Tristia* (1.67–68; 1.111–116; 9.55–64), the exile now states very clearly—it sounds as if he were quoting from the indictment—that the work was found to be indecent and that its author was accused of teaching brazen adultery (2.211–222). He details his position on this charge, whereas, in the letter to Augustus, he makes only one more brief comment on his inadvertent offense (207–210). Better than half the elegy, which fills an entire book, is given over to an attempt to convince the emperor that he has misjudged the *Ars amatoria* and has therefore unjustly concluded that authorship of it constitutes grounds for banishment (213–546).

It should be clear from what we have seen of the *Tristia* so far that the exile interweaves his themes in such a way as to point his reader in a particular direction. I have shown this with respect to the series of themes built up from statements on the speaker's place of exile, his inadvertent offense, and his *Art of Love*. Each of these three thematic strands in the poem is introduced by a hint that raises a question which goes answered, leaving the reader in suspense. After being tantalized with further hints, she is finally conducted to a point in the text at which she is provided fuller information. In the case of the first and second themes, however, she is told so little even at this point that she can by no means be said to have received a satisfactory answer. The exile's description of his place of banishment in his letter to Augustus makes it sound truly wild: he is to go live in the far north, where it is freezing cold and his life is threatened by hostile barbarians (187–206). One would like to hear more about this in the remaining three books of the *Tristia*, and about his unintentional act of lese majesty (103–108) as well. But, on the latter subject, the only other thing the exile says in his letter to the emperor is that he shall say nothing more, because he does not want to grieve Augustus all over again (207–210). And he keeps his resolution in all the subsequent passages of the elegies of exile in which his "error" is mentioned.

Unlike the first and second thematic strands, the third, about the art of love and the banishment decree, culminates, in the letter to Augustus, in a genuine answer to the question posed at the beginning of the *Tristia*. This answer too is provided with an eye to guiding the reader's reception of the poem. To begin with, the reader is led toward a pause in the narrative. For the first time, after a long wait for the answer to a question, her patience is amply rewarded. Simultaneously, she is given the impression that it matters a great deal to the exile to provide an exhaustive answer to this question here, and accordingly attaches special importance to what the exile now goes on to say on this score. Moreover, the content of what she is told in over three hundred lines differs sharply from what she has read so far. In previous passages, she learned about the experiences and thoughts of someone bound for his place of banishment, and then listened as, in humble tones, he addressed the person who banished him. Now, however, she is suddenly presented with a treatise on the *Ars amatoria,* written in the style of Horace's verse letters on poetics, and is positively overwhelmed by the arguments that are piled up to refute the idea that *Ars* constitutes grounds for banishment. Thus, for example, the exile tries to prove, by way of a rapid review of the history of Greek and Roman poetry, that many erotic poems like the *Ars* have been composed ever since Homer's day (361–470). Ultimately, one so completely loses sight of the question of lese majesty for all these "scholarly" explanations as to suppose that the *Art of Love* is the sole reason for its author's banishment and that he is the hapless victim of a miscarriage of justice. Thus, by the end of the letter addressed to him, Augustus emerges as an arbitrary ruler who has punished a poet for one of his works not only severely, but without real justification. The exile accordingly appears as a victim of political censorship.

Alongside the image of a ruler who treats a poet unjustly, the *Tristia* forges—again, by way of a thematic strand in the poem—the image of an emperor-god who wrathfully persecutes a mere mortal and will not be placated. Ovid's readers were familiar with the resulting situation from epic, especially Homer's, which recounts the persecution of Odysseus by the wrathful god Poseidon, and Virgil's, in which Aeneas is pursued by Juno's wrath. Thus the exile becomes a self-styled epic hero victimized by the wrath of the "god" Augustus. He draws frequent parallels between his own predicament and Odysseus': for example, in a catalog of their similarities in *Tristia* 1.5 (57–84), which recalls the comparison between Augustus and Romulus in the *Fasti* (2.133–144; see pp. 156f.). Just as, in the *Fasti,* arguments are marshaled in support of the claim that the emperor is a greater ruler than the city's founder, so, in the *Tristia,* the exile sets out to prove that his lot is in many respects harder than that of Odysseus, famed for his patience under adversity. And, in the first poem he composes after reaching Tomis—the second in Book 3, preceded by a prologue uttered by the book that is arriving in Rome—the exile looks back upon his journey to his place of banishment in a line that contains an unmistakable allusion to a famous one in the proem to the *Odyssey.* The line from Homer reads, "But, at sea, he endured many pains in his heart" (1.4). Of himself, the exile says, "But I endured very many perils at sea and on land (plurima sed pelago terraque pericula passum)" (3.2.7).

If, following the well-taken suggestion of a number of scholars, we treat Elegy 4.47–78 as Elegy 4b (5), then Book 3 of the *Tristia* contains fifteen elegies. Poetics is the subject matter of three of them: the prologue to the book (1), a letter to the poetess Perilla, in which the exile predicts fame for his poetry after his death (7 or 8), and the epilogue, addressed to an unnamed friend, from whom the poet begs indulgence for the deficiencies of his new poetic work (14 or 15). As the letter to Perilla makes up the middle section of the book, there are as many elegies between it and the prologue as there are in the group of elegies framed by this letter and the epilogue. Each of the two series of poems has its overarching theme. In Elegies 2–6 (7), the exile affords the reader a glimpse of his inner life and emotions during the first part of his stay in Tomis; in Elegies 8 (9)–13 (14), he essays a preliminary description of the place and people.

After declaring, in Elegy 2, that he was overcome by despair and longed for death after arriving in his place of banishment, the exile informs his wife in Elegy 3, an elegy he expressly calls a letter, that he is seriously ill. The report on the state of his health modulates into instructions that his wife is to follow if he dies. Lamenting, in advance, her absence in his dying hour, he says that she should have his bones brought to Italy and interred near Rome. Here is the epitaph he chooses for himself:

> hic ego qui iaceo tenerorum lusor amorum
>   ingenio perii Naso poeta meo.
> at tibi qui transis ne sit grave quisquis amasti
>   dicere Nasonis molliter ossa cubent

> Here I lie, the playful author [*lusor*] of delicate love poetry,
> I, Naso, the poet who went to ruin because of his verse.

But you who pass by, if you have ever loved, may it not be hard for you
to say: may Naso's bones rest softly!

(73–76)

The poem contains a great many allusions to erotic elegies, including
Tibullus 1.3. There the *poeta/amator* is lying ill on the island of Corfu,
far from his *puella;* fearing that, if he should die, his mother and sister
will not attend his burial, he too composes his own epitaph. If we look
more closely at the way the banished poet adapts elegiac themes such as
this one to his poems of exile, while simultaneously reinterpreting them
in light of his situation (something we shall have to forgo here), we can
again see that he has good reason to call himself a *lusor* (someone who
likes to play) in his epitaph.

The rest of the first series of elegies in Book 3 is addressed to friends. As
in Book 1, the exile does not name them, so as to spare them the kind of
problems that might crop up in their relationship with Augustus if he did.
Speaking of these problems in Elegy 4b (5), he reiterates a theme that he
has already sounded (1.5.37–38) and that he immediately returns to in
the next elegy (5 [6].18). Several thematic strands link Book 3 to Book 1.
Only one new one is introduced early in Book 3: in the second elegy, the
exile makes his first imaginary journey to Rome (21–22) and, from this
point on, often travels there in his imagination. In 3.8 (9) he associates
this theme with a wish that he could fly (1–10). The poem consists mainly
of the exile's report on his mental and physical health; thus it creates the
impression that, after the metapoetical Elegy 7 (8), the exile is developing
the themes of Elegies 2–6 (7). But one couplet makes a veiled reference
to a new theme. Here the exile says: "cumque locum moresque hominum
cultusque sonumque cernimus"; "I long for death" "when I see the place,
the customs of the people, their way of life and their sounds" (37–38).
This is another allusion to a famous line from the beginning of the
Odyssey: "Of many people he saw the cities and became acquainted with
their mentality" (3). The line in Ovid is a cue: the exile will now go on to
describe the region and its inhabitants. The "Odysseus" patient in afflic-
tion gives way to the "Odysseus" who reports his observations of foreign
climes, that is, the land of the Getae.

The exile begins the narrative section of Book 3 with a sort of prologue (9 [10]). He glosses the name "Tomis" in an explanatory legend
which affirms that Tomis derives from the Greek word *tome* (the act of
cutting). We are told that Medea, fleeing her father, murdered her
younger brother Absyrtus on the site of the future city, cutting him up
and scattering his members far and wide to throw her pursuer off the
track. This thrusts us straight back into the world of the *Metamorphoses,*

where we remain in the next elegy as well, which provides a detailed account of Tomis' rigorous winter, so cold that the Black Sea freezes over; of attacks by barbarian hordes who allegedly sweep across the frozen Danube; and of the region's poverty in edible crops (10 [11]).

With its catalog of fabulous curiosities—including wine that, when it freezes, takes the form of the vessel containing it and is not drunk but consumed piece by piece (23–24)—the elegy is reminiscent of Pythagoras' pseudoscientific lecture in the *Metamorphoses* (15.75ff.; see pp. 144ff.). Like Pythagoras, the exile claims, with an emphasis that is as suspicious as it is funny (35–50), to be delivering an eyewitness report. Ovid has here borrowed certain themes from Virgil's excursus on the Scythians in the *Georgics* (3.349ff.), added something of his own, and lightened up the whole with his wit. Two couplets allude to myths that he exploited (perhaps while in exile) in the paired letters of the *Epistulae Heroidum* (18/19 and 20/21; see pp. 87f.). After describing how he stepped out onto the frozen Black Sea, the exile exclaims: "si tibi tale fretum quondam, Leandre, fuisset,/non foret angustae mors tua crimen aquae"; "If you had in times past experienced the sea in this form, Leander,/We could not blame the straits for your death" (41–42). And, on the subject of the region's crops, he remarks, "poma negat regio, nec haberet Acontius in quo/scriberet hic dominae verba legenda suae"; "The land refuses to give apples; Acontius would have nothing/On which to write the words his beloved was to read" (73–74). This is the world of elegy again, which the exile wrenches so thoroughly out of joint that it seems as if there will be no setting it right ever again.

In Elegy 11 (12), the exile again addresses one of his enemies in Rome. Although, from a thematic point of view, this poem is better suited to the atmosphere of the first half of the book, the exile no doubt deliberately places it after the "ethnographic" elegy, since his Roman adversary resembles a cruel tyrant and thus provides living proof that the capital has its own barbarians. There is, on the other hand, a great deal in Rome that Tomis lacks; for instance, a proper springtime, like the one the exile vividly imagines in Elegy 12 (13). Still, the spring thaw is underway in the land of the Getae, ships will soon land on its coasts, and the exile can ask a sailor—assuming he manages to find one who knows Greek or Latin—whether he can tell him anything about Augustus' latest triumph over the Germans. The exile's first spring in Tomis brings a meeting with the god who personifies his birthday (the 20th of March). But the meeting gives him no pleasure, and he voices the wish that it will be his last such encounter in exile (13 [14]).

That his wish is not fulfilled becomes clear, at the latest, by the seventh elegy in Book 4, in which he says that the sun has now come to him twice after a freezing winter (1). Later, in 5.10, he reports that he has now weathered three winters on the Black Sea coast (1–2). Like Book 3, Book 4, with its ten elegies, is framed by two metapoetical poems. We have already looked closely at the epilogue, in which the exile tells his life's story (see pp. 24ff.). As to the prologue, he informs us in the first half of it (1–52) that writing is his way of assuaging the permanent grief of exile. But it is precisely writing that has gotten him into the predicament he is in, he seizes the opportunity to observe, alluding to the fact that the *Art of Love* helped precipitate his exile. On the other hand, he notes, someone in love is also generally unhappy but does not stop loving for all that. The exile too, then, loves the projectile that wounded him.

Be it noted that single-minded devotion to an erotic passion that causes one nothing but grief—in other words, elegiac love—is here equated with single-minded devotion to an activity that met with severe punishment, and that this activity, like the elegiac lover's, consists in writing elegies. Exile again appears as an elegiac world thrown out of joint, as it does all the more forcefully in the second half of 4.1 (53–106), in which, evoking the barbarian attacks on the city of Tomis, the exile says,

> aspera militiae iuvenis certamina fugi,
>   nec nisi lusura movimus arma manu;
> nunc senior gladioque latus scutoque sinistram,
>   canitiem galeae subicioque meam.
> nam dedit e specula custos ubi signa tumultus,
>   induimur trepida protinus arma manu.

> I shunned bitter military struggles as a young man,
> and only set arms [*arma*] in motion with my hand in order to play with them.
> Now, as an older man, I have a sword at my side and a shield in my left hand,
> and press my gray hair under a helmet.
> For when the guard has given the signal of alarm from the tower,
> I immediately put on the weapons with a fearfully trembling hand.

(71–76)

A young elegiac *amator* who was a soldier only in love—*arma* in l. 72 again carries sexual connotations—has, in the new elegiac world, become a real fighter, and in his old age at that.

The theme of the poet grown old in exile dominates the second of the two series of elegies in Book 4, each comprising four elegies. The first series (2–5), like the first series of poems in Book 3, is dominated by the exile's reflections on his plight, which are intertwined with imagined journeys to Rome. In Elegy 2, for example, he lets his imagination fly to the capital in order to watch a triumphal procession staged after one of Tiberius' victories over the Germans. Beginning with Elegy 6, however, his thoughts keep turning to the time that is slipping by in his place of banishment, making him ever older. Thus he opens Elegy 8 with the words, "Iam mea cycneas imitantur tempora plumas,/inficit et nigras alba senecta comas"; "Already my temples are beginning to resemble swan's down,/And the white of old age colors my black hair" (1–2). In the next poem but one, we hear this swan's swan song: in a certain sense, the exile is speaking about his approaching death here, as we have already noted (see pp. 24f.). Indeed, the first couplet sounds like the opening of a last will and testament or deathbed speech: "Ille ego qui fuerim, tenerorum lusor amorum,/quem legis, ut noris, accipe posteritas"; "Who I was, I, the playful author of sensitive love poetry,/listen, posterity, so that you will know whom you are reading" (10.1–2).

It might seem plausible to suppose that this poem is the epilogue to Books 1–4 of the *Tristia*. These four books would thus comprise a self-contained tetralogy; detached from the rest, Book 5 would constitute an independent unit. Most Ovid scholars do indeed make precisely that assumption. Two things, however, militate against it. To begin with, 4.10 is, on the structural and thematic planes, very closely bound up with the last book. It fleshes out the contrast, only sketched in 4.1, between the way of life of the young *amator* and the old exile, closing off the series of elegies about growing old. Second, one should keep in mind that the exile, at the point he has reached by 4.10 in the story line of the "epistolary novel," is "dead" only with regard to the poetic career that he began long ago in Rome as a fresh young thing. He lives on as a "mere shadow of what he was," in a locality that he likens to the underworld in several passages in his poems of exile. One of them seems particularly significant to me. It occurs in 5.7, the first poem since 3.10 (11) in which the exile again gives us a detailed description of the region and its inhabitants. In l. 43 he calls the region *inamabilis* (unfriendly); this word, rare in Latin poetry, occurs twice in the *Metamorphoses* (4.477 and 14.590) and occasionally in Virgil's and Horace's descriptions of the underworld (Williams 1994, 13).

Thus Book 5 of the *Tristia* is the section of the "epistolary novel" about life in the underworld. This is a fitting theme for the poetry of a first-person speaker who constantly compares himself to Odysseus, since, in Book 11 of the *Odyssey*, the hero visits the realm of the dead. But Odysseus returns to the world of the living and then to his native land, as the exile does not. Thus the "epistolary" novel lacks the ending that the "Odyssey" it contains leads one to expect; it has an "open-ended" structure, as Gerlinde Bretzigheimer has aptly put it (1991, 57). This open-endedness is further due to the fact that Book 5, unlike the other books containing several elegies (1, 3, and 4), has no proper epilogue. It is true that the last poem in Book 5 and thus in the *Tristia* (5.14) constitutes a conclusion, since it promises the exile's wife that she will win fame thanks to his poetry. But it is hardly memorable, certainly not as memorable as the conspicuously absent ending would be: one in which the exile would report that the hard lot he has bewailed for five books running has in one way or another been made easier.

In most of the manuscripts, Book 5 contains fourteen elegies. One of them may again consist of what was originally two elegies that were fused as the work came down through the centuries; if so, the book actually contains fifteen elegies. However, Ovid may have wanted to signal, by "leaving out" an elegy, that his "epistolary novel" was open-ended. In any event, the book's structure does not bear out the argument that the book should be reconstructed so as to contain fifteen poems. The poems are here organized not in sequences, but according to a principle of alternation: the elegies following the metapoetical prologue addressed to the reader alternate regularly between individual poems addressed to the exile's wife (2, 5, 11, 14) or an enemy (14) on the one hand, and pairs of poems addressed to friends on the other (3/4, 6/7, 9/10, 12/13).

Elegies 7, 10, and 12 offer descriptions of the region and its inhabitants. The exile focuses on the people of Tomis. The men are wild, warlike fellows. As Gareth Williams has pointed out (1994, 19), they carry the same weapons as the followers of an Etruscan leader in Virgil's *Aeneid* (7.15–16/10.168–169). This and other intertextual references to the renowned work put the men of Tomis in the world of epic. Thus they stand in sharp contrast to the elegiac world, insofar as they are utterly uncivilized creatures. For instance, we are told about them that "non coma, non ulla barba resecta manu"; "Neither their hair nor their beard is trimmed by human hand" (7.18), whereas *The Art of Love* tells men "sit coma, sit trita barba resecta manu"; "Let hair and beard be trimmed by an expert hand" (1.518). Because not a single inhabitant of Tomis knows Latin (7.53–54), the exile has either to make himself understood with sign language (10.36) or have a go at speaking the local tongue (7.56). He once describes how this affects him as follows: "I myself, it seems to me, have already forgotten my Latin,/Have already learned to speak Getic and Sarmatian" (12.57–58). This is one of many passages in which the exile claims that he is losing his language as a way of explaining something else he also often affirms, namely, that his writing is not what it was. One need only glance at the original Latin version of the two lines just cited in order to see that he in fact continues to compose his verse with consummate art: the couplet is made to sound like helpless stammering:

Ipse mihi videor iam DEDIDICIsse Latine,
iam DIDICI GetiCE SarmatiCEque loQUI. (Barchiesi 1994, 26–27)

That, then, is what it sounds like when someone has lost his (native Latin) tongue.

Epistulae ex Ponto, Books 1–3: What Losing One's Tongue Leads To, Part 2

The exile's wish that Augustus might allow him to move to a more pleasant place of banishment is an especially frequent theme in the *Tristia.* At the end of the collection of elegies, the exile still does not have the slightest prospect of seeing his wish granted in any way, shape, or form. Thereafter, he continues to compose elegies in which he repeatedly voices the same desire. These new elegies are, once again, assembled in books of poems. Four such books have come down to us in the manuscripts; taken together, they bear the title *Epistulae ex Ponto* (or *Ex Ponto libri,* Books from the Black Sea). But what we have here is manifestly two separate collections. For, as we shall see at somewhat greater length in a moment, Books 1–3 represent a structurally unified whole; Book 4 stands apart, in obvious allusion to the relationship between Propertius' Book 4 and the collection comprised by his Books 1–3. Common to the four books of *Ex Ponto* is the fact that all the elegies they contain are conceived as letters and that the names of the addressees are now stated.

The first three books of *Ex Ponto* contain thirty elegies: there are ten in the first, eleven in the second, and nine in the third. If John Richmond, the editor of the most recent edition (1990), is right to insert 2.11 between 3.4 and 3.5 (so that 3.5–9 become 3.6–10)—and he gives good reasons for his choice—then we may assume that the original edition comprised three books of ten elegies each. Analysis of the structure of the collection, among other things, shows that this is a safe assumption, for the principle of symmetry is clearly at work here. The collection is framed by two letters to a certain Brutus; in both, the exile drops remarks that provide fundamental insights into the origins and nature of his collection (1.1; 3.9 [10]). Most of the other letters are addressed to influential friends in Rome. The exile has assigned certain of these elegies a "place of honor" in the collection because their recipients are people who could be important to him. Thus 1.2 and, probably, 3.8 (9), the penultimate poem, are addressed to Fabius Maximus; Ovid's third wife may have been a member of his family. The collection also assigns a prominent role to Cotta Maximus, one of Valerius Messalla's two sons, who, on the exile's testimony, did a great deal to foster his maiden efforts at poetry (2.3.75–78). It would take us too far afield to show in detail that the letters to Cotta, of which there are six (seven, if he is the Maximus who is addressed in 3.8 [9]), also hold a conspicuously central place in *Ex Ponto;* I therefore refer the reader to Hermann Froesch (1968).

Because the structure of *Ex Ponto* is oriented toward its addressees, it is hardly to be expected that the collection will "tell" a running story like the one we find in the *Tristia.* And, indeed, it does not. It is true that we can make out a rough chronological framework—we shall come back to this point—but, basically, it may be said that Books 1–3 of the *Epistulae ex Ponto,* like the three pentads of the *Epistulae Heroidum,* do not constitute an "epistolary novel," but rather a collection in which each letter stands as an independent whole. Some of these letters stand out from the rest of the collection by dint of their surprising subject matter. They catch the reader unawares, because *Ex Ponto* simply pursues most of the themes found in the *Tristia,* so that, for long stretches of the work, we find nothing but new variations on old themes. Even here, however, as recent analyses have demonstrated, Ovid exhibits the kind of virtuosity we are familiar with by now. The exile continues to affirm that he is losing his command of his native tongue and therefore writing bad verse, while his text continues to give him the lie.

Let us begin with a glance at the gems it has to offer. One is the letter addressed to Severus in Book 1 (1.8), which I shall return to in another connection. Of the two most striking poems in Book 2, the letter to Macer with the description of a journey to Asia Minor and Sicily (10) has already been discussed in Chapter 2 (see pp. 22f.). The other poem in Book 2 that merits a closer look, Letter 8 to Cotta, is prompted by the fact that this friend of the exile's has sent him a silver representation of Augustus, Tiberius, and Livia. Examining this gift, the exile thinks he can see the image of Augustus glowering at him; he thereupon offers up a long prayer to the three "gods" in which he wishes them well and, at the same time, appeals to them to allow him to change his place of banishment (23–70). Then he says:

> aut ego me fallo nimiaque cupidine ludor,
> aut spes exilii commodioris adest.
> nam minus et minus est facies in imagine tristis,
> visaque sunt dictis adnuere ora meis.
> Vera precor fiant timidae praesagia mentis,
> iustaque quamvis est, sit minor ira die.

> Either I am mistaken and am being fooled by an all too violent longing,
> or there is hope for a more agreeable place of banishment.
> For the face in the image is less and less stern,
> and it seems that the countenance is nodding consent to my words.
> May the premonitions of my fearful heart, I pray, come true,
> and, however justified, may the god's wrath abate.
>
> (71–76)

For once, a long elegiac speech suddenly seems to have an effect, and a rather astounding one at that! But, in an elegiac world out of joint, all sorts of things can happen.

Book 3 opens with a set of three elegies. All three are more than one hundred lines long, and each has its special charm. Elegy 1 contains the last words the exile says to his wife in the poetry of exile, mainly instructions on how to conduct herself if she intercedes with Livia, the emperor's wife, on her husband's behalf. What is surprising about this text is that we seem to hear the voice of the *Art of Love*'s *praeceptor amoris* (professor of love) from the moment the exile begins speaking of the part his wife will have to play (42–43); he adds that, whatever she does, people will be watching her on a vast stage (59). Indeed, he proceeds to give her stage directions for her "scene" with the empress, like those the *praeceptor* also often gives his male and female students. For example, he offers her advice as to how to shed tears. The *praeceptor*'s student, we remember, is supposed to fall back on a little artificial stimulation whenever his tears fail to flow naturally (*Ars* 1.661–662; see p. 96). The exile pointedly emphasizes that his wife has reason enough to cry, in view of her husband's wretched plight, and speaks of the "devices" (*opes*) that fate has put in her hands (101–104). Listening to him, we can hardly avoid the impression that he too is playacting in the roles of director and husband.

Assuming that the *Ars amatoria* really was one of the reasons for Ovid's banishment, what was Augustus likely to have thought when he read a poem in which his wife was, as it were, allotted the role of the *puella* who was to be deceived by false appearances? In Elegy 3.3, someone is privy to the emperor's thoughts and plans: Cupid. In this poem, the exile describes how the god of love appeared to him one night and, in response to the reproach that he was ultimately to blame for the banishment order, said, among other things, that chances were the emperor's wrath would soon abate. Cupid should know what he is talking about, since he is related to Augustus through his brother Aeneas (62). The poem in which the god of love makes his appearance clearly recalls the scenes early in the *Amores* and the *Remedia amoris* in which he is also on hand. This poem follows an elegy whose central section may be ranged with the *Metamorphoses* and the *Fasti,* for here a native of the Black Sea region tells the exile the story of Iphigenia among the Tauri (3.2.43–96), going into great detail.

This is, for the exile, a pleasant way of communicating with the "barbarians," and a report on such communication is a new development in the poetry of exile. This brings me to the rough chronological framework I mentioned earlier. It is formed by a number of statements that the exile scatters through Books 1–3 of *Ex Ponto,* to the effect that he has gradually grown accustomed to an environment that was long very alien for him. In 1.5 he says that he is now content to be a poet among the uncivilized Getae (65–66); then, in 1.8, he expresses a desire to engage in an activity that can serve as a metaphor for writing in Augustan poetry—namely, farmwork, such as raising cattle and cultivating crops on his own plot (49–62). He even makes the following wish: "et discam Getici quae norunt verba iuvenci,/adsuetas illis adiciamque minas"; "And I would like to learn the words that Getic cattle understand,/and to add the threats they are familiar with" (55–56). By 2.7, the exile is already reporting that the Getae, the most savage people in the world, have joined him in bewailing his misfortune (31–32). In 2.9, he addresses a letter to a "colleague," King Cotys of Thrace, who lives not very far from Tomis; the king writes verse, as his countryman Orpheus once did. The next contribution to the theme of contact with the surrounding world in *Ex Ponto* 1–3 is the description of the scene in which the exile listens to the native storyteller (3.2).

Thus, to the extent that it discusses the exile's relationship to his new place of residence, the second collection of exile elegies continues the "epistolary novel" begun in the first. Moreover, there are two poems at the end of *Ex Ponto* that, for contemporary readers, must surely have recalled the endings of the elegiac "erotic novels" by Ovid and Propertius: 3.7 (8) and 3.8 (9). In 3.7 (8), a letter to friends in Rome, the exile springs a complete surprise on us: he declares, with all the emotion of an epic hero bowing to his fate, that he is now ashamed of having vainly requested, ad nauseam, the same thing in all his letters. He means, as appears in the course of the poem, permission to move to a more attractive place of banishment, which the intercession of the people to whom he wrote was supposed to induce Augustus to grant. Henceforth what he writes is to have a different content (7: *mutetur scripti sententia*); he also resolves to stop being a burden on his wife. He has long been intimately acquainted with every imaginable kind of woe and is therefore willing to die in the land of the Getae.

Is this a serious testimonial that the exile has been "converted" and has abjured the kind of exile elegy he has so far written? We are warned away from such an interpretation by, among other things, the intertextuality at work in this poem and the indications of ironic intent that it provides. We cannot here discuss the parodic allusions to thematically related declarations by Homer's Odysseus or Virgil's Aeneas about their readiness to stand firm even in the face of death (Galasso 1987). We shall have to content ourselves with a brief reference to *Amores* 3.11, which, like *Ex Ponto* 3.7 (8), is an elegy placed shortly before the end of a collection. There the *poeta/amator* renounces the *puella* he loves and, simultaneously, elegy as a genre. But, after suddenly asserting, in the very same poem, that he is once again prepared to submit to the *puella*'s will—similarly, at the end of *Ex Ponto* 3.7 (8), the exile associates the declaration that he is ready to die bravely in the land of the Getae with a confession that his resolve depends on whether Augustus will look upon him with favor (39–40)—he announces in the last elegy of the *Amores* that he is bidding farewell to this kind of poetry after all. Yet the poet Ovid who plays the role of the *poeta/amator* continues to write elegies; in the exile's role, he does the same thing after *Ex Ponto* 1–3 ends, composing a whole book of new exile elegies in the style of those he has already written.

While it may not be immediately apparent, *Ex Ponto* 3.8 (9) alludes to an elegy placed shortly before the end of Propertius' "erotic novel" (3.23). In Ovid's poem, the exile writes his friend (Fabius?) Maximus that, after thinking about what kind of a present he might send him from Tomis, he has come to the conclusion that nothing will do. He sends him arrows in a Scythian quiver all the same, with the wish that they will be stained red with the blood of Maximus' enemies. Here is what he says about them:

> hos habet haec calamos, hos haec habet ora libellos,
>   haec viget in nostris, Maxime, Musa locis!
> quae quamquam misisse pudet, quia parva videntur,
>   tu tamen haec, quaeso, consule missa boni.

> These reeds [*calamos*], these books [*libellos*] are what this shore has to offer,
> this Muse [*Musa*] thrives in the region I live in, Maximus!
> Although I am ashamed to send this, because it seems so slight,
> please content yourself with what I send you here nevertheless.

(21–24)

Obviously, the gift is supposed to symbolize the place of exile. But more can be made of *calamos* (21). When first reading this line, one takes the word to mean "reed arrows"; soon, however, under the influence of *libellos* and *Musa*, one construes it as "reed pens." Thus the gift also symbolizes the exile's poetic activity. This is confirmed by Propertius 3.23, where the *poeta/ amator* says he has lost his writing tablets, presumably a symbolic way of indicating that his first collection of elegies will soon come to a close. Is the exile implicitly anticipating the end of his collection? Does he even mean to confirm the announcement he makes in 3.7 (8) to the effect that he no longer wants to write poetry of the kind he has produced so far? We have already seen that, between the lines, he casts what he declares in the earlier poem in an ironic light. It is now time to notice that, in 3.8 (9), the reed pens from Tomis can also serve as a metaphor for Getic poetry. Indeed, the exile's desire to take up farming there, expressed in 1.8, can even be construed as a veiled allusion to the fact that he is gradually becoming a Getic poet. And in Book 4 of *Ex Ponto,* he will in fact tell us that he has composed Getic verse.

Epistulae ex Ponto, Book 4: The Sequel to the Sequel

It is generally assumed that the elegies in Book 4 of *Ex Ponto* were collected not by Ovid, but by an anonymous editor after Ovid's death. One argument offered in support of this thesis is that, with its 930 lines, the book is much longer than the other books of exile elegies, all of which contain only 700 to 800 lines. However, like Propertius 4, this book was obviously meant to stand as an independent collection vis-à-vis an already existing trilogy, and Ovid may have sought to bring that out by making it "excessively long." This may also be the explanation for the unusual number of elegies in the book, sixteen rather than fifteen. Propertius 4 contains eleven, that is, one more than ten, which is, like fifteen, a "normal" number for Augustan books of verse. *Tristia* 1 also contains eleven elegies. In the middle of that book is an elegy addressed to the exile's wife (6), so that the "excess" has its justification (as it does in Propertius too, though I cannot go into that here). In *Ex Ponto* 4, the sixteenth elegy is, unmistakably, the extra one. For Elegies 1 and 15, addressed to Sextus Pompeius, frame 2–14: Elegy 1, announced as a "finespun poem" (1: *deductum carmen*)—like, implicitly, the proem to the *Metamorphoses*—includes a lengthy expression of thanks to Pompeius, as does Elegy 15. Thus Elegy 16 comprises a kind of appendix to a "normal" book of fifteen poems. Its contents reflect this. Defending himself against the letter's addressee, who has criticized his verse, the exile here rattles off a long list of contemporary poets and then pats himself on the back for becoming famous despite such stiff "competition."

Another argument often marshaled in support of the thesis that *Ex Ponto* 4 was edited after Ovid's death is that it is the only book of exile elegies to contain poems originating over a four-year period (c. 13–16). But what does "originating" mean? The fact that Elegy 4, looking ahead to the start of the new year, refers to the day when Consul Pompeius will officially assume office by no means dictates the conclusion that the poem originated before Pompeius took office. What *can* be fairly conclusively established, on the other hand, is the structural function of the elegy, one it shares with Elegy 5, which also refers to Pompeius' consulship. For the following elegy, 6, makes a sharp break: it mentions Augustus' death, which occurred during Pompeius' consulship (on 19 August 14). Thus the first pentad of elegies is still "set" during Augustus' reign. All the other elegies, in my view, date from the period of Tiberius' rule; insofar as they can be dated at all, this seems altogether plausible. It would follow that Ovid structured the book with the succession in mind, composing it only after all the events he alludes to had already become history.

The caesura created in *Ex Ponto* 4 by Augustus' death may be likened to the passage in Deianira's *Epistula* in which she learns, while writing to Hercules, that he is dying (9.143–144; see p. 82). Just as this prompts her to adopt a new line of action, so the death of Augustus leads the exile to undertake a new sort of activity (he cannot "do" anything in the true sense of the word) in the sense that he now takes the changed political situation into account, adjusting his efforts to elicit sympathy for his plight and gain the right to move to a more attractive place of exile. The people he now addresses are clearly chosen with this in mind. We shall here have to content ourselves with noting that, of the eleven Romans mentioned by name to whom he writes in *Ex Ponto* 4, only five also appear in Books 1–3.

The fourth book of the *Letters from the Black Sea* is the sequel to a sequel, inasmuch as the thematic strands found in the *Tristia* are drawn out still further here. But we also find poems with surprising themes. Let us single out three. There is, first, the letter to Vestalis (7), a Roman military leader who has fought in a campaign against the Getae. The exile praises him for his heroism and credits him with deeds of the sort one usually reads about only in epics. Once again, this produces an extremely curious effect in an elegy. One more genre comes into play in Elegy 10: the exile tries his hand as a didactic poet, explaining in a lengthy passage that the Black Sea freezes over because of its low salt content, which he attributes to the large number of fresh-water rivers that empty into it. This passage can hardly be intended seriously either. The exile is obviously joking in Letter 12 to Tuticanus: because the name does not fit elegiac meter, he weighs the possibility of dividing it between two lines of a couplet or changing the length of its syllables.

Once again, his witty wordplay unambiguously belies the assertion, which he makes in *Ex Ponto* 4 as well, that his creative talent is waning. In the elegy on the theme of diminishing talent (2), the exile declares that Homer too would have become a Getan if he had been plopped down in the region of Tomis (21–22). This provides a cue for further remarks about his ever greater integration into the society of his place of exile. In Elegy 9, we learn that the people of Tomis want to keep him with them, although they understand his desire to leave (99–100), and that they have even honored him. He has been praised by official decree and exempted from paying taxes (101–102). Indeed, as Elegy 14 adds, a holy garland has even been laid about his temples (55–56). In response, he tells us in Elegy 13, he has composed a work in Getic too. What is it about?—about the apotheosis of Augustus, and about Tiberius, Livia, and the new emperor's sons (13.19–32). Thus a Roman heart continues to beat in his breast, and that too, of course, deserves recognition:

> haec ubi non patria perlegi scripta Camena,
>   venit et ad digitos ultima charta meos,
> et caput et plenas omnes movere pharetras,
>   et longum Getico murmur in ore fuit.
> atque aliquis "scribas haec cum de Caesare," dixit,
>   "Caesaris imperio restituendus eras."

> When I had read this work, written in the words of the foreign Muse,
> and to my fingers had come the last page,
> all shook their heads and their full quivers,
> and a long murmur was in the Getan mouth.
> And someone said: "Since you write that about Caesar,
> you should have been fetched back on Caesar's orders."

> (33–38)

Right he is, the worthy Getan! The emperor should have rewarded his subject for writing the work if only because it was by no means easy to become familiar with foreign prosody and foreign ways of looking at things. But that too is possible in an elegiac world thrown out of joint.

The metamorphosis into a Getan poet is doubtless the last one that Ovid underwent as a poetic speaker. But it obviously mattered a great deal to him that his fictive double should stress that he had, at the same time, remained a Roman poet. For in the last elegy in *Ex Ponto* 4, conspicuous by dint of its placement in the book, the exile ranges his own name alongside those of fellow poets in contemporary Rome (16).

Perhaps Ovid had an inkling that, among the poets he lists here, none was so important that he could expect to enjoy lasting fame. Ovid could, and he surely knew it.

But That Is Hardly Enough to Shake a Naso

The basic question that anyone interpreting Ovid's elegies of exile has to answer is, how deeply did the peculiar situation in which the poet wrote influence the matter and manner of this poetry? Biographical criticism offers the easy answer that what we hear in this verse is the voice of a man deeply shaken by the exile's existence that fate has reserved for him: when such a voice rings out, we are told, one cannot put aesthetic demands on the way it sounds or expect it to utter anything more than variations on "I want out of here!" In contrast, those who read Ovid's poems of exile as literary texts, as we have done in this chapter—in other words, those who distinguish the real author's voice from that of the speaker of these poems and treat the speaker's situation as an essentially fictive one—have a harder time of it. They must address the problem posed by nine books containing some one hundred poems in which the author's characteristically playful transformation of his pretexts and genres is continued even as a relatively small number of themes, all directly bound up with exile, are sounded again and again.

As to the thematic strands thus generated, we have seen that they may well have been inspired by a related genre, the Greek epistolary novel. Examining three such strands, I have tried to show that Ovid, like the Greek authors, uses them to construct a plot. But that only explains the function of those thematic strands in the first books of the *Tristia*. To explain the matter further, we need to consider the unique position that the *Tristia* and *Ex Ponto* hold as a result of the special conditions surrounding their publication. As with all his other works, Ovid was writing for a small circle of aristocratic, educated Romans. Now, however, he was no longer in a position to read aloud to them; he could reach them only in writing. That must have been one of the main reasons that this poetry does not systematically refrain from addressing specific readers, as Ovid's previous work generally had—the only exceptions are *Amores* 1.9, 2.10, and 2.18, as well as Books 1 and 2 of the *Fasti*—but, indeed, depends for its very life on personal address. In evaluating the literary qualities of the *Tristia* and *Ex Ponto*, therefore, we need to keep two things in mind. First, the circumstance that the exile directly addresses a great many of his friends leads him to repeat certain basic themes, all of which involve one special concern. Second, certain of the allusions associated with the variation of a basic theme doubtless escape us; they were probably best, or indeed only, understood by the individual addressees.

Of course, this justification for the recurrence of a small number of themes will not do for those involving the princeps, Augustus, which return with monotonous regularity in the elegies of exile. Nonetheless, the frequent appeals to his mercy, the accolades to his leadership, and the comparisons of the sovereign to a wrathful god do not only reflect the exile's efforts to better his lot. As we have seen, the emperor also has a role to play in the elegiac world that Ovid constructs in the poetry of exile. Indeed, he is better integrated into this world than that of the *Fasti*. In the latter poem, the devotion to the emperor that is juxtaposed to the playful treatment of myth breeds a tension that threatens to wreck the unity of the work. Here, on the other hand, the game could quite simply not be played without the piece represented by the emperor. For, as unbending sovereign, Augustus, in a certain sense, assumes the role assigned to the hardhearted *puella* in love elegy. As such, he is both reason for, and addressee of, the stock lament. To what extent assigning the emperor this role implies criticism of him is another question. Biographical interpretation naturally detects opposition to the principate here. But critics who interpret the text this way rarely bother to stop and ask whether it made sense for someone who allegedly only rings changes on the theme "I want out of here!" incessantly to attack the one person capable of granting his wish—and to unmask him into the bargain. It must be repeated that, today, we cannot establish a clear picture of Ovid's attitude toward Augustus from poetic texts of this kind.

Let us turn back to the question I posed at the outset. It will have become clear by now that the repetition of certain themes finds its explanation at a metapoetical level. But that in no way alters the fact that the general conception informing Ovid's poetry of exile arises from his situation as an exile. However, the work that came into being on the basis of this general conception was not merely the product of a "because of all that," but, much more, the product of a "despite it all." By itself, the justification just offered for Ovid's use of thematic repetition as a mode of representation shows that he made the best of the conditions imposed on him by the situation in which he wrote. This holds in even greater measure for his use of the literary techniques we have focused on in our discussion of the poetry of exile. The poet exploited the thematic potential of his situation to pursue his playful treatment of the elegiac system, on the one hand, and, on the other, to fashion a new subgenre. Unfolding in three episodes, the story of the exile who, from a seafaring, patient Odysseus learning the ways of a remote land, becomes, after undergoing a living death, a new member of a barbaric people, is something unique in ancient literature, both formally—the story is, after all, presented first in the guise of an "epistolary novel" and then in two collections of letters—and thematically.

The high literary quality of his poetry of exile is Publius Ovidius Naso's way of declaring that he refuses to let the situation shake him— refuses, at least, to let it shake the poet in him. That he has here adopted "despite all" as his motto first becomes apparent in his letter to Augustus, in which the exile indirectly presents the emperor as a prototype of the ruler who subjects poets to political censorship. Another, explicit formulation of this "despite all" is also aimed at Augustus. It occurs in the letter addressed to Perilla, *Tristia* 3.7; like the concluding lines of the *Metamorphoses*, it contains the prophecy that the poet will be transformed into a book:

> en ego, cum patria caream vobisque domoque,
> > demptaque sint, demi quae potuere mihi,
> ingenio tamen ipse meo comitorque fruorque:
> > Caesar in hoc potuit iuris habere nihil.
> quilibet hanc saevo vitam mihi finiat ense,
> > me tamen extincto fama superstes erit,
> dumque suis victrix omnem de montibus orbem
> > prospiciet domitum Martia Roma, legar.

> Look at me: though I must renounce my native land, you, and my house
> and though whatever could be taken from me has been,
> I am nonetheless accompanied by my talent and use it;
> Caesar could have no power over that!
> Anyone can put an end to my life with a cruel sword,
> but, when I have been snuffed out, my fame will nevertheless live on;
> and as long as she, the victorious one, looks down from her seven hills
> on the conquered world—Roma, the city of Mars—I shall be read.

(45–52)

Glossary

aition: explanatory myth
amata: beloved woman
amator: lover (masculine)
amatrix: lover (feminine)
Amores: Experiences of Love
Ars amatoria: Art of Love
ars fallendi: art of deception
carmen: poem
crimen: crime
cultus: civilized mode of life; bodily hygiene
domina: mistress, beloved
dura puella: hard-hearted beloved
elegiac couplet: a couplet consisting of a line of hexameter followed by a line of pentameter
emendation: correction of a text transmitted in manuscript form
Epistulae ex Ponto: Letters from the Black Sea
Epistulae Heroidum: Letters by Heroines (Mythical Women)
Fasti: Festival Calendar
fides: fidelity
Floralia: festival in honor of Flora, goddess of bloom
foedus aeternum: everlasting love bond
imperator: military commander
Janus: in *Remedia amoris* 561, a passage leading to the Forum Romanum, where bankers and money-changers did business
kalends: the first of the month, when interest came due
lex Iulia de adulteriis: a law enacted by Augustus that made adultery a punishable offense
"major" poetry: epic and tragedy

Mamuralia: a festival commemorating King Numa's blacksmith Mamurius
militia amoris: erotic military service (metaphor)
"minor" poetry: genres treating subjects of little gravity, such as elegy and epigram
otium: idleness
paraklausithyron: lament sung at a door
pentad: a unit consisting of five poems or books
poesis: poetry
poeta doctus: learned poet
poetria: poet (feminine)
praecepta: teachings
praeceptor amoris: professor of love
puella: (young) women, beloved
Puteal: a place in Rome where financial transactions were conducted
recusatio: refusal to write "major" poetry
relegatio: a mild form of banishment
Remedia amoris: Love Therapy (literally, remedies for love)
Robigalia: festival to ward off the personification of crop mildew (Robigo)
servitium amoris: erotic servitude (metaphor)
triptychon: tripartite work of art, triptych
Tristia: Elegies of Lament
Vestalia: festival of Vesta, goddess of the hearth
Vinalia: festival of the new wine

Bibliography

Allen, Peter L. 1992. *The Art of Love: Amatory fiction from Ovid to the "Romance of the Rose."* Middle Ages Series. Philadelphia.

Anderson, Billie Teresa. 1986. The grotesque in Ovid's *Metamorphoses*. Diss., University of Iowa.

Arnaud, Daniel Leonard. 1967. Aspects of wit and humor in Ovid's *Metamorphoses*. Diss., Stanford.

Athanassaki, Lucia 1992. The triumph of love and elegy in Ovid's *Amores* 1.2. *Materiali e discussioni per l'analisi dei testi classici* 28:125–141.

Baldo, Gianluigi. 1995. *Dall'Eneide alle Metamorfosi: Il codice epico di Ovidio.* Studi testi documenti, no. 7. Padua.

Barchiesi, Alessandro. 1986. Problemi d'interpretazione in Ovidio: Continuità delle storie, continuazione dei testi. *Materiali e discussioni per l'analisi dei testi classici* 16:77–107.

——. 1989. Voci e istanze narrative nelle *Metamorfosi* di Ovidio. *Materiali e discussioni per l'analisi dei testi classici* 23:55–97.

——. 1991. Discordant muses. *Proceedings of the Cambridge Philological Society* 37:1–21.

——. 1992. *P. Ovidii Nasonis "Epistulae Heroidum" 1–3.* Biblioteca Nazionale, serie dei classici greci e latini, testi con commento filologico, no. 1. Florence.

——. 1993a. Insegnare ad Augusto: Orazio, Epistole 2.1 e Ovidio, *Tristia* 2. *Materiali e discussioni per l'analisi dei testi classici* 31:149–184.

——. 1993b. Future reflexive: Two modes of allusion and Ovid's *Heroides*. *Harvard Studies in Classical Philology* 95:333–365.

——. 1994. *Il poeta e il principe: Ovidio e il discorso augusteo.* Collezione storica. Rome and Bari. Trans. *The Poet and the Prince: Ovid and Augustan Discourse.* Berkeley and Los Angeles, 1997.

Beard, Mary. 1987. A complex of times: No more sheep on Romulus' birthday. *Proceedings of the Cambridge Philological Society* 33:1–15.

Bernbeck, Ernst Jürgen. 1967. Beobachtungen zur Darstellungsart in Ovids *Metamorphosen*. Zetemata 43. Munich.

Bömer, Franz. 1957–1958. *P. Ovidius Naso, "Die Fasten."* 2 vols. Heidelberg.

———. 1969–1986. *P. Ovidius Naso, "Metamorphosen."* *Kommentar.* 7 vols. Heidelberg.

Booth, Joan, ed. and trans. 1991. *Ovid, the Second Book of "Amores."* Warminster.

Boyd, Barbara Weiden. 1997. *Ovid's Literary Loves: Influence and Innovation in the "Amores."* Ann Arbor.

Bretzigheimer, Gerlinde. 1981. See Wellmann-Bretzigheimer.

———. 1991. Exul ludens: Zur Rolle von *relegans* und *relegatus* in Ovids *Tristien.* *Gymnasium* 98:39–76.

———. 1993. Jupiter Tonans in Ovids *Metamorphosen.* *Gymnasium* 100:19–47.

———. 1994. Diana in Ovids *Metamorphosen.* *Gymnasium* 101:506–546.

Brown, Robert. 1987. The palace of the sun in Ovid's *Metamorphoses.* In *Homo viator: Classical Essays for John Bramble,* ed. Michael Whitby, Philip Hardie, and Mary Whitby. Bristol, 211–20.

Buchan, Mark. 1995. Ovidius imperamator: Beginnings and endings of love poems and empire in the *Amores.* *Arethusa* 28:53–85.

Casali, Sergio. 1995a. *P. Ovidii Nasonis "Heroidum Epistula" 9: Deianira herculi.* Biblioteca Nazionale, serie dei classici greci e latini, testi con commento filologico, no. 3. Florence.

———. 1995b. Strategies of tension: Ovid, *Heroides* 4. *Proceedings of the Cambridge Philological Society* 41:1–15.

———. 1995c. Tragic irony in Ovid, *Heroides* 9 and 11. *Classical Quarterly* 45:505–511.

Claassen, Jo-Marie. 1990. Ovid's poetic Pontus. *Papers of the Leeds International Latin Seminar* 6:65–94.

Clauss, James J. 1989. The episode of the Lycian farmers in Ovid's *Metamorphoses.* *Harvard Studies in Classical Philology* 92:297–314.

Conte, Gian Biagio. 1989. Love without elegy: The *Remedia amoris* and the logic of a genre. *Poetics Today* 10:441–469.

Crabbe, Anna. 1981. Structure and content in Ovid's *Metamorphoses.* *Aufstieg und Niedergang der römischen Welt* ii 31.4:2274–2327.

Curran, Leo C. 1972. Transformation and anti-Augustanism in Ovid's *Metamorphoses.* *Arethusa* 5:71–91.

———. 1984. Rape and rape victims in the *Metamorphoses.* In *Women in the Ancient World: The Arethusa Papers,* ed. John Peradotto and J. P. Sullivan. Albany, 1984, 263–286. Originally published in *Arethusa* 11 (1978):213–241.

Davis, Noel Gregson Graham. 1969. Studies in the narrative economy of Ovid's *Metamorphoses.* Diss., University of California, Berkeley.

———. 1980. The problem of closure in a Carmen perpetuum: Aspects of thematic recapitulation in Ovid *Met.* 15. *Grazer Beiträge* 9:123–132.

———. 1983. *The Death of Procris: Amor and the Hunt in Ovid's "Metamorphoses."* Rome.

Davisson, Mary Thomsen. 1982. *Duritia* and creativity in exile: *Epistulae ex Ponto* 4.10. *Classical Antiquity* 1:28–42.

———. 1984. *Magna tibi imposita est nostris persona libellis:* Playwright and actor in Ovid's *Epistulae ex Ponto* 3.1. *Classical Journal* 79:324–339.

Doblhofer, Georg. 1994. *Vergewaltigung in der Antike.* Beiträge zur Altertumskunde, no. 46. Stuttgart and Leipzig.

Döpp, Siegmar. 1991. Vergilrezeption in der Ovidischen "Aeneis." *Rheinisches Museum für Philologie* 134:327–346.

———. 1992. *Werke Ovids: Eine Einführung.* dtv Wissenschaft, no. 4587. Munich.

Downing, Eric. 1990. Anti-Pygmalion: The praeceptor in *Ars amatoria*, Book 3. *Helios* 17:237–249.

Due, Otto Steen. 1974. *Changing Forms: Studies in the "Metamorphoses" of Ovid.* Classica et Mediaevalia, Dissertationes, no. 10 Copenhagen.

Ehlers, Widu-Wolfgang. 1988. Poet und Exil. Zum Verständnis der Exildichtung Ovids. *Antike und Abendland* 34:144–157.

Ellsworth, James D. 1980. Ovid's *Iliad: Metamorphoses* 12.1–13.622. *Prudentia* 12:23–29.

———. 1986. Ovid's "*Aeneid*" Reconsidered: *Met.* 13.623–14.608. *Vergilius* 32:27–32.

———. 1988a. The episode of the Sybil in Ovid's *Metamorphoses* 14.103–56. In *East Meets West: Homage to Edgar C. Knowlton, Jr.,* ed. Roger L. Hadlich and J. D. Ellsworth. Honolulu, 47–55.

———. 1988b. Ovid's "*Odyssey*": *Met.* 13.623–14.608. *Mnemosyne* 41:333–340.

Fairweather, Janet. 1987. Ovid's autobiographical poem, *Tristia* 4.10. *Classical Quarterly* 37:181–196.

Feeney, D. C. 1991. *The Gods in Epic: Poets and Critics of the Classical Tradition.* Oxford.

———. 1992. *Si licet et fas est:* Ovid's *Fasti* and the problem of free speech under the principate. In *Roman Poetry and Propaganda in the Age of Augustus,* ed. Anton Powell. London, 1–25.

Fränkel, Hermann. 1945. *Ovid: A Poet between Two Worlds.* Sather Classical Lectures, no. 18. Berkeley and Los Angeles.

Fredericks, B. R. 1976. *Tristia* 4.10: Poet's autobiography and poetic autobiography. *Transactions of the American Philological Association* 106:139–154.

Froesch, Hermann Hartmut. 1968. Ovids *Epistulae ex Ponto* 1–3 als Gedichtsammlung. Diss. Bonn.

Fruhstorfer, Martin. 1986. *Fores perfringere*—eine Metapher in der erotischen Dichtung? *Rheinisches Museum für Philologie* 129:54–56.

Galasso, Luigi. 1995. *P. Ovidii Nasonis "Epistularum ex Ponto" liber 2.* Biblioteca Nazionale, serie dei classici greci e latini, testi con commento filologico, no. 2. Florence.

Galinsky, G. Karl. 1975. *Ovid's "Metamorphoses": An Introduction to the Basic Aspects.* Oxford and Berkeley.

Gamel, Mary-Kay. 1989. *Non sine caede:* Abortion politics and poetics in Ovid's *Amores. Helios* 16:183–206.

Gentilcore, Roxanne. 1995. The landscape of desire: The tale of Pomona and Vertumnus in Ovid's *Metamorphoses. Phoenix* 49:110–120.

Graf, Fritz. 1988. Ovide, les *Métamorphoses* et la véracité du mythe. In *Métamorphoses du mythe en Grèce antique,* ed. Claude Calame. Geneva, 57–70.

———. 1994. Die Götter, die Menschen und der Erzähler. Zum Göttermythos in Ovids *Metamorphosen.* In *Ovidius Redivivus. Von Ovid zu Dante,* ed. Michelangelo Picone and Bernhard Zimmermann. Stuttgart, 22–42.

Hardie, Philip. 1988. Lucretius and the delusions of Narcissus. *Materiali e discussioni per l'analisi dei testi classici* 20/21:71–89.

——. 1990. Ovid's Theban history: The first 'Anti-*Aeneid*'? *Classical Quarterly* 40:224–235.

——. 1991. The Janus episode in Ovid's *Fasti*. *Materiali e discussioni per l'analisi dei testi classici* 26:47–67.

——. 1992. Augustan poets and the mutability of Rome. In *Roman Poetry and Propaganda in the Age of Augustus*, ed. Anton Powell. London, 59–82.

——. 1995. The speech of Pythagoras in Ovid's *Metamorphoses* 15: Empedoclean epos. *Classical Quarterly* 45:204–214.

Hardie, Philip, Alessandro Barchiesi, and Stephen Hinds, eds. 1999. *Ovidian Transformations: Essays on Ovid's "Metamorphoses" and Its Reception*. Cambridge Philological Society, Suppl. 23. Cambridge.

Hardy, Clara Shaw. 1995. Ecphrasis and the male narrator in Ovid's Arachne. *Helios* 22:140–148.

Harries, Byron. 1989. Causation and the authority of the poet in Ovid's *Fasti*. *Classical Quarterly* 39:164–185.

——. 1990. The spinner and the poet: Arachne in Ovid's *Metamorphoses*. *Proceedings of the Cambridge Philological Society* 36:64–82.

——. 1991. Ovid and the Fabii: *Fasti* 2.193–474. *Classical Quarterly* 41:150–168.

Heinze, Richard. 1972. Ovids elegische Erzählung. In *Vom Geist des Römertums. Ausgewählte Aufsätze*. Darmstadt, 1972, 308–403. Originally published in *Berichte über die Verhandlungen der Sächsischen Akademie der Wissenschaften zu Leipzig, Philologisch-historische Klasse*, no. 71/7 (1919).

Heldmann, Konrad. 1994. Ovids Sabinus-Gedicht *Am.* 2, 18 und die *Epistulae Heroidum*. *Hermes* 122:188–219.

Helzle, Martin. 1989. *Publii Ovidii Nasonis "Epistularum ex Ponto" liber 4: A Commentary on Poems 1 to 7 and 16*. Spudasmata, no. 43. Hildesheim.

Herbert-Brown, Geraldine. 1994. *Ovid and the "Fasti": An Historical Study*. Oxford Classical Monographs. Oxford.

Heyworth, S. J. 1992. Ars moratoria: Ovid, *A.a.* 1.681–704. *Liverpool Classical Monthly* 17:59–61.

Hinds, Stephen. 1985. Booking the return trip: Ovid and *Tristia* 1. *Proceedings of the Cambridge Philological Society* 31:13–32.

——. 1987a. Generalising about Ovid. *Ramus* 16:4–31.

——. 1987b. *The Metamorphosis of Persephone: Ovid and the Self-Conscious Muse*. Cambridge.

——. 1992. *Arma* in Ovid's *Fasti*. Part. 1: Genre and mannerism. Part 2: Genre, Romulean Rome and Augustan ideology. *Arethusa* 25:81–112, 113–153.

——. 1993. Medea in Ovid: Scenes from the life of an intertextual heroine. *Materiali e discussioni per l'analisi dei testi classici* 30:9–47.

Hofmann, Heinz. 1985. Ovid's *Metamorphoses: Carmen perpetuum, carmen deductum*. *Papers of the Liverpool Latin Seminar* 5:223–241.

Holzberg, Niklas, ed. 1994. *Der griechische Briefroman. Gattungstypologie und Textanalyse*. With the collaboration of Stefan Merkle. Classica Monacensia, no. 8. Tübingen.

——. 1997. Playing with his life: Ovid's "autobiographical" references. *Lampas* 30:4–19.

———. 1998. Ter quinque volumina as carmen perpetuum: The division into books in Ovid's *Metamorphoses*. *Materiali e discussioni per l'analisi die testi classici* 40:77–98.

Horsfall, Nicholas. 1979. Epic and burlesque in Ovid, *Met.* 7.260ff. *Classical Journal* 74:319–332.

Jacobsen, Garrett A. 1984. Apollo and Tereus: Parallel motifs in Ovid's *Metamorphoses*. *Classical Journal* 80:45–52.

Jacobson, Howard. 1974. *Ovid's "Heroides."* Princeton.

Jäkel, Siegfried. 1970. Beobachtungen zur dramatischen Komposition von Ovids *Amores*. *Antike und Abendland* 16:12–28.

Jones, David. 1997. *Enjoinder and Argument in Ovid's "Remedia amoris."* Hermes Einzelschriften, no. 77. Stuttgart.

Keith, A. M. 1992a. *Amores* 1.1: Propertius and the Ovidian programme. In *Studies in Latin Literature and Roman History*, no. 6, ed. Carl Deroux. Collection Latomus, no. 217. Brussels, 327–344.

———. 1992b. *The Play of Fictions: Studies in Ovid's "Metamorphoses,"* Book 2. Ann Arbor.

———. 1994/95. *Corpus eroticum:* Elegiac poetics and elegiac *puellae* in Ovid's *Amores*. *Classical World* 88:27–40.

Kennedy, Duncan F. 1984. The epistolary mode and the first of Ovid's *Heroides*. *Classical Quarterly* 34:413–422.

———. 1993. *The Arts of Love: Five Studies in the Discourse of Roman Love Elegy*. Roman Literature and Its Contexts. Cambridge.

Kenney, E. J. 1976. Ovidius prooemians. *Proceedings of the Cambridge Philological Society* 22:46–53.

———. 1982. Books and readers in the Roman world. In *Latin Literature*. Vol. 2 of *The Cambridge History of Classical Literature*, ed. E. J. Kenney. Cambridge, 3–32.

Knox, Peter E. 1986. *Ovid's "Metamorphoses" and the Traditions of Augustan Poetry*. Cambridge Philological Society, Suppl. 11. Cambridge.

Kraus, Walter. 1968. Ovidius Naso. In *Ovid*, ed. Michael v. Albrecht and Ernst Zinn. Wege der Forschung, no. 92. Darmstadt, 67–166.

Labate, Mario. 1984. *L'arte di farsi amare: Modelli culturali e progetto didascalico nell'elegia ovidiana*. Biblioteca di Materiali e discussioni per l'analisi dei testi classici. Pisa.

Latacz, Joachim. 1994. Ovids *Metamorphosen* als Spiel mit der Tradition. In *Erschließung der Antike: Kleine Schriften zur Literatur der Griechen und Römer*, ed. Joachim Latacz. Stuttgart and Leipzig, 569–602.

Lateiner, Donald. 1978. Ovid's homage to Callimachus and Alexandrian poetic theory: *Am.* 2, 19. *Hermes* 106:188–196.

Leach, Eleanor Winsor. 1974. Ekphrasis and the theme of artistic failure in Ovid's *Metamorphoses*. *Ramus* 3:102–142.

Loehr, Johanna. 1996. *Ovids Mehrfacherklärungen in der Tradition aitiologischen Dichtens*. Beiträge zur Altertumskunde, no. 74. Stuttgart and Leipzig.

Luck, Georg, ed. and trans. 1967–1977. *P. Ovidius Naso, "Tristia."* 2 vols. Heidelberg.

Lucke, Christina. 1982. *P. Ovidius Naso, "Remedia amoris": Kommentar zu Vers 397–814*. Habelts Dissertationsdrucke, Reihe Klassische Philologie, no. 33. Bonn.

Ludwig, Walther. 1965. *Struktur und Einheit der "Metamorphosen" Ovids*. Berlin.

McKeown, J. C. 1984. *Fabula proposito nulla tegenda meo:* Ovid's *Fasti* and Augustan politics. In *Poetry and Politics in the Age of Augustus,* ed. Tony Woodman and David West. Cambridge, 169–187.

——. 1987–1998. *Ovid, "Amores." Text, Prolegomena and Commentary in Four Volumes.* Vol. 1: *Text and Prolegomena.* Vol. 2: *A Commentary on Book One.* Vol. 3: *A Commentary on Book Two.* Arca, nos. 20, 22, and 36. Leeds.

Miller, John F. 1982. Callimachus and the Augustan aetiological elegy. *Aufstieg und Niedergang der römischen Welt,* ii 30.1, 371–417.

——. 1991. *Ovid's Elegiac Festivals: Studies in the "Fasti."* Studien zur klassischen Philologie, no. 55. Frankfurt.

——. 1992. The *Fasti* and Hellenistic didactic: Ovid's variant aetiologies. *Arethusa* 25:11–31.

——. 1993a. Ovidian allusion and the vocabulary of memory. *Materiali e discussioni per l'analisi dei testi classici* 30:153–164.

——. 1993b. Apostrophe, aside, and the didactic addressee: Poetic strategies in *Ars amatoria* 3. *Materiali e discussioni per l'analisi dei testi classici* 31:231–241.

——. 1994. The memories of Ovid's Pythagoras. *Mnemosyne* 47:473–487.

Moles, John 1991. The dramatic coherence of Ovid, *Amores* 1.1 and 1.2. *Classical Quarterly* 41:551–554.

Morgan, Kathleen. 1977. *Ovid's Art of Imitation: Propertius in the "Amores."* Mnemosyne Supplementum, no. 47. Leiden.

Morrison, James V. 1992. Literary reference and generic transgression in Ovid, *Amores* 1.7: Lover, poet, and *furor. Latomus* 51:571–589.

Myerowitz, Molly. 1985. *Ovid's Games of Love.* Detroit.

——. 1992. The domestication of desire: Ovid's *Parva tabella* and the theater of love. In *Pornography and Representation in Greece and Rome,* ed. Amy Richlin. New York and Oxford, 131–157.

Myers, K. Sara. 1990. Ovid's *Tecta ars: Amores* 2.6, "Programmatics and the parrot." *Echos du Monde Classique* 34:367–374.

——. 1994. *Ovid's Causes: Cosmogony and Aetiology in the "Metamorphoses."* Ann Arbor.

——. 1996. The poet and the procuress: The *Lena* in Latin love elegy. *Journal of Roman Studies* 86:1–21.

——. 1999. The metamorphosis of a poet: Recent work on Ovid. *Journal of Roman Studies* 89:190–204.

Nagle, Betty Rose. 1980. *The Poetics of Exile: Program and Polemic in the "Tristia" and "Epistulae ex Ponto" of Ovid.* Collection Latomus, no. 170. Brussels.

——. 1988a. Ovid's reticent heroes. *Helios* 15:23–39.

——. 1988b. Two miniature Carmina perpetua in the *Metamorphoses:* Calliope and Orpheus. *Grazer Beiträge* 15:99–125.

——. 1989. Ovid's *Metamorphoses:* A narratological catalogue. *Syllecta Classica* 1:97–125.

Neumeister, Christoff. 1986. Orpheus und Eurydike. Eine Vergil-Parodie Ovids, Ov. Met. 10.1–11.66 und Verg. Georg. 4.457–527. *Würzburger Jahrbücher für die Altertums-wissenschaft* 12:169–181.

Newlands, Carole Elizabeth. 1984. The transformation of the *Locus amoenus* in Roman poetry. Diss., University of California, Berkeley.

———. 1986. The simile of the fractured pipe in Ovid's *Metamorphoses* 4. *Ramus* 15:143–153.

———. 1991. Ovid's ravenous raven. *Classical Journal* 86:244–255.

———. 1992. Ovid's narrator in the *Fasti*. *Arethusa* 25:33–54.

———. 1994. The ending of Ovid's *Fasti*. *Ramus* 23:129–143.

———. 1995. *Playing with Time: Ovid and the "Fasti."* Ithaca and London.

Nicoll, W. S. M. 1980. Cupid, Apollo, and Daphne: Ovid, *Met.* 1.452ff. *Classical Quarterly* 30:174–182.

Olstein, Katherine. 1975. *Amores* 1.3 and duplicity as a way of love. *Transactions of the American Philological Association* 105:241–257.

Parker, Holt N. 1992. Love's body anatomized: The ancient erotic handbooks and the rhetoric of sexuality. In *Pornography and Representation in Greece and Rome,* ed. Amy Richlin. New York and Oxford, 90–111.

Pulbrook, Martin. 1987. *The Original Published Form of Ovid's "Heroides."* Studies in Greek and Latin Authors, no. 1. Maynooth, 9–24. Originally published in *Hermathena* 122 (1977):29–45.

Quinn, Kenneth. 1982. The poet and his audience in the Augustan age. *Aufstieg und Niedergang der römischen Welt* ii 30.1, 75–180.

Rahn, Helmut. 1968. Ovids elegische Epistel. In *Ovid,* ed. Michael v. Albrecht and Ernst Zinn. Wege der Forschung, no. 92. Darmstadt, 476–501. Originally published in *Antike und Abendland* 7 (1958):105–120.

Richlin, Amy. 1992. Reading Ovid's rapes. In *Pornography and Representation in Greece and Rome,* ed. Amy Richlin. New York and Oxford, 158–179.

Richmond, John. 1981. Doubtful works ascribed to Ovid. *Aufstieg und Niedergang der römischen Welt* ii 31.4, 2744–2783.

Richmond, John. 1990. *P. Ovidi Nasonis Ex Ponto, libri quattuor/recensuit.* Leipzig.

Rieks, Rudolf. 1980. Zum Aufbau von Ovids *Metamorphosen.* *Würzburger Jahrbücher für die Altertumswissenschaft* 6b:85–103.

Rosati, Gianpiero. 1979. L'esistenza letteraria: Ovidio e l'autocoscienza della poesia. *Materiali e discussioni per l'analisi dei testi classici* 2:101–136.

———. 1983. *Narciso e Pigmalione: Illusione e spettacolo nelle "Metamorfosi" di Ovidio.* Con un saggio di Antonio La Penna. Florence.

———. 1985. *Ovidio, i cosmetici delle donne.* Il convivio. Collana di classici greci e latini. Venice.

———. 1992. L'elegia al femminile: Le *Heroides* di Ovidio e altre heroides. *Materiali e discussioni per l'analisi dei testi classici* 29:71–94.

———. 1994. *Ovidio, le "Metamorfosi." Introduzione, traduzione e note.* Biblioteca Universale Rizzoli. Milan.

———. 1996a. *P. Ovidii Nasonis "Heroidum Epistulae" 18–19: Leander Heroni. Hero Leandro.* Biblioteca Nazionale, serie dei classici greci e latini, testi con commento filologico, no. 4. Florence.

———. 1996b. Sabinus, the *Heroides* and the poet-nightingale. Some observations on the authenticity of the *Epistula Sapphus. Classical Quarterly* 46:207–216.

Rüpke, Jörg. 1994. Ovids Kalenderkommentar: Zur Gattung der libri fastorum. *Antike und Abendland* 40:125–136.

———. 1995. *Kalender und Öffentlichkeit: Die Geschichte der Repräsentation und religiösen Qualifikation von Zeit in Rom.* Religionsgeschichtliche Versuche und Vorarbeiten, no. 40. Berlin and New York.

Rutledge, Eleanor S. 1973. The style and composition of Ovid's *Fasti.* Diss., University of North Carolina at Chapel Hill.

Schmidt, Ernst A. 1991. *Ovids poetische Menschenwelt. Die "Metamorphosen" als Metapher und Symphonie.* Sitzungsberichte der Heidelberger Akademie der Wissenschaften, Philosophisch-historische Klasse, no. 2. Heidelberg.

Schmitzer, Ulrich. 1990. *Zeitgeschichte in Ovids "Metamorphosen:" Mythologische Dichtung unter politischem Anspruch.* Beiträge zur Altertumskunde, no. 4. Stuttgart.

Schubert, Werner, ed. 1999. *Ovid: Werk und Wirkung. Festgabe für Michael von Albrecht zum 65. Geburtstag.* Studien zur klassischen Philologie, no. 100. Frankfurt.

Seeck, Gustav Adolf. 1975. Ich-Erzähler und Erzähler-Ich in Ovids *Heroides.* Zur Entstehung des neuzeitlichen literarischen Menschen. In *Monumentum Chiloniense: Studien zur augusteischen Zeit. Kieler Festschrift für Erich Burck zum 70. Geburtstag,* ed. Eckard Lefèvre. Amsterdam, 436–470.

Segal, Charles. 1969. Myth and philosophy in the *Metamorphoses:* Ovid's Augustanism and the Augustan conclusion of Book 15. *American Journal of Philology* 90:257–292.

———. 1992. Philomela's web and the pleasures of the text: Ovid's myth of Tereus in the *Metamorphoses.* In *The Two Worlds of the Poet: New Perspectives on Vergil,* ed. Robert M. Wilhelm and Howard Jones. Detroit, 281–295.

Semmlinger, Lothar. 1988. Zur Echtheit der Elegie 'De somnio' = Ovid, *Amores* 3.5. In *Festschrift für Paul Klopsch,* ed. Udo Kindermann, Wolfgang Maaz, and Fritz Wagner. Göppinger Arbeiten zur Gemanistik, no. 492. Göppingen, 455–475.

Sharrock, Alison R. 1991a. The love of creation. *Ramus* 20:169–182.

———. 1991b. Womanufacture. *Journal of Roman Studies* 81:36–49.

———. 1994a. Ovid and the politics of reading. *Materiali e discussioni per l'analisi dei testi classici* 33:97–122.

———. 1994b. *Seduction and Repetition in Ovid's "Ars amatoria" 2.* Oxford.

———. 1995. The drooping rose: Elegiac failure in *Amores* 3.7. *Ramus* 24:152–180.

Smith, Riggs Alden. 1997. *Poetic Allusion and Poetic Embrace in Ovid and Virgil.* Ann Arbor. Revised ed. of Allusion of grandeur: Studies in the intertextuality of the *Metamorphoses* and the *Aeneid.* Diss., University of Pennsylvania, 1990.

Spoth, Friedrich. 1992a. Hohe Epik als Liebeswerbung? Zweifel an der Authentizität von Ovid, *Ars* 3.335–338. *Museum Helveticum* 49:201–205.

———. 1992b. *Ovids "Heroides" als Elegien.* Zetemata, no. 89. Munich.

———. 1993. Ovids Ariadne-Brief *Her.* 10 und die römische Liebeselegie. *Würzburger Jahrbücher für die Altertumswissenschaft* 19:239–260.

Starr, Raymond. 1987. The circulation of literary texts in the Roman world. *Classical Quarterly* 37:213–223.

———. 1991. Reading aloud: *Lectores* and Roman reading. *Classical Journal* 86:337–343.

Stroh, Wilfried. 1969. *Ovid im Urteil der Nachwelt: Eine Testimoniensammlung.* Darmstadt.

———. 1971. *Die römische Liebeselegie als werbende Dichtung.* Amsterdam.

———. 1979a. Ovids Liebeskunst und die Ehegesetze des Augustus. *Gymnasium* 86:323–352.

——. 1979b. Rhetorik und Erotik: Eine Studie zu Ovids liebesdidaktischen Gedichten. *Würzburger Jahrbücher für die Altertumswissenschaft* 5:117–132.

——. 1981. Tröstende Musen: Zur literarhistorischen Stellung und Bedeutung von Ovids Exilgedichten. *Aufstieg und Niedergang der römischen Welt* ii 31.4, 2638–2684.

——. 1983. Die Ursprünge der römischen Liebeselegie: Ein altes Problem im Licht eines neuen Fundes. *Poetica* 15:205–246.

——. 1991. Heroides Ovidianae cur epistulas scribant. In *Ovidio poeta della memoria: Atti del Convegno Internazionale di Studi, Sulmona, 19–21 ottobre 1989*, ed. Giuseppe Papponetti. Rome, 201–244.

Tarrant, Richard J. 1983. Ovid. In *Texts and Transmission: A Survey of the Latin Classics*, ed. L. D. Reynolds. Oxford, 257–286.

——. 1995. Ovid and the failure of rhetoric. In *Ethics and Rhetoric: Classical Essays for Donald Russel on His Seventy-Fifth Birthday*, ed. Doreen Innes, Harry Hine, and Christopher Pelling. Oxford, 63–74.

Tissol, Gareth. 1997. *The Face of Nature: Wit, Narrative, and Cosmic Origins in Ovid's "Metamorphoses."* Princeton.

Verducci, Florence. 1980. The contest of rational libertinism and imaginative license in Ovid's *Ars amatoria. Pacific Coast Philology* 15/2:29–39.

——. 1985. *Ovid's Toyshop of the Heart: "Epistulae Heroidum."* Princeton.

Volk, Katharina. 1996. Hero und Leander in Ovids Doppelbriefen epist. 18 und 19. *Gymnasium* 103:95–106.

Wallace-Hadrill, Andrew. 1987. Time for Augustus: Ovid, Augustus, and the *Fasti*. In *Homo viator: Classical Essays for John Bramble*, ed. Michael Whitby, Philip Hardie, and Mary Whitby. Bristol, 221–230.

Watkins, O. D. 1983. Ovid, *Metamorphoses* 8.365–68. *Latomus* 42:135–138.

Watson, Patricia. 1982. Ovid and *cultus: Ars amatoria* 3.113–28. *Transactions and Proceedings of the American Philological Association* 112:237–244.

——. 1984. Love as a civilizer: Ovid, *Ars amatoria*, 2.467–92. *Latomus* 43:389–395.

Wayne, Philip, trans. 1949. Johann Wolfgang von Goethe, *Faust*, Part 1. Harmondsworth, Great Britain.

Wellmann-Bretzigheimer, Gerlinde. 1981. Ovids "Ars amatoria." In *Europäische Lehrdichtung: Festschrift für Walter Naumann zum 70. Geburtstag*, ed. Hans Gerd Rötzer and Herbert Walz. Darmstadt, 1–32.

Wheeler, Stephen Michael. 1992. Repetition, continuity, and closure in Ovid's *Metamorphoses*. Diss., Princeton. Revised as *Narrative Dynamics in Ovid's "Metamorphoses."* Classica Monacensia, no. 20. Tübingen. 2000.

——. 1995. *Imago mundi:* Another view of the creation in Ovid's *Metamorphoses. American Journal of Philology* 116:95–121.

——. 1999. *A Discourse of Wonders: Audience and Performance in Ovid's Metamorphoses.* Philadelphia.

White, Peter. 1993. *Promised Verse: Poets in the Society of Augustan Rome.* Cambridge, Mass., and London.

Wiedemann, Thomas. 1975. The political background to Ovid's *Tristia* 2. *Classical Quarterly* 25:264–271.

Wildberger, Jula. 1998. *Ovids Schule der elegischen Liebe: Erotodidaxe und Psychagogie in der "Ars amatoria."* Studien zur klassischen Philologie, no. 112. Frankfurt.

Williams, Gareth D. 1991. Vocal variations and narrative complexity in Ovid's Vestalia: *Fasti* 6.249–468. *Ramus* 20:183–204.

———. 1992. Representations of the book-roll in Latin poetry: Ovid, *Tr.* 1.1.3–14 and related texts. *Mnemosyne* 45:178–189.

———. 1994. *Banished Voices: Readings in Ovid's Exile Poetry.* Cambridge.

———. 1996. *The Curse of Exile: A study of Ovid's Ibis.* Cambridge Philological Society. Suppl. 19. Cambridge.

Wright, Ellen F. 1984. Profanum sunt genus: The Poets of the *Ars amatoria. Philological Quarterly* 63:1–15.

Wyke, Maria. 1989. Reading female flesh: *Amores* 3.1. In *History as Text: The Writing of Ancient History,* ed. Averil Cameron. London, 111–143.

———. 1994. Taking the woman's part: Engendering Roman love elegy. *Ramus* 23:110–128.

Zanker, Paul. 1987. *Augustus und die Macht der Bilder.* Munich. Trans. *The Power of Images in the Age of Augustus.* Ann Arbor, 1988.

Zimmermann, Bernhard. 1994. *Ille ego qui fuerim, tenerorum lusor amorum.* Zur Poetik der Liebesdichtung Ovids. In *Ovidius redivivus: Von Ovid zu Dante,* ed. Michelangelo Picone and Bernhard Zimmermann. Stuttgart, 1–21.

Zumwalt, Nancy. 1977. *Fama subversa:* Theme and structure in Ovid's *Metamorphoses* 12. *California Studies in Classical Antiquity* 10:209–222.

Index